Paul Rambali was a rock journalist for the *NME* during the Punk era and editor of *The Face* from 1980 to 1987. The author of two books about France and works including *It's All True – in the Cities and Jungles of Brazil*, a personal odyssey exploring issues of politics and culture in the Developing World, he also ghost-wrote *I, Phoolan Devi*, the autobiography of India's Bandit Queen, which has been published in twenty-six countries.

A complete catalogue record for this book can
be obtained from the British Library on request

The right of Paul Rambali to be identified as the author
of this work has been asserted by him in accordance with
the Copyright, Designs and Patents Act 1988

Copyright © 2006 Paul Rambali

First published in 2006 by Serpent's Tail,
4 Blackstock Mews, London N4 2BT
website: www.serpentstail.com

ISBN: 1 85242 904 6
ISBN: 978 1 85242 904 1

Designed and typeset by Sue Lamble
Printed by Mackays of Chatham, plc

10 9 8 7 6 5 4 3 2 1

Barefoot Runner

The Life of Marathon Champion Abebe Bikila

Paul Rambali

1

Abebe had never been aware of his legs until then. You are not aware of your body, only the sensations it affords. When you touch someone, you are not aware of your hand; likewise, you can't really feel your legs, only the movement they bring. He looked down at his legs under the white bed sheet, immobile like the half-buried roots of a tree, and tried to recall how it was to run.

He remembered what it was like to run until his legs ached, and then to run farther still. There was no ache in his legs now, not as there used to be, the permanent agony that came from running and which went away only if he ran again. He wanted to believe what the doctors said, that feeling would gradually return and that he would be able to walk again – and even run, they promised. He tried to put his faith in the doctors' science. He wanted to trust them. But he knew that he had somehow offended God and there would be nothing they could do. He feared that the Almighty had deprived him of the use of his legs as a punishment for his conceit, for his pride in once being able to run farther, faster and for longer than any man on earth.

As a boy, he used to wonder whether he could run as far as the horizon, if he could reach it before the sun set. He was convinced that if he could run for long enough, he could race the sun that moved so slowly across the sky and be the first to reach the distant mountains. He imagined that if he could keep running, following the sun, the day would last for ever – or at least until he grew tired and went to sleep. When he asked his parents about this, his father laughed. He said there was nothing beyond the mountains; the day ended and with it the world when the sun went down, bloated like a juicy mango, between the dark mountain slopes, and it began again when the sun rose refreshed over the plains. His father knew nothing of the aeroplanes that carried you high up, high as the sun, and beyond the edge of the world. If someone had told Abebe of such possibilities then, he would not have believed them. As far as he knew, everything ended with the jagged peaks burned red by the morning sun, like the teeth of the old betel-chewing women squatting by the well who laughed at his incessant scurrying.

Where was he going in such a rush?

The old women shouted the question at him as he passed. He was always running, it was true. If he didn't answer them, it wasn't because he was out of breath, for he was never out of breath. If he didn't stop to reply, it was because he hadn't heard them, or if he had, it was already too late; his legs had carried him on. He was lost in his thoughts, wondering whether the sun extinguished itself every night in a beautiful lake, as his father said, or whether it slept in the bosom of the earth; the mountains rose so high they embraced it, like a mother a returning child.

Propped up in the hospital bed, he could see through the wall of glass to the gardens outside. The first few mornings, he had woken dreaming that he had been sleeping in the clouds. The hospital was a sterile heaven smelling of bleach, filled with steel instruments and plastic cups and little tablets to swallow, with nurses in white for angels. It was the cleanliness of this developed world which had always amazed him, even more than the food and the clothes and the profusion of goods and the fact that everything was finished, old, permanent, and not forever in the process of becoming, or falling apart.

The tablets would reduce the inflammation, the doctors had told him, and that would ease the pain. He had imbibed them dutifully, trusting the doctors the way he trusted the major. After all, the major's science had made him a champion. But the truth was he could no longer feel any pain. At first, yes, there was pain, and humiliation when he woke up and tried to lift his body and found he couldn't, but now he didn't feel anything at all, only a twinge at the base of his spine like the twinge he got sometimes from running in ill-fitting shoes. One of the nurses told him that it was because he had been sitting up too long in bed watching television. She chided him, saying he was a naughty boy and he was making her vexed, but she came back regularly to move him, and she told him he could call her Rita. He didn't know how to tell her. There was no more pain, only discomfort, only bedsores and sadness.

The doctors discussed with each other when he would begin his re-education. One of them, a woman, had turned him over and massaged his back the way he had seen American athletes being massaged. He would have to learn to walk again, they said, like a child. The doctors smiled and said that once the swelling had gone down they could begin the programme. The hospital had a pool, they said, and Rita said he would be spending a lot of time in it. She laughed and told him not to worry when he confided to her afterwards that he couldn't swim. 'Is not a deep pool,' she said. 'All you must do is relax.' The water would take away all his problems.

Abebe turned his gaze from the sullen fields beyond the glass wall and searched under the bed for the cord with the television controls. It was midday and he liked to watch the daily news programme. Though everyone had transistor radios in Addis, no one, apart from His Imperial Majesty, as far as he knew, had a television set. He had watched over and over again the astronauts leaping effortlessly on the surface of the moon, and he wondered how it would be to be weightless, the way it once was for him to run without effort.

Around the world, there was smoke and looting in the cities and youths demonstrating like the students in Addis.

That day, the newsman was talking about a skull. He said that the skull had been found in the Afar triangle. It belonged to man's oldest ancestor, *Homo afarensis*. Her name, he said, was Lucy.

Abebe knew the Afar region, which lay north-east of Addis, beyond the Mountain of Light. It was a desolate plain, a furnace in which everything, even the rocks, had been baked to dust. No one could possibly have lived there, he thought, yet the reporter was talking excitedly to a rugged-faced man in his fifties wearing a cowboy hat. The pockets of his khaki bush jacket were full of penknives and pipes. The man's name was Professor Carleton Coon. He was holding a human skull, examining it closely. The head was small, the front of the cranium flat. Staring into the empty eye sockets of what was once a person, the professor emitted a satisfied grunt. He said he wasn't sure yet where she fitted in, but Lucy might just be our oldest relative.

Two men were sifting through the dust behind him, tiny figures undaunted by the immensity of the landscape, unhurried by the enormity of their task. They were searching with toothbrushes for bone fragments, said the reporter, searching pebble by pebble for the beginning of human time. Near by, a camp was pitched, a huddle of canvas and rope.

As the reporter talked, the image changed to show a runner, long limbed and dark and wearing a single white cloth wound about his waist and thrown over his shoulder. He was running with his arm held high, the way Abebe had seen men running by his village, and he knew he was wearing a special bracelet on the arm, with a compartment for messages. The raised arm was a signal that he should not be hampered. Behind him were the jagged red peaks of the Afar mountains, the fortress massif that runs southwards from the Red Sea.

Abebe watched the porter jogging steadily away, his arm still held aloft as though carrying a torch. He was thrilled to see something he recognised among all the strange places and events he had seen on the television. Often, he was told by people that they had seen him on television, running in Japan or Mexico, images he himself had never seen.

On the screen, Professor Coon was squinting upwards at the bright hot sky where the vultures circled. He held up the skull and turned it around in the sun, admiring its proportions, the early human form that had endured so long. He said that Ethiopia was probably the cradle of humanity.

Elsewhere in Africa, the newsman said, there had been no let-up in fighting in the civil war in Biafra, and abruptly Abebe was staring into the hollow, pleading eyes of hungry children, still standing somehow on their bony legs with their bloated protruding bellies.

'What you looking at this for?' asked Rita.

The nurse had entered without him noticing, carrying a lunch tray. 'Is a terrible thing. Poor people starving and dying and nobody lift a finger to help them!'

They both looked at the tray. On it was a plate of food and a saucer of pills. He set the tray on his lap and, thanking the nurse profusely – the custom in his country, though it always made her smile – began soaking up the gravy with the bread. It was square and white, so perfect yet it had no flavour, and he missed the sourness of *injera*. He had already scooped up the stew with the bread and put it in his mouth before he remembered the cutlery. He had to remind himself again which hand held the fork and which the knife. The first time he had been given such things, in a restaurant in Rome, Kidanah had told him what to do while everyone stared. His discomfort was spared this time, however, as Rita had become hypnotised by the television pictures.

'The poor people…' she muttered.

She tore herself away with a shudder.

'They tell me in reception you going to get a visitor this afternoon,' she said brightly.

She paused, looking at him wide eyed.

'A royal visitor!' she added, lolling her head to one side and smoothing her uniform at the hips as though preparing to curtsy.

Abebe stopped eating.

'His Majesty Haile Selassie I is coming to the clinic.'

Abebe gulped, swallowing the mouthful of food. His body straightened.

'What's the matter? Like you have a fright or something.'

'Not afraid. I have always been the loyal servant of His Imperial Majesty.'

'I suppose you must be feeling nervous, then. I know I would be if I was getting a visit from royalty.'

'No, I am not nervous. My life belongs to His Imperial Majesty,' said Abebe. 'If I am here, it is because of His Majesty, if I have brought glory to Ethiopia, it is because of him. I have nothing more to fear. I have been waiting.'

'Well then, you better get yourself prepared.'

Abebe pushed the plate of food away and then, remembering where he was, pulled it back towards him and resumed eating.

Rita took the cord with the controls and turned the television off. The image of the starving child lingered like a ghost on the dark screen.

2

The boy squatted under a vast baobab guarding some scrawny goats, the only traces of life on the vast plain. Barefoot, wearing only a white *shamma*, he scratched at the dry, sandy ground with his fingers. Like the goats that nibbled at the earth, Abebe was searching for the still-moist blades that had sprung up in the cool night. He pulled up a meagre shoot of grass and stuffed it into a ragged jute sack tied at his waist, listening all the while to the sounds of the empty highlands: the rats in their holes and the buzzards wheeling above.

Suddenly he tensed, aware of a low rumbling.

He thought at first the sound was coming from the mountains, but then he looked in the opposite direction, along the road that ran straight across the wide plateau, and saw dust rising up, a yellow swirl in the blue, cloudless sky.

As he watched the spreading sandstorm, he heard a rumble of thunder and realised that the cause of the noise and the dust – whatever it was – was coming closer to him, coming along the road. Panicking, he glanced about frantically for somewhere to hide, but there were only a few clumps of dry scrub near the tree.

The boy crouched down behind one of them as the crows scattered from the branches, flapping their dark wings and rising slowly upwards.

The first vehicle to pass was a motorcycle, ridden by a man in uniform with buttons that shone in the sun like tiny jewels. The man was wearing goggles, though the boy took this to be that he had the eyes of an owl. The second vehicle was a purple carriage with long running boards like the outstretched legs of a leopard. As it passed, the boy rose from behind the bush, forgetting his fear and gaping in astonishment. He saw, sitting upright in the back, a man wearing on his head a tall crest of long black feathers.

Almost as soon as he glimpsed the man-eagle, a second car passed, leaving the air thick with the hot sweet smell of exhaust fumes. He watched the convoy speeding on towards the mountains. Then he backed away from the roadside and began to run.

He ran, forgetting the goats that had scattered in fright across the plateau.

He ran until he reached the perimeter of the village. And then he continued to run, weaving around the circular huts, unable to stop. Bony hens scattered in fright as he burst through a wooden gate, almost trampling the few struggling plants as he crossed the vegetable patch.

Inside the hut, he halted, panting, breathing in the reassuring cool of the mud walls. His mother was seated at the wooden loom, passing the shuttle with a wide sweep of her arm and pedalling softly in the obscurity. His father was lying on a blanket spread on a ridge of hard earth.

'I saw him!' cried the boy.

'Who did you see?' asked his father.

'The *Negus Negasta*!'

His mother stopped pedalling.

'In his chariot!'

He trembled as his father rose, gathering his dusty white *shamma* over his forearm. He pulled the sack from the boy's waist and turned it upside down.

A few clumps of grass fell out.

'Is that all you have? Where are the animals?'

It was only then that Abebe remembered the goats...

'Go and bring the animals back!' said his father. He threw his *shamma* over his shoulder and left the hut.

Abebe's mother fixed her gaze on him.

'You must do as your father says.'

Outside the hut, neighbours had congregated, already aware of the family's distress. The men had watched Bikila pass, drawing across their faces – to spare his dignity – the white scarves they wore twisted into turbans. When after a few minutes the boy emerged, they fell silent, studying him intensely.

Abebe was conscious only of the stares of the other boys, who proceeded to follow him silently through the village. Finally, one of them spoke, saying Abebe had better find the animals before nightfall, otherwise he would have to fight off the wolves and jackals!

He broke into a run as he reached the fields, leaving his friends behind. Abebe ran, trying to keep a steady pace, trying not to exhaust himself; he knew he would need all his reserves, but he knew too that he must run as fast as he could. He was spurred on by a stabbing in his side, a pain born of fear that he knew he would have to find the courage to surmount.

Abebe's mother returned to her work, pedalling slowly. But she couldn't concentrate. She looked up and saw her neighbours crowding at the entrance to the hut, peering in wonder. The nosy villagers wouldn't go away. She pedalled faster but she only succeeded in snapping the thread.

'Get away from here,' she yelled. 'If he says it's true, it's true!'

She snatched the curtain across the doorway and continued her weaving by the glow of the oil lamp.

Meanwhile, Abebe's father had gone to the centre of the village, where he found the elders sitting in the shelter of the broad tree in front of the church. He squatted down to confer with them and they all agreed that what he had done was right. Apart from the loom, the animals were all the family possessed. The milk from the goats was their only livelihood. Without them, they would have nothing to eat.

The priest stood aside outside the church, listening. Finally, he beckoned Bikila inside.

The church was the largest building in the village, a circular adobe hut with a conical roof topped by a *Maskal* cross. Hanging from the thatched rafters was a large iron bell. The priest followed Bikila. While the worried father knelt at the wooden pew, he untied the heavy rope that hung from the rafters and pulled it with all his weight, causing the bell to sway until it rang loud and deep.

The sound echoed across the highlands, growing faint until it found an echo: the reply of another bell in another church in another village, and another, tolling in the encroaching night.

The purple Rolls-Royce Silver Phantom climbed slowly, winding its way upwards from the plateau and through a mountain pass. The figure in the back remained bolt upright, looking neither right nor left. The emperor was returning from Tigray, where he had gone to see for himself the damage done by British air strikes, a bombardment he had requested to help put down the rebellion in the northern province.

More than ever, His Majesty was convinced of Ethiopia's need for modern aviation. Now that the war in Europe was over, the Allies were seeking to reinforce their positions in the Horn of Africa. The Americans wanted to take over the Italian radio transmitters. Perhaps they would supply planes? The Swedes had kindly offered to train pilots.

He was now able to cross the country swiftly on the roads the Italians had built during their five-year occupation. Goods too travelled more rapidly by lorry instead of donkey train, and the profits from the government ventures he had created to trade in coffee and hides were flowing, profits that excited jealousies...

Since his return from exile, he had been obliged to execute the Dejazmach of Gojam, whose treachery – encouraged, no doubt, by his popularity as a patriot leader – had led him to declare that he was unwilling to serve a monarch who had deserted his country! Treasonous words from someone Selassie himself had ennobled! The emperor was weighing the fate of others he had imprisoned for criticising the government's supposed favouritism. He could not allow sentiment to cloud his judgement. He had to remain firm. He couldn't show any sign of weakness. He remained parade-ground straight in the back of the limousine. Luckily, the Rolls-Royce absorbed all but the worst bumps from the shell craters on the road.

Reaching a pass in the mountain range, the purple Rolls-Royce rounded a sharp bend that led down into a lush green valley. In the distance a lake shone orange in the early morning light. A shepherd saw the imperial vehicle approach, headlamps glinting magically, and fell to his knees, pressing his forehead in the dust.

A cheer went up from the villagers when they saw first the scampering goats and then Abebe returning. Hearing them, the priest released the bell cord and came out. He raised his right hand, palm outwards, and gazed up at the heavens.

'It is the will of God!' he announced. 'On this day, Abebe looked upon the King of Kings, whose existence gives us light. Abebe has been blessed.'

Abebe walked through the village with his father at his side. From the little white huts, the remaining villagers, who had abandoned their chores, emerged to admire the fortunate boy.

Abebe had seen the emperor! Each week, during his sermon, the priest repeated the litany, enumerating the titles of His Imperial Majesty, Lion of Judah, *Negus Negasta*, the true and noble descendant of Menelik I, who was the son of King Solomon and the Queen of Sheba, and who brought the Ark of the Covenant, containing God's law, to Ethiopia! So it was written in the Book of Kings.

Abebe had seen him.

3

The clubhouse was a simple wooden pavilion painted ochre red, perched on a hill beside an oval running track. Standing on the steps outside, Niskanen inhaled deeply, drawing the clean, sweet air of the pine forest in through his nose for five seconds and then breathing out for twice as long.

Oxygen, he thought. That was the key!

He turned his attention to the athletes gathered around the starting blocks, studying their torsos as they limbered up. He observed the arching of their backs, the puffing of their chests and the clouds of their breath as they exhaled in the crisp, cold air. From a distance, he could gauge their respiratory forces, measure their lung capacities. He marched on to the field, the grass crunching under his boots, and his approach caused the athletes to tense in readiness.

'Right,' he said. 'Let's get to work. Fifteen hundred, OK?'

The men dropped to their positions in the starting blocks, one knee down, heads lowered and necks screwed tight in anticipation.

Niskanen fired his starting pistol into the air and the report echoed like ice cracking across the lakes. The runners streaked forwards and he glanced at his stopwatch. Six runners, 1,500 metres; anything under five minutes would be acceptable.

He watched them moving, willing them to get up on their toes instead of landing flat. He was looking for a good stride: upper body relaxed, breathing easy. With the selection approaching, they were striving to outdo each other. He was waiting to see who would break away, who would find the extra wind, the final burst of speed that could make all the difference, but they stayed tightly grouped till the finish. It was a good sign. They would push each other harder than he could ever push them.

When he came to them, they were still panting, flushed and elated from their run yet looking hungrily at him for affirmation. Niskanen made a point of congratulating them all but cautioned that there were still things they each had to work on. Now that they had learned to run, they had fallen into a trap: they had become self-conscious. They were running like runners, or what they had seen of runners. They were merely copying; none of them had any form, any personal gait, the mark of a true runner. And they were all running too stiffly.

'Remember what I told you: the torso must be upright. Running tall extends the legs through the full range of motion. But not stiff like this' – he stood parade-ground straight and pulled his shoulders back – 'I don't see the sergeant out here on the track!'

The teenage conscripts relaxed at his joke. Running for them was a welcome relief from the routine of national service. Niskanen knew how to play on this.

'A runner whose posture is too tight reduces his stride, wasting energy by running upwards rather than forwards,' he explained. 'When there is too much tension in the shoulders and arms, you don't run so fast. If the posture is relaxed, the stride will flow.'

Flow was important. It was part of the technique of running but also part of the grace. 'A good runner should be relaxed without slouching,' Niskanen stated. He flexed his shoulders, pausing for a moment for them to absorb what he had said before suggesting another heat. 'And remember, I want to see you running tall, shoulders loose. Three thousand metres this time, eh?'

As they ran, spreading out over the longer distance, he began to see the individual coaching they were each going to need. They had just started running seriously; they were still landing on their heels or simply landing flat and, because of this, their stride length and turnover were poor.

Winter night came quickly, cutting short their afternoon. The sky had turned ashen and snowflakes floated gently in the air. But it was only after they had completed another 2,000 metre run, when they were slowing from fatigue and couldn't stretch themselves any further, that he told the servicemen they had accomplished enough for the day.

Together, they walked back to the clubhouse in silence. Though he wasn't the one who had been doing the running, Niskanen shared their exhausted contentment, their physical satisfaction.

When they passed the reception desk inside, the secretary interrupted them.

'Onni,' she said loudly. 'There's a letter for you.'

She made a show of sorting through the small bundle of correspondence before handing it to him officiously. On the back of the envelope was a seal with two lions and a crown. He told the men to go on ahead of him to the sauna and opened the letter.

'Good news?' she enquired.

'Indeed,' he replied, placing the letter in his pocket. 'But I'm afraid it means you won't be seeing so much of me for a while,' he added.

'I didn't know it was Major Niskanen,' she said, looking admiringly at his shoulders, as though she had never noticed them before.

'There are a lot of things you don't know about me.'

He took the locker key from her and, with a wink, left her to puzzle while he headed downstairs to the sauna. He was glad to have piqued her curiosity, not about his military status – he knew that women liked rank – but because the rumour of his enigmatic disappearance would surely get back to his wife and perhaps that would make her call him at least.

In the changing room, Niskanen removed his heavy coat and then took off his army jersey. He folded it carefully so as not to pleat the chevrons on the upper arms and smoothed down the stars on the epaulettes. Then he took a towel from the pile and placed it around his shoulders, pulling on each end as he twisted his head. There was always a heaviness when it was about to snow.

Inside the wooden cabin, wreathed in steam, he could sense his pores opening as his heart beat faster and his blood pressure fell. He wondered whether it would be as hot in Ethiopia as it was in the sauna. At any rate, he knew there would be no possibility of stepping outside into the snow to cool off.

The servicemen came from the showers and joined him, and soon they were reliving the day's heats, the conversation moving as it always did from their own achievements to the absolute, Olympian summits. In that soothed state that came after a good day's practice, they listened to Niskanen describe again the styles of the great Finnish marathonians, staunch men like Nurmi who brought back gold medals for the trophy cases of their clubhouses. The Swedes liked to hear Coach Niskanen telling of the victories of these Scandinavian heroes, record-breakers who came from villages just like their own. He had been a small child when his parents had emigrated from Finland. The Swedes treated the poor Finns like country bumpkins and the Finnish distance runners – the Flying Finns, as they were called – were the only thing about Finland of which he could be proud. He had run too, of course, but mainly at club level. The national heats were very competitive – he liked to joke that the Swedes had finally caught up with the Finns. Now, at the age of thirty-six, with his muscles losing their once endless force, his competitive running days were over. When he ran now, it was just for pleasure, and to remind himself he could still do it.

After a while, the rising temperature caused a lull in their talk, a reverie interrupted by the hiss of steam as Niskanen ladled more water on the coals, announcing that he had some important news. He told them he would soon be leaving them. He was going to Africa to be an instructor there.

There was no reaction. The wood-panelled room was now thick with steam, isolating everyone. Niskanen couldn't see their expressions and the continuing silence made him uneasy.

'Don't worry,' he said, 'I'm not going to be eaten by cannibals!'

There was a little chuckle at his attempt at humour.

'Ethiopia is a Christian country! I hear it's very pleasant.'

Finally, one of them spoke.

'Sir,' he asked, 'does this mean you are going to be teaching Africans?'

'I expect so. Ethiopia is in Africa, after all.'

'Teaching them to run, sir?'

He liked the fact that they permitted themselves to speak

informally with him. He was nearly twice their age but he looked younger and he was still fit. Even though he ranked as their superior, he was like one of them, and they were fond of him the way you could only be of a coach. Unlike other teachers, sports instructors don't measure you against an intellectual ideal; they know your physical limits and they pit you against yourself. Niskanen had expected the conscripts to be perturbed – he would be abandoning them just as he had begun to show them their possibilities, after all – but he realised now there was something else. It hadn't occurred to him until then: what was the point of teaching Africans to run?

It was something they could barely imagine – though, of course, blacks must run. Everybody runs, Africans probably more than most. But real running, track and field? Everyone had seen the newsreels of Jesse Owens, a heavy, compact bundle of ebony muscle scoring four gold medals in Berlin in front of an irritated Chancellor Hitler. Owens broke the 100 metres record and won the 200 by a distance of 4 metres, but he was an American. It had been a year since the war ended, and the Americans had become almost like gods.

'Yes, teaching them to run, among other things. I'll be in charge of a general programme of fitness and training for His Majesty's Imperial Bodyguard.'

In fact, Niskanen had not given it any thought. When Count von Rosen suggested he apply, it had seemed like an opportunity to do something, to use his skills. He knew how to impose a training schedule, how to keep discipline; he was sure he could get them organised. And it went without saying that he would be able to raise their standards, did it not? Everyone knew the count had been achieving great things in the Horn of Africa and Niskanen was honoured that the renowned aviator had invited him to participate.

'Anyway,' he added, 'sport is universal, is it not?'

There were nods of polite agreement. Physical competition was as natural as breathing, he believed.

'But if that is so,' said one of the young Swedes, 'why are there no African sportsmen?'

4

The emperor's motorcade advanced slowly to avoid accidents; people coming from the countryside to the Mercato were unused to traffic and sometimes wandered in front of the cars. Also, they had to allow the few other drivers on the road enough time to pull over and get out of their vehicles so as to be able to bow as the emperor passed, and for the trains of pack animals to shuffle by.

The royal procession finally turned into Churchill Avenue. During the Italian occupation, the emperor had been given refuge by the royal family of Great Britain. Afterwards, His Majesty renamed the central avenue after the British prime minister. He had passed the war in the city of Bath, and the royal spa town surrounded by green hills reminded him of Addis. It was the emperor's wish that the Ethiopian capital should have a similar Elysian aspect. But this meant development, an end to backwardness; and therefore, on his triumphant return, His Majesty had allowed the British to run the Commercial School.

At the top of Churchill Avenue, near the former piazza – which he had also renamed, but after French president de Gaulle – was St George's cathedral. The great cathedral had been built to commemorate the rout of the first Italian invasion at Adwa in 1896 by Emperor Menelik, the first time an imperialist army had been repulsed from Africa. No longer merely a spear-carrying warrior in Europe's eyes, Menelik shed his pelts and adorned himself instead with imperialist pomp. It was a taste Selassie had inherited, and it had been sharpened and polished by his French Jesuit tutors, who showed him how to put such prestige to use.

They turned right and approached the Guennet Lal Palace. There were hardly any cars now, and cows and goats grazed on the grassy banks to each side. Their owners, nomads with their tents, should not have been there, but there was nothing the police could do. Along the pavement women walked by, some with their faces covered, most carrying baskets on their heads. Men passed on heavily laden bicycles, pedalling slowly.

Outside the stone walls of the palace grounds, flanked by impassive guardsmen, a crowd of men had gathered. There were fifty or more and, as they did every day, they were standing on the grass verges under the trees, debating earnestly. Some wore old, dirty *shammas*, while others had washed and pressed their white robes. The shabbier men clutched sheaves of papers in their hands; the better dressed carried briefcases or folders tied with ribbon. As the royal procession neared, the iron gates swung open, galvanising the swarm; the men jockeyed for positions close to the entrance, and soon enough more guardsmen emerged from the palace to shove them aside, followed by an official in a suit.

The motorbikes drew up, with, behind them, the purple Rolls-Royce, now covered in dust, and the supplicants ceased to shove and shout and instead fell to their knees, bowing low with their foreheads to the ground. They twisted their necks in discomfort as, with their faces in the dust, they simultaneously tried to catch a glimpse of the emperor. The haughty profile – their only hope of justice – was visible for just an instant as the Rolls-Royce glided through the gates and up the driveway. The supplicants dared to lift their heads only after the vehicle had passed. They sprang to their feet waving their bundles of papers and folders as the guardsmen held them back. From behind the guardsmen's shoulders, the official in the suit collected some of the papers from the clamouring men, choosing with indifference from those who happened to be nearest to him, before retreating inside the palace.

The supplicants pressed their faces to the iron gates, watching the Rolls-Royce slip silently away. Many of them had waited weeks for that moment, sleeping outside the palace, and now they didn't know when they would have another chance to press their cases.

They saw the official follow the vehicle, squaring the papers he had gathered into a neat pile and seeming to take an interest in one or two of the plaints.

Inside the grounds, a troop of bodyguards rushed forward, hastily presenting arms. Down the steps of the palace another group of men emerged, dignitaries in Western-style suits. There were almost as many of these as there were supplicants outside the gates. They hurriedly took position in three descending rows, fussing with their ties and the buttons of their jackets. The dignitaries were more orderly but they still jostled like the supplicants beyond the gates, struggling for prominent and thus advantageous positions. The welcoming committee was in place just as the Rolls-Royce came to a halt at the foot of the steps.

The figure in the back remained sitting stiffly, waiting for the last of the ministers and vice-ministers to smooth their jackets and tighten their ties. A bodyguard rushed to open the door of the vehicle and froze with one hand on the handle and the other fixed in a salute. His Imperial Majesty nodded slightly, and the guardsman pulled the door open with relief.

Preceded by his plumed hat, the emperor descended from the car. A short man with a stiff bearing, he tugged at his tunic and straightened his sword before advancing between the two rows of guardsmen and up the palace steps.

The palace had been built less than two decades before. With his coronation imminent, the future Emperor Haile Selassie had decided he was unsatisfied with the old palace, constructed of iron and timber by Menelik II. He desired a residence that would reflect his glory, made of stone, solid and imposing but modern in style; thus the broken pediments over the entrances were surmounted by granite lions and gas lamps. The palace was finally completed in time for the visit of the Swedish crown prince in 1934, a visit Mussolini had tried to disrupt with his illegal and belligerent incursions.

Ethiopia was in those years a forward redoubt against Catholic fascism. His Majesty had stood in the League of Nations and demanded justice, but he was not the one who was appeased. The only help came from the missions of the Swedes; the Lutherans shared with the Copts a dislike of Rome that made them true allies, while the British and the French, who pretended to be concerned, were really interested only in outmanoeuvring each other. And now it was the Russians and the Americans who came offering favours. Selassie accepted them all equally, the way a monarch should receive tribute.

The emperor kept his gaze fixed ahead of him, and did not appear to notice the dignitaries fidgeting near by; nor did he see, to the right and the left, in front and behind, near and far, in the doorways and windows of the palace, on the paths, in the grounds – everywhere in fact – a multitude of lackeys, kitchen staff, servants, gardeners, cleaners and policemen pushing their faces forth to be noticed too.

Watching His Majesty ascend the steps, the crowd of supplicants, their faces still pressed against the iron gates, slumped in dejection. When the emperor disappeared inside, they turned away and immediately some of them began to argue, excited to have been, however briefly, in the presence of the King of Kings, of supreme judgement. The exchanges grew heated and scuffling broke out, soon developing into a fight between two of the men. Other supplicants managed to subdue the two opponents, but when they tried to separate them they found it was impossible to pull the men apart. The two men were chained together at the ankles. They had been dragging their iron shackles around for several years, ever since they had been joined to one another by a regional court until their case could be heard.

At the top of the steps, waiting in the shade inside the palace, was a young dignitary with a neatly trimmed moustache. Aklilou had the bronze complexion and Roman nose of the privileged Amhars who comprised most of the government staff. He stiffened and then bowed low as the emperor passed. But His Majesty acknowledged no one except Kassa, the chief of the Rasses, who observed Aklilou with an eagle stare.

Ras Kassa was a tall, bearded aristocrat who wore a white linen *shamma* embroidered in gold, and over it a black cloak fastened with gold clasps in the shape of lions' heads. The emperor paused before him, and the Ras bowed deeply, his left leg stretched out straight behind him, his shoulder bent forward until it touched his right knee, his forehead inclined towards the heavily carpeted floor. Behind him stood twelve other Rasses, members of the Crown Council, all wearing embroidered white *shammas*. They each bowed in turn, the crest of a rolling wave of fealty that extended through his provincial governors, the Rasses, to all the emperor's subjects in all the villages of the kingdom.

Without a word, the emperor advanced towards the large doors leading to the interior of the palace. Just as he approached, the doors parted as if by divine hand, opened from behind by servants listening for the imperial footfalls. Beyond was a second pair of doors, and these too swung back in the royal path, and then a third pair of doors opened. His Majesty finally vanished inside the Hall of Audience, and the three pairs of doors closed, one after the other.

Bowing to him, the official presented Aklilou with the briefs he had taken from the supplicants, neatly gathered in a folder. As Vice-Minister of the Pen, it would in due course be Aklilou's job to present certain cases to His Highness, with a suggestion for the course of action to be taken.

Night fell, the stars sparkling and the air becoming thin with the cold but sweet with the smell of eucalyptus. Inside the palace, the electric lights went off with a buzz. In the gardens, straining against their chains, the imperial lions growled. Outside, a guard played a torch over the supplicants beyond the railings. The chained pair slept side by side in the darkness, waiting for justice.

5

Abebe was sorting *teff*, carefully separating the grains from the chaff so as not to lose even one, and he didn't notice the sound at first. From outside the hut, far off in the distance, came a rhythmic slapping. He stopped working and listened. The sound grew louder, coming nearer – *thud, thud* – until it broke stride, becoming a shuffle, and then suddenly stopping dead.

There was a tense silence. Abebe moved cautiously to the doorway and peered out under the cloth. He saw a row of bare feet with staffs and rifle butts between them. Lifting his gaze, he saw that the feet and the guns belonged to soldiers standing in line in their tunics with brightly polished buttons. Despite the dust, they were resplendent in their uniforms; they were more than human, like strange birds in their plumed hats, their chests puffed out proudly, their eyes fixed on a distant prey. Beyond them, the villagers were huddling together.

The sergeant nodded to a soldier carrying a drum and the soldier played a roll. The noise frightened the villagers and sent them scurrying backwards. Fascinated, Abebe crept out of the hut and noticed that, while most of the villagers had drawn back, his father and some of the other men had remained where they were. Like the soldiers, they were standing stiffly to attention.

Bikila Demssie had been a soldier. Abebe was a small boy when his father had answered the great war drum that thundered from the palace, more than a hundred miles away. He had fought valiantly with the army at Dese but they had been forced to retreat as the Italians advanced from the north through Tigray, fleeing clouds of poison gas and Oromo brigands taking shots at them with Italian rifles. After the emperor left to go into exile, Bikila continued to fight the occupiers. He had been cunning, as His Majesty had commanded. A farmer by day, Abebe's father ceased wearing white and going to Mass, and became by night one of the *Arbenyotch*. Even though the gas had weakened him and he had not been able to do much to help the resistance, his father was proud to have served the emperor, to have fought for their country and for their religion, without which, he said, they would be like the people of Somalia and Eritrea – mere serfs.

Abebe saw his father standing expectantly before the soldiers as though awaiting an order, and he feared that a new war had begun, and that his father would have to leave them again. If that was the case, he decided, he would go to fight in his father's stead.

Then the sergeant unfurled a document and began to speak.

'In the name of His Imperial Highness, Haile Selassie I, Lion of Judah, *Negus Negasta*, the Minister of the Purse has been authorised to collect a new tax.'

There was consternation among the villagers. A disrespectful grumble went around and the sergeant paused, waiting for quiet.

'Families with less than five oxen must contribute one sack of grain. All families with more than five oxen are to contribute two sacks of grain.'

The village men standing to attention looked at one another in confusion.

'Families with more than five oxen last year that find they have fewer animals this year will nonetheless have to pay two sacks of grain.'

The sergeant handed the paper he was reading from to the headman, who scrutinised the writing and verified the imperial seal. He nodded gravely, confirming to the other villagers that it was true.

Abebe's father was still standing to attention.

'The grain is to be delivered immediately,' added the sergeant.

His words prompted an outburst from the headman.

'But how can we pay this new *asrat*? The harvest has been poor and we barely have enough for our families!'

The sergeant apparently had no intention of arguing with the headman. He said they had been to a dozen villages that day and in each the reaction had been the same. What did the sergeant care? He hadn't joined the army to starve. As long as there were supplies in the garrison, that was all that mattered. 'If we have to return to collect the levy,' he reminded the headman, 'there will be penalties.'

The sergeant stepped back and saluted the headman, signalling that the exchange was over. Then he turned and saluted the men of the village, a gesture of respect towards Abebe's father and the others which caused the adolescent boy's chest to swell. His father returned the salute, and to Abebe it was as if between military men there was a bond that transcended the liens of family and village. They, after all, had shared the honour of serving the emperor, whose blood was the blood of King Solomon, whose glory was the glory of Ethiopia.

The sergeant barked an order at his men, who turned in a single file and marched from the village square. They lifted their knees high as they marched, prancing like horses and stamping on the ground, raising clouds of dust with their bare feet.

For months now, the village had been full of the dust that swirled and settled, covering everything in a pale red veil. It blew into the huts, though the winds that raised it brought only sporadic rain. This rain turned the dust to mud and then the sun baked the mud hard, so that when the rain fell again, it washed over the dry ground, vanishing in a trickle in the river beds. With so little rain the countryside had turned barren, the patches of grass yellowing like scabs and contracting, leaving nothing but pale, cracked earth. Because they had no grass to eat, the oxen were growing weak. Already, they were so feeble they could hardly draw the ploughs any more, and soon they would begin to fall sick and die. And without the oxen, the villagers wouldn't be able to plant enough seed in readiness for the next growing season, when the rains would surely fall in abundance.

'His Highness knows what is right,' said Abebe's father. 'There must be reasons that we cannot understand.'

The headman and the other villagers nodded, but they were wondering how they would be able to cope. How were they going to be able to feed their families and the animals and pay the *asrat*? The sergeant had said there would be penalties. This could mean anything, the headman warned, for punishments and exactions were a matter of local justice, entirely at the whim of the Dejazmach.

Abebe's father silenced them, saying that they should put their faith in the emperor. All this talk was disloyal, he declared. At that instant, there was a loud growl, what sounded like a distant cloudburst; but when the villagers looked up, the skies were still clear overhead. No one knew what to make of this omen, but they hoped it meant that the strong September rains would soon come. While they pondered their burdens, the headman declared that Bikila Demssie was right. They must have faith in God and in H.I.M., the Elect of God.

Abebe followed his father back through the village. He saw that, despite his show of fortitude before the villagers, his father was pale and thin and walked with difficulty.

The village had changed. The mud walls of the huts were falling away, as though no one had the courage or the strength to repair them. The straw on the rooftops was drying out, and on some of the huts it had half blown away. There were few animals to be seen, and the villagers remained inside, conserving their strength and waiting for rain. The fences that once rimmed each garden had fallen into disrepair. Nobody feared any more that their vegetables would be trampled or eaten by animals since there was nothing much left to eat, and the few chickens and goats that remained were watched over jealously night and day.

Abebe was bursting to tell his mother about seeing the soldiers but he was forced to listen respectfully as his father told her the news of the tithes they would have to pay. He saw his mother's features, already pale and hollow cheeked, crease with dismay.

Once they were back inside the hut, however, she became angry.

'Why must we be treated like this?' she moaned. She complained that the emperor didn't understand their woes. And if he did, as Abebe's father promised, then it must be that His Majesty simply didn't care about them. Why had he summoned the old governor, who had fought so loyally against the occupiers, to Addis and then thrown him in jail? What had been his crime? she asked.

Bikila Demssie lowered his face. Abebe's father had fought alongside the man and knew he was a patriot.

And if His Majesty knew of their difficulties, why did he appoint a new Dejazmach, she went on, a man from Addis who was greedy and ambitious? 'He has no sooner settled in the post than he goes about enriching himself as quickly as he can,' said Abebe's mother. 'I suppose he is afraid that he too will be thrown in jail!' she added.

'You are speaking words of treason, Widnesh,' said Abebe's father. 'I will not hear them.'

Abebe's mother shook her head and sighed. Luckily, as a former *Arbenyotch*, Bikila Demssie had certain privileges. They would be exempted from paying part of the new tax. But they were still in difficulty. It was the second year running that the rains had failed.

'Very well,' she said to her husband. 'But who will help us? We have to start planting now, and you are not strong enough, my husband.' If the rains were coming, they would have to plant quickly. But Bikila was too weak to hold the plough for the long days of sowing.

She looked at Abebe.

'Abebe will have to do the work in the field,' she decided.

Abebe nodded. He had finished his *Qes* schooling, and like any thirteen-year-old boy who could recite the names of the kings from the *Kebra Negast* and write his own name and count to ten, he would have to start work. Except that Abebe did not want to work in the fields steering the plough or guarding sheep.

'Abba, Amma, I will do as you ask,' he announced, 'but when the field is sown and the grain is growing, I am going to Addis to become a soldier!'

His father took a deep breath. He looked at his son sternly and then beamed with satisfaction. 'Abebe will be an Imperial Bodyguard!' he declared. 'He will stand before the Guennet Lal Palace and defend the *Negus Negasta*!'

His mother scoffed. 'We'll see,' she said.

'He will wear a uniform instead of a *shamma*, sleep in a brick house and always have enough food to eat!'

'First,' she said, 'he must finish his chores.'

Abebe returned to the task of sorting the *teff*.

He would prove to them that he could be as brave as his father. He would fight in wars! He would win honours! He would come back to the village bent double with the riches bestowed on him by His Majesty!

6

Niskanen entered his apartment and, hanging his coat on the empty rail, he saw suddenly how bare it was, just a chair, a pine table and a bed. He had few belongings; all the things that clutter a home belonged to his wife, and when she left they vanished with her, leaving him in his frugal, practical world devoid of decoration apart from, on the mantelpiece, his cups and trophies and a framed photograph lying face down.

Walking home from the club, he had passed the little church where the wedding had been. He would have avoided doing so normally, but the snow was coming down heavily and he wondered how it would be if he went inside. He was testing himself, he knew, defying himself to feel any more self-pity. Kneeling at the pew in the candlelit silence, however, he became unexpectedly elated. He had asked as usual for pardon, and prayed for release from the feelings of unworthiness that had haunted him since his wife had gone; but this time he also prayed gratefully for the strength to accomplish the mission he had been given, to be able to help and, doing so, be released.

He took the letter from his pocket and opened it again. It was from General Abaye Abebe, commander-in-chief of the Imperial Bodyguard, on behalf of His Imperial Highness Haile Selassie I, notifying him of his successful application for the post of sports officer at the Cadet School of the Imperial Bodyguard. He had used the club's address, telling himself he spent most of his time there anyway, although the truth was he had wanted to give a good impression – and he had signed himself major, his rank in the Red

Cross. It had been a rapid promotion, which in truth he had more or less awarded to himself, but the Soviet Army had invaded in the east of Finland and they needed to get organised quickly. If he had deceived the Ethiopians, it was too late to worry about it now. What mattered was that he was going to be teaching African soldiers to keep fit. In the Red Cross, you heard a lot about disease in Africa and fitness was essential to proper health. There would be plenty to keep him occupied and that was a prospect he relished.

Niskanen had been expecting the letter. He had been informed that the post was vacant by Count von Rosen, and it flattered him to think that he might have put a word in for him; apparently, Count von Rosen had a great deal of influence with Ethiopia's emperor. After hearing from missionaries about the plight of the Ethiopians during the Italian occupation, the count had placed his legendary Heinkel at the disposition of the Red Cross there, undertaking many dangerous mercy flights. Niskanen had become acquainted with the great Finnish aviator during the war, and recently, at a fund-raising dinner, Count von Rosen had encouraged him to apply. The Ethiopians were a polite and civilised lot, he said, and Ethiopia was a very fine country. Niskanen had been surprised to hear the count enthuse about how fresh and beautiful it was. He imagined it to be hot and dangerous, a desert or a jungle, anything but a paradise, as the count described it, 'like the Garden of Eden'. And Niskanen had felt like a schoolboy to hear him tell of the lands he saw from his cockpit: the hills carpeted emerald green and strewn in October with fragrant yellow daisies called *Maskal* flowers, the red-brown torrents rushing down from the mountains in spring, the pretty tapestry of lakes and churches.

With the war ended in Europe, the count had returned to set up the Ethiopian Aviation Academy and, as Niskanen understood it, the sports facilities were located at the aerodrome. He was pleased that he would be around fly-boys again. Perhaps even more than a distance runner, he would have liked to have been a pilot, but his parents were too modest to aspire to such things. Aviation was reserved for bluebloods like the count, and Niskanen admired him greatly. Count von Rosen was a national hero for the Finns because of his efforts on behalf of his people during the war. When Stalin's army invaded Finland in 1939, Niskanen had become involved with the Red Cross in Sweden to help others in the same situation as the Ethiopians, people driven from their homes by war, and he was proud to have been able to help his countrymen during that difficult time.

When poor Finland eventually sided with Germany against the Soviet Union, nobody said anything – they accepted what was called in Finland the 'separate war' against the Bolsheviks; in neutral Sweden too, many people were more afraid of Bolshevism than they were of National Socialism. Now, with the war ended, everyone knew what the Nazis had done, how they had sought to exterminate peoples they held to be inferior. The Finns had simply been trying to save their country, but now they were tarred with the same brush.

Niskanen was relieved to be going somewhere new, where none of this mattered, and he began to think of packing his belongings. He had been meaning to put away the photograph for some time. It showed him arm in arm with some friends after a cross-country heat. They were younger than him, just boys, sturdy, vigorous and stripped to the waist, and he had been running with them. They knew all about the Flying Finns and they were a little bit in awe of the Red Cross major. Afterwards, one of them had sent him the photograph, but it was awkward when people asked who they were and he had to say they were German soldiers stationed in Finland, taking a break before returning to the front.

The next day, Niskanen went to the public library and opened the big Bonniers atlas. The map showed a range of mountains running north–south down the Horn of Africa, bordered by Egypt and Sudan to the north and Kenya and Somaliland to the south. This was Ethiopia. Some of the country's borders – drawn, he assumed, by politicians – ran in perfectly straight lines. Ignoring all frontiers, the Blue Nile laced around the mountains towards its sister from its source in Ethiopia's Lake Tana; and there was a single railway line that ran eastwards from the capital, Addis Ababa, to the port of Djibouti on the Gulf of Aden. Across the Red Sea from there lay Saudi Arabia and Yemen. These were the principal features. The name Ethiopia came from Greek, and meant 'burnt faces'. The history of the country, even the dry, potted version in the atlas, was a saga of blood and miracles that read like a missing chapter of the Old Testament. According to the Ethiopian Book of Kings, Menelik I, the son of King Solomon and the Queen of Sheba, brought the Ark of the Covenant to Ethiopia and founded the royal dynasty. Once a year, the Ark is carried from the crypt of the Church of St Mariam of Zion at Axum, the ancient capital, and paraded before the multitudes. No one may see the Ark, however, since it is carried under a heavy cloth. Nevertheless, possession of it is held to be proof that the Ethiopians are the chosen people.

The Axumites converted to Christianity in the third century, and it surprised Niskanen to learn that this was not the work of missionaries. Two Christian sailors from Syria were shipwrecked on the coast of the Red Sea and enslaved in the royal court, where they became valued advisers to Prince Ezanas and ultimately convinced him to accept their faith. Though in time they came to be surrounded by Islamic peoples, the Ethiopians remained devout believers in Christ. Portuguese Jesuits in the fifteenth century tried to convert them to Catholicism, but complained that the Abyssinians, as they were known to the West – derived from the Arabic word for 'mixed' that referred to the many ethnic groups – were stubbornly attached to their church.

It mystified him, however, to read that the Ethiopian Orthodox Church is monophysite, its priests maintaining that Christ had but one nature, at once human and divine.

He tried to grasp this, pondering the implications. As a Protestant, he believed God dwelled in his heart; He could read what troubled his conscience, while he, Niskanen, remained human; as such he was fallen, fallible. For the Copts, he surmised, it was different. There was no need to ask forgiveness from God; if we were both human and divine, we might pardon ourselves. It seemed like a state of grace and, the more he thought about it, a possibility that he came to envy.

7

Abebe was crouching alone under the vast tree on the empty plateau. He had his knees drawn up and his head buried between them; the old tree was withered and dry, but still gave some shade. He thought he sensed someone pass like a ghost with his arm held high but when he lifted his head there was no one. Fear seized Abebe. The Oromo knew that if the runner passed, death would come: this was the message he carried in the bracelet on his wrist. At that instant, Abebe realised he was clutching something in his hand. When he opened his palm he saw it was a brass button that glinted in the sun.

The drought had gone on for more than a year, and in the second year hunger and death had stalked the village... Finally, the rains had returned, but only for a season.

Near the tree, in a cleft between two hills, a trickle of water seeped from the ground, but you had to wait the whole day for enough to fill a gourd. You had to shade the source from the heat, too, because the water evaporated as fast as it emerged, and you had to resist the urge to drink it right away, otherwise there wouldn't be enough to quench your thirst. But if you persisted, if you waited, you would have a cup of water, and you might survive.

His father had asked the priest to write to the royal palace and, a year later, they had received a reply saying that Abebe, son of His Majesty's loyal subject Bikila Demssie, should present himself to the sergeant at arms at the imperial barracks, where his induction would be considered. The letter conferred a great honour on Abebe and the village. God be thanked, the harvests had improved; his father had recovered his strength and they had at last been able to store enough *teff*. It was decided then that Abebe should leave.

He had lost count of the days since he had departed from the village carrying his belongings tied in a cloth on a pole. He walked all day long and slept by night under the cold stars. When at last he came to the road, it was deserted and there was no one to ask the way. Luckily he knew where the animals drank from the ground and he had waited there, growing weaker each day.

An old man had come to the village once, a wanderer who had no home. It was impossible to guess how old he was; he was bald and what was left of his hair was thick and grey and flew wildly from the sides of his head. Despite his journeying, the man's *shamma* was crisp and fresh smelling when he arrived in the village, and his appearance pleased the women, who whispered among themselves and spent a long time powdering their faces and decorating their hair. The old man had a kind face and a full-lipped smile, as though he had acquired secrets in his wandering. He carried with him a wooden instrument, a harp as tall as he was that he called a *beguena*. He said the harp had once belonged to King David, and that it had been entrusted to him. The old man went from village to village with his *beguena* and, once night had fallen, after he had been given food and gifts, he sat under the great tree with the instrument on his knee and sang. He sang in a quiet voice, hardly audible, like the whispering spirit of an ancestor, as, with his eyes closed, his finger-tips caressed the harp. Though he barely seemed to touch them, the strings buzzed and resonated along with his words.

He sang about Mariam, mother of Christ; about a royal hunting party that failed to find any game; about Death, who comes for us all; and about a hermit who chose to live far from everyone so as to be able to return unnoticed one day to the earth. In one song, he told of faraway countries called Africa, Britain and Israel, celebrating their greatness.

Afterwards, Abebe found out that the eerie drone of the instrument came from the strings made of sheep's entrails, and that Africa was where they all lived.

He hoped he might meet the old man again, so he could ask him the way to Addis.

***

Finally a donkey cart came by piled high with straw and the driver asked him where he was going. Abebe replied that he was going to Addis to join the Imperial Bodyguard and the man laughed and told him to climb on the back of the cart.

They travelled all day, and just before the sun set the man with the cart left him at the edge of the town and Abebe walked on, not knowing whether it was Addis or not, amazed at the crowds of people. He had never seen so many people – though they seemed not to notice him. They jostled him without turning or saying a word, as though he was invisible to them, was insignificant, as though he didn't even exist.

Abebe staggered through the town, too amazed to remember how exhausted he was. He had never seen so many people before, so busy, so excited, so full of energy, but it was an agitation that came of desperation. He could feel the violence chafing all around him. It seemed that if they didn't accomplish their business that day, these people would not have another chance. It wasn't like this in the village, where each task took the time it required and there was time enough for everything. Finally, he asked an old man whether they were in Addis and at first he couldn't make himself understood. But eventually the old man laughed and said it was not Addis, it was called Axum.

He walked until he came to the marketplace, where he was bewildered by the stalls piled high with things he had never seen. As well as blankets, *shammas*, pots and pans, ploughs and tools, there was glassware and copper jewellery and mechanical contraptions the uses of which he couldn't guess. Men sat at sewing machines or hammered at bicycle frames and wrenched at umbrellas with their tools, shouting as they worked. He had only ever seen one car before, the Rolls-Royce that belonged to the emperor. Now he saw several. But this was not what excited Abebe. What astonished him was that, in the marketplace, there was food in abundance. There were merchants sitting on sacks of grain and women selling bananas and eggs. There were hens in cages and goats tied to posts. Amid so much wonder he had forgotten his pangs of hunger. Now his mouth began to water. He had eaten only a few grains in the past few days and he was suddenly weak and dizzy.

In the middle of the market filled with more food than he had ever imagined, he halted, staring up at a tall stone obelisk covered in strange inscriptions. The monument, taller than any house or church he had ever seen, rose like a giant phallus, rounded at the head. He tried to imagine what its purpose might be. Though he couldn't read the old language, he guessed the inscriptions told of bravery and conquest. So tall and imposing was it that he forgot about the abundant food for a moment.

As he stared, he felt someone shoving him. Some men grabbed him, pinning his arms back behind him and pushing him into the centre of a space formed by the crowd that had fallen back, forming a circular wall of glaring faces.

He was surrounded. There was a lot of shouting and Abebe tried to struggle free but found he was being held tight. Then he saw the youth waving his arms wildly. The youth was glassy eyed; he trembled, foaming at the mouth. Some men grabbed the youth and forced him to drink from a gourd, whispering something in his ear as he gulped. As soon as he swallowed, the youth wrenched himself away and began spinning insanely and waving his arms. He spiralled around the gathering, the spectators reeling back as he passed, trying to get away but at the same time transfixed.

Finally, he came to a halt in front of Abebe.

Abebe could see that, despite his delirium, the youth had noticed that he was a stranger. He sensed him calculating for just an instant. Then the youth began to dance even more wildly, in front of Abebe this time.

It was a signal. A man approached Abebe carrying a machete loosely at his side.

'Thief! Thief!' the onlookers cried.

Abebe froze.

Suddenly, the youth began shaking and spluttering again. He spun once more, turning around and around as the people gasped, until he halted in front of a middle-aged man.

A look of terror overcame the man. He tried to back into the crowd, but he found that the onlookers had spread out, distancing themselves from him. Whichever way he turned, the crowd shrank away, leaving him exposed. He tried to make a run for it, but now the crowd wouldn't let the man get away. They seemed to be relishing his terror.

'Thief!' they shouted. 'Thief! That's him! He's the one!'

As he tried to push his way out of the circle, the man fell, or perhaps someone tripped him. Abebe saw him try to curl himself into a ball, wailing. The man with the machete rushed up and hacked at his shoulder. Blood showered the onlookers. He held the man's arm and hacked until he had cut through the bone, then he threw the severed arm into the bushes. Instantly, dogs darted for it.

The men who had been holding Abebe released him, but he was too shocked to try to hide. He watched, hypnotised with horror as the shouts of accusation subsided. There were looks of disgust but also satisfaction and even glee on the faces of the savage crowd. The youth who had denounced the thief was shaking and whimpering.

Then Abebe heard a buzzing far off in the sky which became a rumble louder than he had ever heard before, louder than the emperor's Rolls-Royce. He thought it was the roar of an angry God coming to punish the townspeople for the arbitrary vengeance they had just exacted. The noise grew louder until it boomed like thunder, drowning out the screams and the commotion of the marketplace. Finally, Abebe could hear nothing else but the booming sky and, without thinking, he dived to the ground as the great silver aircraft flew over.

8

They had taken off from Cairo and followed the Nile as it slithered in the heat like a green snake across the desert sands, traversing the empty Sudan until the terrain rose steeply and they flew over jagged escarpments to reach the high plateau. This was the fortress kingdom Niskanen had read about, guarded by fierce peaks. Beyond it, gently sloping valleys passed beneath them; streams rushed over cliffs and spilled into silver lakes. In the middle of nowhere, he saw an obelisk ten storeys high, as tall as the monuments of the pharaohs he had seen in the Valley of the Kings during the stopover in Egypt. It seemed that in every green dale there was a huddle of white huts clustered around a little church topped by an equilateral cross, like the cross of St John. For the knights of the Crusades, Abyssinia was the mythical realm of Prester John, reputedly a prosperous, devout Christian kingdom strategically situated to help them outflank Muslim Arabia.

The aeroplane descended gently over the lush, wooded hillsides until the capital came into view, a sprawl of tin-walled, straw-roofed hamlets and, here and there, empty roundabouts alongside defiantly modern towers. The brand-new Air Ethiopia Douglas Corporation airliner landed smoothly; they taxied to a halt and the Swedish pilot cut the engines. Niskanen watched the propellers spinning slowly to a halt with a sense that time too had slipped out of gear and was coming to a stop.

The passengers disembarking down the steps and on to the cracked concrete were a mix of Africans, Egyptians, Indians and Europeans – mostly British and Swedish: nurses on their way to tours of duty with Dr Norup at the Haile Selassie I Hospital and two young priests, members of the Swedish Evangelical Mission. Niskanen had fallen in with one of the Scandinavians, a flying instructor recruited by Count von Rosen for the Imperial Ethiopian Air Force. They had stopped off in Cairo to visit the pyramids in the company of two of the nurses and now, inside the small terminal, Niskanen was surprised to be surrounded by the same placid, smiling faces he had seen on the bas-reliefs in the Valley of the Kings: the Ethiopians were fine featured, with long, thin noses and untroubled expressions, as though possessed of a secret that lent them a serene, haughty distance.

They were met by a junior officer in a crisp new air force uniform. He was about Niskanen's age and he clicked his heels as he saluted them, a sign Niskanen would come to recognise of a spell at a foreign military academy. The junior officer was accompanied by another Ethiopian holding a card with their names shakily written but correctly spelled. The officer introduced himself as Lieutenant Mengistu Neway and invited them to follow. Without halting, he led them past the customs officers busily questioning the Syrian businessmen arriving with empty suitcases. 'They're looking for cash,' said Niskanen's compatriot. 'They know they have money because they're coming to trade. So they'll have to pay.' Outside the terminal, a large American station wagon waited at the kerb. The driver took Niskanen's baggage and loaded it while another Ethiopian opened a black parasol and held it over them. The sun was hot but the air was cool, a welcome surprise after the humid furnace of Cairo.

Lieutenant Neway indicated for them to sit in the back while he got in the front.

'Have you ever been to Africa before, Major?' he asked as the driver pulled out. He was observing Niskanen in the rear-view mirror.

'This is my first visit.'

'I'm afraid you may find it something of a shock.'

'Why is that?'

'People come here with certain expectations, but they can't imagine what it's really like. The distance that separates us is much greater than you think.'

The Swedish instructor spoke up. 'I'm sure that, in time, you'll reach our standards.'

In the mirror, Niskanen saw the lieutenant smiling to himself. 'What do you think, Major?' he asked.

'With time, everything is possible, I suppose.'

The lieutenant nodded. 'Quite,' he said.

Niskanen watched the people at the roadside walking slowly by with their heavy bundles. It was as though the car were rushing past a tableau from a far-off, distant age. The Ethiopians with their white robes and scarves wound like turbans around their heads reminded him of illustrations in the Bible he had as a child. In the fields, men with whips drove oxen that pulled wooden ploughs. As they approached the city, ever increasing hordes blocked the advance of the vehicle, as if they had no idea it was there. Women advanced at a regal gait, balancing great bundles on their heads. Swarming bicycles had to give way to goats being driven, he guessed, to market. Some of the people, it seemed, had given up hope of ever reaching this market and had simply set up their stalls at the roadside. As the car slowed, Niskanen could see their wares spread out on the ground by the side of the road: torn books, dented teapots, rusty pans, scraps of twisted metal, bent spoons, soap and matches. Haggling everywhere was a teeming population, hot, weary and dust-covered.

'Where do they all come from?' Niskanen wondered aloud.

'Where? From the villages, from all around. I don't know. They have always been there,' said the lieutenant.

The car had been advancing gradually because of the animals and the crowds and soon came to a dead stop, unable to make any more headway through the throng. Niskanen became increasingly uneasy at the stares from all the dark faces. The older ones remained aloof, glancing surreptitiously at the occupants of the car as they pretended to be going about their business, while the younger ones pressed their noses against the glass, staring with frank curiosity.

'I'm afraid it is you who are the shock to them,' said Lieutenant Neway. His saturnine features grinned at this reversal of the colonialist order. 'They don't know what to make of you. They know you are not a Turk, or a Muslim. You are not Syrian or Armenian or Greek, not a merchant. They think perhaps you are a "red", an Englishman, with your pink skin and hair the colour of straw. Most of them have probably never seen a blond European before.'

Niskanen had not anticipated that, in Africa, he would be the object of curiosity. In time, he would get used to being stared at endlessly, to being alien, mysterious and frightening.

The driver got out of the car and with his stick started thrashing angrily at the crowd. Niskanen was disconcerted as much by the docility of the people cowering at the soldier's baton as by the arrogance of the soldier, who yelled contemptuously. They drew back, allowing the car to pass.

'Don't be surprised,' said the lieutenant. 'I told you things are not as simple as you think.' He looked at the passengers coldly. 'Our standards are not the same as yours. Perhaps one day they will be...' He paused, looking at the instructor. 'In the meantime, we could be stuck here for ever!'

Soon they were out on the open road, traversing an empty plain, barren except for shepherds waiting with their goats. They were on their way to Debre Zeit, Lieutenant Neway informed them. He didn't say anything more, other than, when they arrived at the air force base, to wish them a pleasant stay.

The party was already under way at Tore's house when Niskanen arrived. Tore was in the construction business and it was his custom to welcome new arrivals from Scandinavia with cocktails. Most of the guests were men and women in their mid-thirties, like himself. Expatriates, he noted, were men with lives to build – or to rebuild.

Apart from the servants carrying trays of snacks and drinks, only two of those present were Ethiopian, and both of them wore Western-style suits rather than *shammas*. Niskanen had learned that educated Ethiopians preferred suits or military uniforms, anything but their traditional robes. Several of the Westerners were wearing uniforms, which made him more comfortable. Politicians with their shifting allegiances made him circumspect, and politicians from Africa, if that was what the Ethiopian guests were, represented an unknown quantity.

The women wore evening gowns, even though there would be no theatre or dancing later. There wasn't much in the way of cultural activity in Addis, Niskanen had discovered. It was a provincial place, it seemed to him, even if there were more cinemas than in most Swedish towns. In the weeks since he had been there, he had kept the company of his fellow countrymen for the most part. He had even seen one of the nurses from the plane. They had dined out at a hotel full of Scandinavians, and it was almost like being in Sweden. The Ethiopians in the restaurant had watched them with what he thought at first was suspicion, although he had come to understand that it was simply silent affront at the boisterousness of foreigners. In time, he would even begin to share their disquiet. He would become a stranger to his own people.

On the plane, he had told the nurse that his wife would be joining him. This time, still unadjusted to the intoxication of the altitude, he freely admitted she had left him. She never gave an explanation, he told the nurse, but she did send a note wishing him well in his new post. The nurse looked at him as though trying to read his bedside chart, wondering presumably how he had failed this wife, or whether she had failed him somehow. Afterwards, he had kissed her fervently, but a few days later she called to say she was going to work in a hospital in Axum, and didn't propose another meeting.

He moved stiffly through the gathering with a tumbler of whisky in his hand, the ice melting fast in the heat.

Tore grabbed him by the sleeve. 'Hey, Onni. Hey, hey! *Willkommen in Ethiopien!*'

He was talking with a young couple, and Niskanen guessed that they were probably American. He had encountered several Americans since he had arrived, employees of the bank where he had been obliged to open an expatriate account. The woman was dressed in an elegant black gown and wore a necklace of translucent green stones that reflected the emerald shards in her eyes. The man's tie was loose, an informality that Niskanen had only ever seen in the films.

Tore switched to English to introduce him to the couple. 'This is Ben Wright. Ben is with the American Council. He's here on a technical mission, they call it.'

'Pleasure to meet you, Major. My wife, Helen.'

Niskanen took her hand and kissed the back, clicking his heels slightly. He noticed her thin blue veins and the nails, bitten and varnished.

'So, are you stationed out at Debre Zeit with the rest of your fly-guys?' asked her husband.

Niskanen suspected his answer would be another sheaf in an intelligence file and tried to reply as neutrally as possible.

'We're training out there for the facilities, but I'm not an airman. I'm just a PE instructor, physical education. I'm here to train the Imperial Bodyguard.'

'Oh, so you'll be at the palace. Have you met His Imperial Majesty yet?'

'I haven't had the pleasure.'

'Quite a fellow, the emperor. Keeps us *and* the Soviets dangling while he plays the leader of the non-aligned cause. That's why he likes having you Swedes here.'

'Why is that?'

'Because you're non-aligned, like him.'

'Ben!' Helen interjected, annoyed. But Ben ignored her. Niskanen noticed that his glass was already empty.

'Sometimes I think the reason he's always out of the country on a state visit somewhere is so's he can get his chamberlain to answer the phone. That way, he doesn't have to commit himself to anything.'

'Perhaps you have nothing in particular that he wants,' suggested Niskanen.

'Don't you believe it! No, he's shrewd. He's always calling on the UN to right the wrongs the world has done to Ethiopia, but he drives a hard bargain. The only reason he let us take over the Italian transmitter at Kagnew is because we said we would back his claim on Eritrea.'

They were joined by a tall man whom Niskanen took to be a European despite his deep tan. He eyed Ben with wary amusement.

'Spencer,' exclaimed Ben. 'You old bulldog, you! Meet Major Onni Niskanen. He's another one of them. Says he's a PE instructor. What do you think?'

Spencer didn't answer. 'My pleasure, Major,' he said, shaking Niskanen's hand firmly.

'Spencer here is a Brit,' Ben interjected for Niskanen's benefit, 'but he works for the Ethiopian government. You'll get used to it. Most of His Majesty's foreign advisers went to the Sorbonne, like our Spencer here.'

'Hello, Ben,' said Spencer. 'Found any reds under your bed lately?'

'At least they weren't *in* my bed!' retorted Ben happily.

Spencer smiled. 'Ben has a puritanical view of world affairs, I'm afraid. He thinks his country can do what it pleases, and I'm here to set him straight. But along with the pens and books, he does have cases of Bourbon at his disposal.'

'We ship them in the trunks of the big cars for His Majesty.'

Spencer seemed to tire of the conversation. He turned to Niskanen.

'Major, was it?' he queried, studying the Scandinavian. 'So you're not with the air force…'

'No. I'm here in a training capacity only.'

Niskanen saw that Spencer was expecting to hear more, but he said nothing.

'I wish you success,' Spencer continued. 'The Ethiopians are a hardy people. During the war, the Italians used Ypron. It's a chemical that burns the skin horribly. They dropped it from planes in canisters, spread it everywhere. The thing is, the Ethiopian troops were barefoot…'

He waited for Niskanen to react.

'The ones who could still walk carried their comrades; three months from the front to Addis. They deposited the wounded, turned around and went back. There were only two ambulances – sent by you Swedes. The League of Nations had turned a blind eye to appease the Duce.'

Ben had been waiting for Spencer to finish.

'And where was His Majesty in this dark hour of his country's history?' he asked. 'He was in England, the illustrious guest of the British royal family!'

One of the Ethiopians had been listening to their conversation.

'I'm sorry. I couldn't help overhearing, and I must remind you that His Majesty had no choice,' he protested. 'It was the decision of the Crown Council. They sent His Imperial Majesty to safety. With our emperor in exile, Ethiopia would remain a sovereign state even if it was under foreign occupation.'

He gave a warm smile as he sipped his martini, carefully holding the napkin in place under the glass. The delicate gesture was inconsistent with his powerful, stocky physique.

'There you are, Ben,' said Spencer. 'Things here are never quite as simple as they seem, eh?'

Spencer introduced the Ethiopian to Niskanen.

'*Ato*. Tessema is the secretary-general of the Football Federation. He's also in charge of the Sports Office at the Ministry of Information. I dare say you two will be seeing a lot of each other.'

Yidnekachew Tessema was not a politician as such – though he told Niskanen later that, until the war interrupted, his parents had intended for him to study law in Paris. He was a footballer, the first Ethiopian soccer player to wear cleats on the field, and he played every weekend as the captain of St George, the local team. But he was the son of a poet and he could see the poetry in sport.

He told Niskanen how, during the Italian occupation, he had been employed by the Native Sports Office to translate the rules of soccer into Amharic. 'Even if they didn't think we were up to much, the Italians wouldn't let us play against them,' he recalled. 'But once the occupation was over, we played against a team of Italian locals and beat them!'

He explained how the Italians had encouraged clubs to form along racial and tribal lines, 'dividing us to conquer us in the classic colonialist way'. Tessema became animated as he related his conviction that sport should be a shared ideal, irrespective of race, tribe, religion or political affiliation. 'It is a way for us to overcome these differences.'

Niskanen was happy to discover that Tessema knew about distance running too. Soon enough, while the others had gone back to the question of which concessions His Majesty would be granting, they were discussing track and field and callisthenics. It hardly crossed the minds of Ben the intelligence agent, or Spencer the diplomat, or Tore the building contractor, that sport would offer the most important prize of all.

9

Kneeling by the lake, Abebe plunged his tired, dirty, bloodstained head under the water and lifted it out, revived. He heard the sound of drums booming across the water, and the bells tolling in the great church on the island. In the shimmering distance, the cathedral floated like a paradisaical vision suspended in the silvery water.

He stared at his reflection in the clear water. His eyes had dark rings around them, his cheekbones protruded, making him seem older than his fifteen years, and his nostrils quivered, excited by the smells of the fresh grass on the lakeside. He had discovered that things grew in some parts of the country when elsewhere there was nothing. In some parts, people ate while elsewhere they starved. That was why people were always walking, going somewhere – they were looking for food.

Leaving the lake, he set off again, becoming one of the people walking the empty roads. He wandered, hungry and tired, until he was beyond hunger and tiredness, until, following the road and then the human tide, he came to another city.

This one was bigger than the last, but offered the same profusion of things he knew and much more with which he was unfamiliar.

He saw, in the middle of the intersection of two wide avenues, a man with a white hat and white gloves waving his arms and blowing a whistle. At the shrill blast, the lorries would halt, swaying like overloaded elephants while black bicycles swarmed like cranes around them, and then more lorries belching clouds of foul-smelling smoke would begin their slow advance from the other direction.

The streets were thronging with people. Traders had spread blankets on the ground and sat in jealous guard over their wares: arrays of pots and pans, heaps of *shammas* and blankets and other things too – astonishing objects like the radios that emitted a harsh music. Some of the traders waited with quiet desperation over their goods, things that Abebe couldn't identify, broken and incomplete. Others shouted at Abebe, imploring him to make an offer for their toothbrushes and matches.

Women in colourful dresses sat large and immobile like queens surrounded by their vegetables, talking loudly among themselves.

They looked at Abebe scornfully.

Then he came upon the palace. It was made of stone and sat high on a hill, like a cathedral. Surrounding it was an iron fence.

Through the tall railings aligned like spears, Abebe saw rows of soldiers, the same barefoot soldiers with the heads of eagles and the brass-buttoned tunics he had seen in the village.

He watched as a column of soldiers marched to the centre of the parade ground, halted and turned to form a line in front of another row of waiting soldiers. They saluted each other and held out their rifles, their arms straight.

Abebe approached the main gates.

The guard on duty outside stared directly ahead, his eyes fixed somewhere in the far distance. Mesmerised by the guard's immobility, not knowing whether he was real or just a statue like the figures he had seen in the squares, Abebe didn't notice the gates opening and he was caught by surprise as a lorry surged inside right alongside him.

The lorry was uncovered at the back, and sitting in it, uncomfortable and acutely self-conscious, were a dozen young men.

Abebe scrutinised the men.

He was weary and bedraggled and he had lost his belongings, but he was transfixed by them. If he could become like them, his miseries would be over. He moved along the iron fence following the exercising soldiers as they advanced, lifting their knees like horses performing a curious, exaggerated trot.

Without realising it, he came to the entrance to the parade ground and a guard challenged him, lowering his bayoneted rifle and pointing it at him.

'What is your business?'

Confused and frightened by the glinting blade, Abebe pointed inside the base. He was only admiring the soldiers, he wanted to say, but no words came out.

The guard jabbed the bayonet towards him.

'Get away from here!'

He realised that he had reached the capital, Addis Ababa, and that his journey was at an end.

10

Cocktail parties were a pleasant part of the routine that Niskanen established. Twice a week, he went out to the air force base at Debre Zeit, some 40 miles north-west of the capital, to put the Ethiopian pilots and the Swedish staff through some basic exercises. In the evenings, he would stay and socialise with his fellow expatriates. The rest of the week he was billeted at the Cadet School, a single-storey concrete building with a tin roof adjoining the barracks of the Imperial Bodyguard, next to the royal palace.

Each morning, he put the guardsmen through their paces on the parade ground. Several times over the months he noticed the emperor staring from the windows of his apartments, an immobile, upright figure contemplating not the guardsmen or the gardens but the city and the hills beyond.

The Imperial Bodyguard were the elite of the Ethiopian army, the best soldiers in the whole of Africa, according to Count von Rosen. They turned out to be ragged but eager recruits picked from the army ranks for their physical form. They were taller than most Amhars, as the people of the Ethiopian highlands were called. Because they were attached to the palace, they enjoyed privileged treatment: they were better fed than the regular army, with whom they rarely came into contact except on ceremonial review. The emperor was proud of his praetorian guard and counted on their loyalty. Niskanen had grasped that Haile Selassie I needed to be sure of their obedience: though he could claim descent from King Solomon, the young Ras Tafari, as he was, had seized the throne by force.

Most of the military staff had been trained outside of Africa. Mengistu Neway and the others bore the hallmarks of the British academies: the shoes and buttons shone, the parade lines were straight. The day's routine was regulated like clockwork, as the British said. This was fine with Niskanen; a basic discipline had been instilled in the guardsmen which he was able to build on.

Physically, though, he detected a legacy of poor nutrition. He recognised it at once in the hollow cheeks that were the sign of vitamin deficiency in infant life; that same fierce, rickety look the poor people had in Finland. It wasn't so bad for his purposes; the guardsmen had youthful stamina and they were resilient enough. He had no way of knowing, however, if there would be more serious consequences such as problems later with fragile bones.

He considered these aspects as he prepared his training programme. The Ethiopians on the whole were smaller than Europeans – certainly northern Europeans – and that meant they had a shorter stride. He wondered how that would affect their times. Would their lower body weight make them faster none the less? He noticed too an antagonism between the Amharic peoples and the recruits from other ethnic groups, an undercurrent of resentment that he hoped might profitably be channelled into competition on the field.

As for the climate, the heat of the day had seemed fierce to him at first but it was mitigated by the freshness of the mornings, a cycle of afternoon torpor and nocturnal cool so marked it made each new day feel like the beginning of the world. It was nothing like the sweltering heat of a jungle or desert, as he had feared, however, more like a daily burst of enveloping warmth. Niskanen adapted his programme to get most of the training done in the mornings. He gave the men a break in the early afternoon and sometimes finished off with a cross-country run before dusk, when the eucalyptus trees filled the air with their oily, soothing scent.

In the tropics, he discovered, night came quickly, falling in an instant like a heavy veil – so unlike the lingering sunsets he was accustomed to in Scandinavia, and which he would never be able to forget.

***

As he did every morning, Niskanen saluted the men before commencing. A hundred soldiers in shorts and singlets returned the salute.

'One, two, three, four; *toes*, two, three, four...'

Niskanen took them through the standard exercises. He made them jump rhythmically, landing with their legs apart and then together, simultaneously clapping their hands above their heads and then bringing their outstretched arms back down, palms flat against their sides. They performed the movements exactly as they had been taught, and in perfect synchronisation. They followed up by touching their toes with the fingers of one hand while holding the other arm stretched upwards. Niskanen was pleased to see that the rows of uplifted arms were almost parallel, the harmonious expression of a physical music. Their white vests were clean and, as yet, barely wet with perspiration. If there was anything to distinguish them from a group of similar young men elsewhere in the world, it was not their physiques, nor their clothing, nor even their aptitude, but their bare feet.

There was not money for such things as plimsolls, Tessema had told him, and he had resolved to try to organise some kind of collection via the Red Cross or the Scouts back home. Used shoes would be better than nothing.

Finally, Niskanen ordered the men to attention. They stood erect, their muscles tensed, their dark skin glistening, their proud regard stern and steady. They were a corps of men now, literally like one body, and this physical communion gave both Niskanen and the Ethiopians satisfaction.

Niskanen saluted them and took a step back.

Mengistu Neway was waiting behind him. The lieutenant who had driven him from the airport had been made a corporal, a rapid ascension that seemed to be the rule rather than the exception. The emperor was apparently in a hurry to renew the administration.

Niskanen turned and saluted the corporal with his bright new stripes, then he stood back and waited as Mengistu made his inspection. The corporal walked slowly up and down the line of men, taking his time to scrutinise each of them. Niskanen was certain he was measuring them against his own experience at some military academy. He had come to realise that, among certain Ethiopians, everything, even attitudes, was imported. He imagined the drill sergeants at Sandhurst or West Point inspecting Mengistu, looking for the smallest fault, a collar half buttoned in haste or a smudge of grease on a rifle. The corporal was now turning the same rigorous, cold gaze on his own men.

'Very good, Major. Very impressive.' He nodded. 'His Majesty will be satisfied.' He turned from the parade line. 'Incidentally, I have a message for you – from the palace,' he added casually. 'His Imperial Majesty requires the presence of his chief sports officer. That means at once, you understand. My jeep is waiting, if you like.'

Niskanen saluted him again and stepped back.

Corporal Mengistu Neway returned the salute and then waited as Niskanen dismissed the men.

Although the palace was adjacent to the barracks and Niskanen could easily have walked there, they took the jeep with the driver. To arrive by foot would, he imagined, have been a sign that he hadn't responded with the proper haste to the emperor's summons.

In the jeep, Niskanen mentioned to Mengistu that he had met his brother Germame, who was a student at the Haile Selassie I Secondary School. Niskanen had been made PE instructor there, a duty that had been added to his roster by the ministry and which he had accepted graciously. He already knew that there would always be further demands, they would always be asking for more from him, though they were too proud to actually voice their needs. Rather, they would offer you a post with an important title or simply wait for you to realise what was lacking and decide to do something about it yourself.

Mengistu was aware of Niskanen's new duties. He said Germame was the intellectual of the family and that he would be going to study at a college in the United States. 'My family were officials in Menelik's government. They decided that, as the eldest, I should be the soldier, and Germame would be the politician. He must know everything about political theory, as I have learnt about military strategy. Only then shall we be able to serve our country fully.'

Mengistu Neway drove through the gates and left Niskanen at the steps, stepping out to open his door and salute him. Niskanen mounted the stairway and entered the palace.

A long arcade ran from the entrance to the Hall of Audience, open to the gardens along one side. A wooden trellis allowed the breeze to enter, cooling the offices but obscuring the view of the grounds. Beyond the fine filigree carvings of orchids and cranes it was difficult to see clearly who was conversing with whom as they walked between the hedges and pools: which Ras was conferring with which minister, which member of the administration was exchanging views with which member of the armed forces.

Doors to ministerial offices lined the other side and the arcade thronged with men in *shammas* congregating, talking or pressing for admittance to the chambers, the dim rooms from which other men – secretaries and advisers wearing Western-style suits – came and went with a preoccupied air of overwork. The imperial functionaries were burdened with dossiers and manifestly were not to be interrupted in their urgent business.

Niskanen waited on a bench, observing the bustle. He thought he detected the repeated enunciation of titles, the exchange of elaborate greetings; he heard the sweet lilt of flattery and the simpering of abasement. It struck him that it was like a European court, but in medieval times. He felt he was witnessing a performance, a representation of European customs in part, but with each performer meshing perfectly as in a complex tribal dance.

'I imagine it's not like this at Drottningholm,' ventured a man seated at his side.

He was surprised to hear the name of the royal palace in Stockholm enunciated so precisely. He turned to see an Ethiopian wearing a black gown over his *shamma* and sitting stiffly with a neat pile of folders on his lap.

'Oh, it's not so different,' he replied. He wondered how it was he had not noticed the man when he sat down.

'Then you have been inside the Swedish palace?' queried his neighbour.

'On ceremonial occasions only.'

'I see.'

From his black gown, Niskanen guessed that the man must be a lawyer. His casual question was designed to elicit more information.

Yet the man seemed excited by Niskanen's reply.

'I imagine it's rather splendid,' he said.

'Oh, indeed it is. '

'I thought so,' said the man. 'It must be very big, very grand.'

'It's quite large, yes.'

Niskanen was used to this sort of exchange. He had learned that there was little point in trying to downplay the imagined glories of European civilisation. Far from being reassured, the Ethiopians were disappointed and sometimes, fearful of being patronised, they even reacted angrily. On the other hand, a portrayal more lavish than their imaginings might have the effect of making them irate.

A court official approached them and the lawyer stopped, eyes wide with expectation and surprise.

'Major Niskanen,' said the official. 'His Highness will see you now.'

11

Before he left his village, Abebe was told about an uncle in Addis, a man who lived near the Mercato, who would take him in. All he had to do was find this uncle, whose name was Mirus. But the city was larger than anyone in his village had ever imagined. On the top of each hill was a house larger than any he had ever seen before or a church taller than he had ever dreamed of, and over the brow was always yet another hill. The city stretched out for ever, spreading uncontrollably over the rolling terrain, vibrating with noise and energy.

When he asked directions to the Mercato, people just laughed and told him to keep going, that he would be sure to find it.

When at last he came to the bustling, noisy market, he discovered it was really another, immense city inside the city. There were more people in the Mercato than Abebe had ever seen in one place before. He didn't know where to even begin looking for this uncle. Everybody, it seemed, was way too busy to take notice of him, or, if they did, it was because they knew already what he wanted.

He was hungry. He had long ago eaten the last of his grain and there was nothing that grew here to sustain him, no shoots he could eat. He only had left a few of the coins he had been given when he set out from the village. And he was afraid. He had seen the bodies of thieves hanging from the great sycamore tree at the gates of the city. He was sure that everyone could see his hunger, that they could detect his fear and his helplessness, and that they were watching him, waiting for the rash, desperate instant when hunger would propel him to act, so they could catch him and then gleefully dismember him as they had the man in the other city.

The first night, he joined a group of men who lay under a tree and slept fitfully clutching his purse under his *shamma*, wondering whether he would be woken in the dark by the cold touch of a knife at his throat. The men slept together like that for protection, he realised. They feared each other, but hoped that together they would be safe.

In the morning, he was woken by a terrible clamour, the noise of the lorries revving their engines. He watched the lumbering beasts with their huge wheels manoeuvring amid the throng. He was cold and damp from the dew, but he was alive and the activity erupting around him gave him courage. He was soon lost in the labyrinth of streets and alleys that comprised the huge bazaar. He wandered along entire streets of blacksmiths, their forges spewing smoke and flame, their hands black and their faces red like demons'. He saw the streets where the tanners sat with their piles of hides and furs and fresh skins hung up to dry, still crusted with blood. Only people of the lowest castes would be involved in such foul and fearful occupations, and it was unlikely that he would locate his uncle among them. He walked on, searching in the faces of the shoeshine boys and the porters carrying heavy sacks or bundles of firewood bigger than themselves, looking for a flicker of recognition.

He had to find someone from his district, perhaps even from his village or one of the villages near by, a relation who could lead him to his uncle. But when he asked the men cutting rocks or trimming vegetables if they knew anyone from his district, they just shrugged or looked down and carried on with what they were doing, as though they heard the question a hundred times a day from bewildered boys who had recently come from the country.

He didn't even dare to ask the innkeepers or the butchers who waited in their little shops. They were proud and well fed but he could tell from their faces that they were people like himself. One of them surely knew the whereabouts of his uncle. If he approached, however, their expressions grew hard and stony. The shopkeepers had learned to see only customers.

He had been straying back and forth all morning without ever returning to a place in the Mercato he recognised. It all looked confusingly similar, and he was beginning to feel the sharp pangs of hunger. He hadn't eaten anything that day, nor the day before. Although he was almost down to the last of his coins, the tumult of the market was so exhausting, and its displays so enticing, that he decided to buy a piece of bread and a bowl of gravy from one of the women sitting under a parasol.

The food warmed him and, as the spices pricked his tongue, his spirits revived. He found the courage to ask the woman sitting behind her cooking pot whether she knew where he might find his uncle. After all, he had purchased her food. She owed him a response at least.

The woman looked at Abebe. 'What does he do, this uncle of yours?' she asked.

If only he could remember what his uncle's occupation was, but it hadn't seemed important in the village, where everyone shared in each activity according to the season. They all worked in the fields when there was grain to harvest; all the women wove cloth while the men repaired the mud walls or threshed stalks to make a roof. In Addis, everyone had a speciality, something they excelled at that enabled them to live and even made them rich.

'I don't know,' he replied.

The woman snorted and the people standing around the stall eating her *injera* glanced at Abebe doubtfully.

'How are you going to find him if you don't know what he does?' the woman asked.

She dunked a roll of the flat bread into a bowl of stew and brought it to her lips, biting scornfully.

There were nods of agreement. The question appeared obvious now. It hadn't seemed so important in the village and its surroundings, where everyone knew his father. Here, nobody knew anybody. But he was desperate.

'His name is Mirus. He lives by the Mercato.'

'Mercato is big, you know.'

There were more chuckles.

'He's from the north, from Shewa.'

'I know a man from Shewa,' one of the diners said.

Abebe looked up hopefully.

'He's a rock cutter. Sometimes he works as a porter. But his name is Haylu.'

They were making fun of him. They didn't care about his plight at all. Dejectedly, he finished his food and took a cup of water. At least he was no longer hungry. But his situation was more urgent than ever. He had to find his uncle. He thought about going home, but that was out of the question. It had taken him months to get there on foot.

He watched a lorry reversing noisily to discharge its load, thinking that perhaps the driver might give him a ride... The lorry was moving slowly backwards and the driver had the door open, looking around. He was a well-fed man with a haughty air. The big vehicle gave him importance; Abebe had seen people imploring lorry drivers to take pity on them at the roadside and he knew he would have no chance unless he could pay.

The driver barked at the people around the lorry, ordering them to get away. He didn't see the stack of wire cages full of hens that a woman had brought to market until he had reversed into it, knocking them over. Suddenly, the air was full of feathers and fumes from the engine. People shouted, trying to grab the hysterical birds, who scattered in a final bid for freedom before they finished in a cooking pot.

Soon enough, all of the hens had been rounded up except one, a large, determined rooster. Whenever the woman caught up with him, he scurried farther away, and each time her curses grew louder. She called him by name and swore it was the last time he would get the better of her.

'Truly, the city is a miraculous place,' said Abebe. 'Where I come from, it is the cock who must do the chasing, not the hen!'

The people at the stall laughed. Their stony expressions softened. 'No, country boy,' said one of the men, 'don't be misled. Usually it is like that here too!'

The woman had stopped trying to catch the rooster and was cursing the lorry driver who had stepped from his cab to see what had happened. She was pointing at the cock and demanding that he catch him, or else he would have to pay.

'See what I mean!' said the man.

Abebe laughed, and in their amused complicity the man seemed to take a liking to Abebe. He asked his name.

'Abebe, son of Bikila.'

The man responded by telling Abebe his name and that of his father, and soon they were embarked on a customary mutual exploration of genealogies that was designed, hopefully, to unearth a common ancestor.

'You are from Neta Denba? But that's where my wife's cousin is from! Her husband is a weaver.'

That was it! Abebe's uncle was a weaver! He wove cloth for *shammas*. The fear and hunger had made him forget, but he was sure he would find the uncle now.

'They live not far from here. Perhaps they know your uncle. Meet me here when I finish my work and I'll take you there.'

Abebe waited the entire afternoon, not moving from the stall in case he was unable to trace his way back. The woman told him that all the weavers had their shops in a certain street and he decided that, if his new friend didn't return, he would go there himself. One of the weavers was bound to know his uncle. But the man did return as he had promised and he led Abebe through the alleys and along the streets as the Mercato grew dark.

In the flickering light of the fires from the braziers, he saw the faces of people returning to their homes. They looked tired and haggard, whether they had earned enough to eat or not. The lucky ones paused in the bars and restaurants. The rest trudged on back to their mud huts and wooden shacks. Hungry or satisfied, rich or poor, they would recommence their struggles the next day. For now, the city let them rest.

That night, Abebe slept on the floor of a warm room with a dozen other people, the relations of his new friend. The next day, he shared in their activities – breaking rocks at a construction site – and in the evening he shared their food. 'You know what they say,' Abebe's new friend responded when he expressed his gratitude. 'He who opens the throat will not let the night pass without closing it.'

The following day, he was introduced to a shopkeeper who knew a weaver named Mirus, and the day after that he and his new friend and the man's wife were received by Abebe's uncle and his family with abundant hospitality.

12

Three pairs of doors opened silently as Niskanen approached, drawn back one after the other by invisible hands.

Niskanen saw first the shoes, a row of polished black Oxfords. His eyes were drawn to them by the agitation of a small dog, a miniature oriental breed, which scampered between the feet of the dignitaries, pausing here and there to urinate on a heel or a toe.

The dignitaries didn't flinch, however. If they felt the wetness seeping through their socks and their feet getting warm, they registered nothing, not even surprise.

Their expressions remained clenched as, from behind their feet, an arm extended, belonging to a man kneeling on the floor and wiping the urine with a cloth. The servant was trying to follow the dog and at the same time doing his best to remain hidden. He hesitated, drawing back as the dog reached the end of the line and leapt up on to a dais, where a pair of immaculate black brogues rested on a velvet cushion.

The dog, whose name was Lulu, did not try to urinate on these, but sat beside their owner.

The emperor was perched, rigid and motionless, on his throne, the cushion under his feet. Clearly, the imperial shoes did not emit the same enticing odours as those of mere mortals, Niskanen noted. His Majesty seemed quite aloof, poised on a tall-backed gilt-edged throne draped with fine cloths. To Niskanen, there was a dark, Byzantine richness to the room, with its layers of carpets and walls laden with tapestries, like being folded in velvet. Everything was finely woven or threaded with gold brocade, but muted by the daylight that filtered in dimly through the dust that hung in the air.

The antics of the dog had punctured the stiffness of the court, however, and Niskanen had to compose himself to make the customary three bows, once at the door, again halfway to the throne, and a third time before the emperor.

'Ah, Major. We are pleased you were able to come. We're sure you must be very busy.'

The voice was low and rasping. It sounded to Niskanen deliberately faint, as though worn out by the chore of deigning to express what was or should be known. And there was a minor, melancholy note that hinted at sadness and fatigue.

'There is something we would like to discuss,' said the emperor. 'Please, this way.'

As Selassie descended from the throne, another servant drew near the dais on his knees and discreetly pulled the cushion from under his feet. Niskanen felt suddenly uncomfortable to be towering physically over the emperor, as though he were committing an affront to royal dignity. He wondered what the protocol was to avoid drawing notice to the emperor's diminutive stature, but found unexpectedly that he was the one who was diminished. The imperial bearing was erect and there was a punishing glint in Selassie's carbon-black eyes. He was the centre of a concentrated attention from his court, a compound of fear, ambition and awe that made him appear much larger.

He turned and walked to one side of the Hall of Audience, and Niskanen followed.

As the emperor approached the doors to his private offices, these too opened as if by the force of imperial will, and remained open for Niskanen to pass.

The room was spacious and sumptuously decorated in a style that reminded Niskanen of the private apartments at Drottningholm, a cosy blend of floral wallpaper and chintz upholstery. There were copies of *Tatler* and *Country Life* on the table, English magazines with, on their covers, pictures of thoroughbreds and debutantes. The decor was more Victorian than Gustavanian, a deep regal red rather than light blue. Heavy net curtains obscured the view and hid the sun.

It was only when the doors were closed behind them that Selassie relaxed slightly and Niskanen noticed that he wore ordinary attire, a black pinstriped suit with a black silk tie. His beard and his temples were greying and his brow was set in an expression of constant concern. He smiled cordially at Niskanen, however, and waved his hand to offer him a seat on the sofa.

'Would you like coffee?' he asked.

'Thank you, Your Highness,' replied Niskanen. He bowed slightly, standing in front of the sofa.

'Please, sit down.'

Immediately, a servant entered carrying a silver coffee pot on a silver tray. He served them coffee and Niskanen watched Selassie delicately stirring the contents of the porcelain cup before raising it to his lips, his little finger in the air.

'We would like to thank you for the work you are doing at the Cadet School,' said the emperor. 'And we are extremely grateful for the time you have been able to devote to physical instruction at our secondary school.'

Niskanen realised that the emperor was using the royal plural. When he said we, he was speaking as the embodiment of the entire nation.

'It is my honour to be of service, Your Majesty.'

The emperor nodded graciously.

'Now, tell me, what do you think of our cadets?' he asked.

'They are fine young men,' said Niskanen, 'with a very high level of discipline. I think His Majesty will be most satisfied.'

'I mean their physical abilities,' said the emperor. 'Have we any good athletes here in Ethiopia?'

'Athletes?'

'Yes.'

'Physically, the cadets are quite capable,' said Niskanen, unsure of what Selassie wanted to hear.

'You see, we want you to develop and train Ethiopian athletes to compete in international sporting competition.' He stood and walked over to the window, peering out for an instant from behind a net curtain. 'Compete – at the highest level,' he added.

He turned to Niskanen and his expression hardened. 'Have you ever attended the Olympic Games, Major?'

Niskanen replied that he had never had the opportunity.

'We attended the Games once, as prince regent, in 1924. We were invited as an observer. It was most edifying. But when we applied for affiliation for the games in Amsterdam two years later, they said that Africans were not ready – they said exactly that – to take part in international sporting competition.'

Selassie walked over to his desk and picked up a letter. He handed it to Niskanen.

'Do you speak French, Major?'

Niskanen scanned the letter. He shook his head.

The emperor quoted from memory the words that had slighted the young regent. *Les africains doivent pratiquer le sport dans leur pays d'abord, pour le comprendre.* He said, 'We shall translate: "Africans should first practise sports in their own countries, to learn them." They said there was no place for Ethiopia. The signature is that of Monsieur Henri de Baillet-Latour, president of the International Olympic Committee.'

Niskanen examined the letter again, and when he glanced up he saw that the emperor had been watching him. Selassie was looking for any hint of the same sentiments in his country's guest.

'It would be extremely gratifying if Ethiopia were to take part in the Games,' he said. In the emperor's eyes Niskanen saw affront – but also a rigid, burning determination. 'Won't you see what you can do?' He smiled.

Niskanen was taken aback. It was an unexpected mission and he wondered whether the emperor was serious, but one glance at the letter from the Olympic Committee told him this was so. The possibility of training the Ethiopians for competition had never crossed his mind, but there was no reason it couldn't be done. Black people could run and win, he thought. Jesse Owens had proved that in Munich. Why not the Ethiopians?

'You can begin by attending the Games in London on our behalf. We're sure it could be arranged so that you have the time. How would that be?'

Niskanen said he would be only too happy to comply. Ever since he was a boy, he had dreamed of witnessing the athletes competing in the Olympic arena.

'Good. You know Yidnekachew Tessema at the Sports Office?'

'I've had the pleasure.'

'*Ato*. Tessema is one of our best footballers! He will see to it you have everything you need.'

13

Abebe found himself in a hall with hundreds of other young men. Some wore *shammas* as ragged and dirty as his own, others were dressed in trousers and shirts like the youths he had seen in the city going to the secondary school, and he envied the modern neatness of their clothes and the advantage that gave them. Some were standing and talking excitedly, but with their voices subdued, awed by their surroundings. Most were squatting or sitting on the ground, silently awaiting their turn.

At the end of the hall was a wide table, and behind it sat a sergeant flanked by two other soldiers in uniform. The sergeant was speaking to one young man who was clearly making an effort to stand excessively straight. He had his hands behind his back, and Abebe could see that the young man could not stop fidgeting as he answered the sergeant's questions.

Edging nervously along the wall, Abebe squatted down and waited.

Eventually, it was his turn to stand before the sergeant with the ledger. He was one of the last, and the hall was nearly empty now apart from some guardsmen standing at attention by the entrance in their white uniforms.

The sergeant had been writing in a large ledger, regularly dipping his quill in black ink.

'Name?' he asked.

'Abebe.'

'Father's name?'

'Bikila.'

'Village?'

'Jirou.'

'School certificate?'

Abebe handed him the piece of paper from the priest that confirmed he had finished his *Qes* schooling in the parish and the sergeant wrote something next to his name. Then he indicated the door to Abebe, as he had done to all the others.

Abebe passed through the doorway and emerged in a courtyard in the afternoon sun. The other recruits were waiting under the trees. They were talking excitedly about their families and their animals, and how impressed the village girls would be when they returned in their white uniforms.

The sergeant ordered them to form long rows, making them reach out to touch the shoulder of the recruit in front and then do the same with the recruit to their right, a way of establishing which of them knew left from right as much as of creating an orderly block of men. He pointed to those who had shown confusion, ordering them to stand by the wall, and then he began walking up and down between the rows of recruits. He paused in front of one and gripped his shoulders, pushing them back. Halting in front of another, he parted the young man's robes with his baton, inspecting his genitals. The sergeant wasn't happy with what he saw. He glanced at the guard accompanying him, who grabbed the recruit by the elbow and pulled him from the ranks, leading him out of the courtyard.

When the sergeant reached Abebe, he halted again.

He lifted Abebe's chin, inspecting his bone structure as one might that of a horse, looking at the profile and then releasing him curtly. The man was a Galla, an Oromo like him, but Abebe sensed in his gestures the disdain of the Amhars. He had learned to imitate them well.

The sergeant nodded and returned to the front of the block of recruits, where a folding chair had been placed. Beside it a guardsman stood holding a wide canvas parasol. The sergeant sat down and crossed his legs, idly swishing his baton. They were going to wait.

It was the hottest part of the afternoon and soon sweat was beading the faces of the recruits. The eyes of some were half closed, as though they were sleeping where they stood, still guarding their flocks. Others tried hard to keep their heads up as they had seen the guardsmen do, but found that it took an effort of concentration to remain immobile. Some started to tremble. One of the recruits could not overcome the need to wave a fly away and the gesture caught the eye of the sergeant. He whispered to a guardsman and there was one less recruit. Soon enough, the rows were full of holes.

A few of the recruits slumped and were made to leave the ranks. Some gave up and skulked away, ignored by the sergeant, until only a quarter of the candidates remained, a few dozen men. The blurry sun moved slowly across the white sky until at last Abebe could feel the cool of the approaching night. He had fought hard to remain motionless and keep his eyes open and focused, and he was relieved when the sergeant stood up and, lifting his head, spoke to the men.

'*Ten-shun!*' he shouted.

Abebe had no idea what the word meant, but he saw the sergeant clicking his heels and did the same.

Later, in the bunkhouse, after they had been made to shower and were given food, Abebe rested quietly, reflecting on what the day had brought.

He was a guardsman now. He would have food and a uniform. His father and mother would be proud.

It was not yet light when he was woken by the sergeant walking along the aisle and banging the iron-framed bunks with his baton.

'Good morning, men,' said the sergeant. Abebe was impressed to see he was already fresh and alert. 'You are guardsmen now. A guardsman must be like the jaguar, watchful even in his sleep.'

Abebe raised himself on his elbow. He could see the dawn breaking outside the windows of the dormitory, proof that he wasn't dreaming.

'Nor does a guardsman keep the corporal waiting.'

Abebe saw his new comrades dragging themselves from their bunks and straightening their robes, and he did the same. They had been given uniforms from the stores and some of them had tried them on before the electric lights were turned off, showing off.

Abebe had been too shy, too thrilled by the smoothness of the machine-woven cloth to do anything other than touch it. Now he donned his uniform for the first time.

He had difficulty with the trousers, however; he had never worn such garments before and someone had to show him how to button the fly. He felt like a different man. The trousers gripped his hips and enveloped his legs. Sheathed in the heavy material, he felt a new sensation, armoured like a warrior.

On the parade ground, Abebe recognised the white officer standing with his feet apart and his hands clasped behind his back. In front of the foreigner, the sergeant was standing at attention in the same spot as the day before. A hundred men had already fallen in, and more were coming from other bunkhouses. The twenty men from Abebe's bunkhouse joined them and a corporal lined up these new recruits at the rear.

Once everyone was in place, the sergeant took a step back. This was the sign for Corporal Mengistu to emerge from an office at the side of the parade ground. He wore several decorations on his resplendent white tunic, which shone in the light. He walked up to the sergeant, who saluted him and stood aside.

Corporal Mengistu approached the men, walking slowly to the back of the squad until he was level with the line of new recruits. Then he turned, returning to where Niskanen stood.

'They're all yours, Major,' he said.

Niskanen saluted him and stepped forward to address the men.

'For those of you who are new here, I'm Major Niskanen. I'm your sports officer.'

The recruits looked at each other in surprise. They had never heard a foreigner speaking Amharic before. Accents and intonations were crucial. Some knew only the dialects of their village or province. Furthermore, they had no idea what a sports officer was.

Niskanen persisted. 'Nis–kan–nen,' he said, pointing at his chest.

Abebe wanted to salute, as he had the day before. But the presence of the corporal persuaded him he should not try to make himself noticed.

'Very good. Now, you men who have just joined us follow the rest.'

While the sergeant interpreted for him, the major took position centrally before the men. Once the sergeant had finished he began the exercises.

'Ready, men? I want you all to copy me...'

Slowly he lifted one knee, pulling it up to his chest. Then he did the same with the other knee and, as he repeated the movement, first one knee then the next, over and over, the guardsmen did the same, and the new recruits did their best to follow.

'Now we shall do some running on the spot.'

He demonstrated, springing from one foot to the other and lifting his knees to waist level. The activity made no sense to Abebe. What was the point of running without going anywhere? Running was a means of locomotion, of journeying. Perhaps, he thought, it was the confinement of the parade ground which forced them to practise this strange ritual.

'One, two. One, two...'

Abebe began to count.

One, two...

Pulling back the curtains over the door, the priest entered Bikila's hut. He saw Abebe's father lying on the wooden cot.

After exchanging the customary greetings, he told the man, 'I have received news of your son.'

A flicker of life crossed Bikila's sullen, weary face. The mother lifted her head from her loom.

The priest opened the letter he had brought with him and read from it.

'Abebe is safe. He says he has joined the Imperial Bodyguard. He sends you love and respect.'

Abebe's mother looked at her husband now, and then at the priest.

'He says that when he is paid he will send money.'

He folded the letter and handed it to Abebe's father, who laid his head down with relief.

The priest turned to address his mother. 'So, now you may make plans for the wedding.'

14

As always, the marathon was the final contest, the culmination of the Olympiad. The marathon was the most arduous sporting trial of all, the longest and the most gruelling of foot races. At the Helsinki Games in 1952, it was no different.

The race was to begin and end in the stadium, taking the runners on a twenty-six-mile course through the green fields surrounding the Finnish capital.

Niskanen settled into his seat to await the start. It was a pleasant, sunny day, not too hot, perfect weather for distance running. He was surrounded by his countrymen sitting upright in neat rows, all of them wearing the pale blue blazers of Finnish sporting clubs, their attention focused on the field of runners and their emotions, like his, welling silently as they relived the glories of thirty years before, when Finnish athletes won successive Olympic marathons. In 1920 Hannes Kölehmainen won in two hours and thirty-two minutes. Four years later, Albin Stenroos won in two hours and forty-one. But for Niskanen and the other Finns, the marathon had a special significance, an importance beyond national pride and simple sporting achievement.

Perhaps it was the contrast between the vast emptiness of the Nordic landscape and the frailty of any human effort to traverse even an infinitesimal part of it, a monumental exertion that defied nature's limits. Was this the real reason Finland's Olympic successes had thrilled them so as youths? The distance runner had found the strength and the will to conquer the empty spaces. For Niskanen, runners transcended human limits to become supermen.

The 1952 Games were almost literally taking place in the shadows of the legendary Finnish runners. Outside the newly built stadium was a life-size statue of the greatest of the Finnish champions. There could be no doubt as to whose body the naked figure was modelled on, nor of the identity of the same iconic athlete on the posters for the XVth Olympiad everywhere around the capital. Niskanen had recognised at once the compact, muscular frame of Paavo Nurmi from newsreels and photographs he had seen as a youth. Nevertheless, he had been surprised to actually see, set in stone, Nurmi's short-legged power, confirming what he had read about the athlete's physique. It was yet another challenge to nature. How could a man with such an evident physical disadvantage become a champion runner? But there had been an even greater surprise in store for Niskanen. The athlete who carried the flaming torch into the stadium for the last leg of its journey from Olympia in Greece was none other than Nurmi himself, an older man now, bald and somewhat paunchy. At school they called him the Flying Finn, but despite the records he had broken, Nurmi was excluded from Olympic competition because he had run for money. Once through the gates and on to the track, he passed the torch to the other Flying Finn, Hannes Kölehmainen, who carried it across the stadium and, under wet, dark skies, touched off an eruption of smoke and flame in the tall sculpted stone brazier. Kölehmainen was the first man to run the 5,000 metres in under fifteen minutes, and won the gold medal in the 1920 marathon. Niskanen couldn't help feeling pity for Nurmi, however. He had not been allowed to approach the brazier. It was against the rules, of course, and contrary to the spirit of the Games to earn money from sport; it meant you were a professional and no longer an amateur. But it was unfair that someone with such talent should have been ostracised like that, just because he needed to earn a living. Sport wasn't only the pursuit of aristocrats.

It had rained on the day of the opening ceremony. Although it was the middle of July, summer was abruptly suspended by a freezing downpour. The stadium was uncovered, a modern design with concrete terraces opening like a Cubist hand of cards, and the shards of icy rain had fallen hard, leaving the spectators drenched and shivering. Niskanen had forgotten how different the rain was in his homeland from the heavy, warm deluge that fell on Addis, just as he had forgotten the stoicism of his compatriots, who remained silent and unmoving under their dripping hat brims, a silence not so different finally from that of the Ethiopians. They both had to wait for the rain to stop – or else get on with it. Since he had been back, he had begun to notice the quirks of his countrymen, while those of his new companions, the Ethiopians – their fondness for umbrellas, for example – had gained his sympathy. He immediately wished he had brought one, though if he had, opening it would have impolitely blocked someone's view. Five years was enough, it transpired, to make you a foreigner.

Happily, on the final day of the Games, the sun miraculously returned and now, as the runners lined up for the marathon, it blazed auspiciously, a good omen for the Finnish entrants.

There had been, however, a last-minute change that had caused consternation among both Niskanen's colleagues and the competitors down on the track. A late entrant from Czechoslovakia had been added to the field, a distance runner, perhaps the best in the world.

That week, they had watched Emil Zatopek preserve his world championship in the 10,000 metres and then go on to win the 5,000 metres with astonishing facility. It was as though he didn't want to – or simply couldn't – stop running. Nobody in the stands could recall him running a marathon in competition before, but now Zatopek was lining up for the start.

Niskanen scrutinised the field, looking for the runner from the communist bloc. Zatopek had a wiry tension in his body, a kind of excitation, an electricity that comes from winning. The 'unstoppable Czech', as the newspapers called him, had won the 5,000 metres just the day before, bursting out to overtake the leading group of three runners at the final bend, the look of agony on his face belying a seemingly effortless reserve of speed. He was a natural distance runner, and Niskanen had twice witnessed him win gold in the 10,000 metres; first in London in 1948 and then again earlier that week. The marathon was another dimension, however, a race more than four times as long.

The start of a marathon was always an anticlimax. At the sound of the pistol, the throng of athletes – more than a hundred runners this time – moved forward hesitantly as the rope snaked wildly, lashing them into reluctant action. They spread out without any noticeable antagonism, without the spark of competition you get in other races, without any sidelong glances to see where the threat was coming from. The challenge of a marathon was nature's as much as it was personal, a challenge to oneself as much as to one's rivals.

The runners completed a lap of the track and, as the last of them left the stadium, the cheers that had filled the air died away, leaving only the words of the commentator echoing from the loudspeakers. Niskanen listened, transfixed by the rasping voice. The commentary transported him inside the runners' bodies and he could feel their ambition, their hope, their cunning, their will, their desperation, their thirst and – most terrifyingly – their fatigue. For, if the start was a shambles, the finish of a marathon was never less than dramatic. It was this that everybody was anticipating now. In just over two hours, only one runner, maybe two or three at best, would return to the stadium in the lead.

Niskanen was not the sort of person to notice changes in himself. He wasn't concerned with his own evolution, with the possible effects on his views and habits of living for several years in a poor African country. It was others who evolved, he thought, while he remained constant. But it had been over five years since he had left Scandinavia and even longer since he had been back to Finland. And so, carried away by the sunshine, by the occasion, by the excitement of the race, his heart beating to the pulse of the runners, he took a moment to consider how far he had come.

He knew he had developed sympathy for the Ethiopians but he also knew how much they hated anything that resembled pity. It was what they feared most in their dealings with him – that he would regard them with pity – and so he was careful to avoid any sentiment, remaining cheerful and enthusiastic about overcoming the obstacles they faced. He had come to admire their fortitude, however, the way humiliation left them indignant but unbowed, and he saw that they deserved respect, not sympathy. He wondered sometimes whether his pity was misplaced: did they really need him – or were they simply exploiting his own needs?

Certainly, the promotions had come faster than he could earn them, a symptom of countries in a hurry, he concluded modestly, rather than a reflection of his true abilities. He had been made head of PE at the Haile Selassie I Secondary School and then director of the Department of Physical Education at the Ministry of Education, though in practice there was so very much to do and very little means to do it. Where was he to find PE teachers? And what need did a country without schoolbooks have of physical education? Nevertheless, he had issued a circular with some simple exercises and recommended that teachers in the village schools devote a few minutes in the week to performing them with their pupils.

He had joined the Ethiopian Football Federation at Tessema's insistence and, though soccer wasn't his favourite sport, he went along to the matches with him. He wished the Ethiopians had shown the same interest in his efforts to get a Scout movement going. The idea of teaching youngsters to survive in the wild was met with incredulous looks at the Ministry of Education; Tessema had remarked dryly that, for the time being, Ethiopians needed to learn more about technology than about nature. At the same time, Niskanen had been appointed general secretary at the Red Cross. Even though this was a voluntary post and supposedly a part-time activity, it was the one that occupied him the most. If there weren't enough schoolbooks, there certainly weren't enough medicines, nor enough nurses or doctors. He had helped get a folk dance festival going to raise funds but it was never enough. In truth, there weren't enough nurses or doctors in the whole of Scandinavia to begin to serve the needs of Ethiopia – and that still left the rest of Africa.

The way he saw it, what the Ethiopian Red Cross needed to do was train its own nurses. But whenever he mentioned this, it was the Europeans' turn to be sceptical. Training Ethiopian women to be nurses was to them an even more unlikely prospect than training more nurses in Sweden. The new doctrine of self-sufficiency promulgated by the Rockefeller Foundation and the World Bank was gaining ground in Ethiopia, but in any case everything depended on education. His Highness trusted the British to build schools. Once there were enough high school graduates, he reasoned, it wouldn't be unfeasible to train nurses.

None of his new responsibilities particularly surprised Niskanen. He had always known what his abilities were and where they might lead him. He was a good organiser: give him training schedules, exercises, and he could implement them. One task had fallen to him that he had never expected, however; he would never have thought of becoming Ethiopian delegate to the Olympic Committee. It wasn't a post he had sought. He knew, too, that some people didn't take it very seriously. Since he had been back home, he had heard the sniggers when he mentioned the possibility of Ethiopian athletes competing in the Games. But these reactions didn't discourage him. He was enjoying the job too much for that.

Niskanen was attending the Olympics for the second time, but his excitement was, if anything, even greater. The emperor had asked him to attend the Games in London four years earlier as an observer on behalf of Ethiopia. It was 1948 – hostilities had barely ended – but the British had built a brand-new stadium bigger than any he had ever seen, reportedly bigger even than the one at Nuremberg. The Allies had won the war, after all, and he supposed the British had the right. The stadium at Wembley was austere nevertheless. At one end was an enormous sign board, on which was written, 'The important thing in the Olympics is not winning but taking part', and then below, 'The important thing in life is not conquering but fighting well'. Niskanen had recognised the words as those of Pierre de Coubertin, the Frenchman who founded the Olympic movement and envisaged a truce through sport. 'The important thing in life is not the triumph but the struggle' – an odd tribute from the victorious British which went almost too far in gentlemanly courtesy.

It was the first time Niskanen had been to England and he found the people expressive, not aloof at all, especially when they complained about the rationing – or the unusually hot weather.

There was an exuberance in London and he sensed that, despite what they said, the English were proud of the surprising lack of goods in the shops. Their liking of sports, he conjectured, was not to do with the human battle so much as with the fair play and endurance they idealised.

There had been no competitors from Germany in London, unsurprisingly, nor from Japan. The Axis powers were being boycotted. Exclusion from the Olympic family meant a country did not meet the ideals of fraternity and equality at the heart of sporting competition. On the starting grid, everyone was equal.

Not quite.

In the sprints, times were coming down. The so-called 'starting blocks' that the British had devised for their Games ensured that everyone toed the line, as they liked to put it; and the new blocks made for faster starts. He had been thrilled to watch Zatopek win a gold medal in the 10,000 metres and then win the silver in the 5,000. Of the sprinters, he was impressed with Arthur Wint, who won the 400 metres with a well-timed last-minute burst. Wint, said the trackside commentator, was 'a colonial boy from one of the Empire's smallest colonies'. He was from Jamaica and, Niskanen couldn't help but notice, not a boy but a tall black fellow with legs so long it seemed he could lengthen his stride at will, stretching it farther when everyone else's was at the limit.

It was the first time he had seen a black person running in competition. Running and winning. Even if, as Tessema pointed out afterwards, Wint was running in the colours of his former slave masters, just like Jesse Owens in Berlin.

Niskanen had profited from his presence at the London Games to sound out feelings over Ethiopia's application for membership of the Olympic Committee. At a reception in the large room overlooking Hyde Park, no one was hostile, though most of the committee members, if they had heard of the country, didn't know where it was. Upon learning that it was in the Horn of Africa, they enquired no further. The application was a formality that would be dealt with in due course, he was told, and for the first time he felt the frustration of the Ethiopians. Naturally, everything depended on the timings, they remarked, and there would be little point in taking things farther if these were not 'dependable'. No point in being over-enthusiastic, someone said, it would only be humiliating in the long run, so to speak. The chuckles in the room at this feeble pun made Niskanen uncomfortable.

In Finland, the response was more encouraging. Sixty-nine nations were present at the Helsinki Games, including, to Niskanen's unease, Finland's former enemies, the Soviets. But there were still no African nations present apart from the Republic of South Africa, and it now struck Niskanen as odd that their athletes were exclusively white. The only black competitors were once again those from America and the British colonies of Jamaica and Trinidad. Wint was back, but his performance this time was erratic. The lanky Jamaican made the final in the 400 metres but was beaten by his own teammate. He put on a strong show in the 400 metres relay, however, running his leg in three minutes and three seconds. Niskanen wondered whether this uneven performance was merely symptomatic of poor training. Wint's preparation in Jamaica may have been less than thorough, but there was also the question of attitude.

Were the committee members right to insist that the results had to be consistent?

Wint's showing in London and then Helsinki had left Niskanen convinced that it was possible for black people to reach the heights of physical achievement. But he wanted to be sure. He wanted to know that the suspicions he still heard voiced among the committee members in Helsinki were unfounded; that results such as those achieved by the Jamaican sprinters were not mere flukes. The measurements would tell him that much at least. But there was another factor, one that he was just beginning to appreciate. It had to do with application. Was there something inherently unreliable about their achievements? Were blacks characteristically unstable, like children, over-emotional and temperamental? Was their attitude not consistent enough, as people inferred; were they really not mature enough?

There was only one way to find out: he had decided to take some Ethiopians to Sweden, where he would be able to put them through a series of physical evaluations. He would test them scientifically. He would find out whether they were physically capable of equalling and – why not? – surpassing white athletes.

He was confident that if the results were consistent, he would be able to instil in them the motivation they needed.

In Helsinki, he had met again with the members of the Olympic Committee to discuss Ethiopia's participation. The country was now officially a membership candidate, and he was told in Helsinki by the committee, assembled in an office in the royal palace, that there was no reason why Ethiopia's attendance would be refused at the next Games – provided the times were there.

Niskanen assured the committee that they would be. In his excitement, he went so far as to suggest they were going to be in for a surprise! He knew he had some promising athletes among the guardsmen and he was confident that the next four years could be put to good use. One of the members, a Swede who knew Niskanen from the Red Cross, warned him afterwards in private not to get too carried away. There was no point in putting your reputation on the line, he said. There was a lot of ground to make up. There's only so much one can do. He was getting used to this kind of talk, he heard it often enough. It was like the question of training nurses. It was possible – theoretically. Niskanen didn't know how to convince them of the capacities of Ethiopians. If he was honest about it, he wasn't entirely sure of their abilities himself.

But he knew that they had to be supported in their attempts to do things for themselves. Helped, but not the way you would help children, that was the tricky thing about it, for they hated condescension even more than they resented pity. He had come to understand that self-sufficiency was the corollary of independence, the source of the Ethiopians' – and the emperor's – self-esteem.

He thought about the emperor riding his horse about Addis, visiting his subjects, and the people who bowed their heads as he passed. His Imperial Majesty was going to be very pleased indeed at the news. He had made it a matter of honour, but it was a question of strategy too. If Ethiopia was accepted into the Olympic fraternity, that would strengthen the emperor's hand. His Majesty was a shrewd politician who balanced the intrigues of the Rasses at his court and knew that the key to independence was tactical allegiances with the foreign powers, the Americans, the British, the Russians and everyone else who wanted to help Ethiopia, whatever their reasons. Occasionally, Niskanen wondered what his own reason was for wanting to help Ethiopia. He was sure that, unlike the great powers, he had no hidden motive. He was happy about his work. He was going to be training athletes for the Olympics. It was an honour and a challenge.

All the while he had been hearing the drone of the commentator, but he had not really been listening, and when a lone runner trotted into the stadium he found himself rising involuntarily with the rest of the spectators; in an instant, the entire stadium was on its feet. The feline stride, the elbows up high – it could only be Zatopek.

A low rumble began, the awe-struck stirrings of a huge exclamation as everyone could finally see with their own eyes what they had been hearing from the commentator: there was no one on his heels. The Czech runner was in the lead, and even more incredible, nobody else was coming through the archway behind him on to the track. Zatopek was alone, lapping the track that belonged uniquely to him now.

As he approached the finish line, the rumble from the crowd exploded like thunder. Zatopek was about to win a third gold medal. When he burst the tape, arms high and head upturned, still alone on the track, Niskanen saw the joy and also the agony on Zatopek's face. He had won a hat-trick. He had become the first person to win the 5,000 metres, the 10,000 metres and the marathon in an Olympic Games. He had become indisputably the greatest runner in the world.

Everybody talked about how hard Zatopek trained. There was something about his determination and his technique that was no longer really amateur. Niskanen had been told by a Finnish athlete that the Czech team had a new concept called interval training. In practice sessions, Zatopek would run at full pace for as long as he could and then slow to a jog for a while and then run at full pace again. That way, apparently, he was able to push himself harder. Niskanen had witnessed the demonstration in the 5,000 metres just the day before, when Zatopek had found the reserves to overtake the leading group of three runners on the outside of the bend before the last straight, a burst of extraordinary energy that had etched itself in Niskanen's memory. He couldn't wait to get back to Addis and try the same techniques.

Before boarding the plane back to Ethiopia, however, Niskanen paid a visit to the Royal Swedish Physical Education Institute in Stockholm. Ostensibly, he wanted to apply for scholarships for Ethiopian instructors. He hoped to enable some of the young men at the Haile Selassie I Secondary School to train as PE teachers. While he was there, he sounded out the possibilities of doing biometric studies of one or two Ethiopian athletes. The results, he hoped, would show once and for all whether there were any physical differences between Africans and runners from the rest of the world.

15

Abebe had been received into the emperor's service, but his troubles were far from over. Indeed, life was much more complicated, for once the news spread, it seemed that all those who had shown him the smallest kindness, who had offered a word of advice, even just directions to an address, let alone those who had shared their food with him or allowed him to sleep under their roof, all of them now sought him out to ask a favour.

It wasn't the solicitations which bore heavily upon him. These were only to be expected, after all. He had been shown hospitality and it was only right that he should show gratitude and generosity in return. No, the problem was the impossibility of satisfying the demands that were made on him.

Sharing a meal was one thing. With his wages, he bought food and drinks; he discovered the restaurants and bars in the Mercato, places he had stared into with apprehension when he first came to the city, whereas now, in his guardsman's uniform, he was received like a Ras in their dark interiors.

His companions drank and talked loudly, and he would willingly have shared his roof, too, with those who had given him shelter, though there was no possibility of this as he was billeted in the imperial barracks. Yet this was not sufficient for some. They would slap him on the back and then, leaning close and speaking in a whisper, ask whether he could do them a small favour, nothing to do with money, they reassured him. What they wanted was for Abebe to put in a word for them at the palace. They imagined he might be able to find them a job, or get them an audience with some official. Lending them money would have been a simple matter, but what they were asking was beyond his ability to grant, for he knew no one in the palace apart from his fellow bodyguards and his superiors, whom he addressed only when they issued an order, and only then to say 'Yes, sir', as he had been taught.

Even more awkward was the reaction of his relations when he was forced to tell them he couldn't fulfil their requests. Disbelief spread across their faces, followed by a sombre cloud of disappointment. Since they knew Abebe to be honest, the realisation followed that their problem was more complex than they had thought, that the palace was more labyrinthine, its workings more intricate, than they had ever guessed. Abebe could confirm this at least. His relations listened intently to his account of life in the barracks. Rations were eaten in the mess hall, he told them, and they were always abundant. He told them about the polish for the buttons of his uniform and the electric lamps that filled the barracks with light before the sun rose, and their expressions would change again, from frustration this time to wonder.

There were more surprises in store. Life as a soldier was not what he had expected. They learned how to dismantle and clean their rifles, and then to reassemble them again. They had to do this as quickly as possible as their lives might depend on it, they were told, though there were no wars to fight, merely exercises in which they pretended to be at war. They learnt about rank and the importance of obeying the orders of their commanding officers, and they spent a lot of time drilling. When he asked other guardsmen what the purpose of this marching dance was, he was told it was for ceremonies, they were learning to march in parades. Nearly every day, too, there were half-hourly training sessions on the parade ground during which they followed the orders of the white sports officer, a hundred bodyguards united in a sometimes comical synchronised dance. It was hard not to feel ridiculous lying on your back pedalling an invisible bicycle, but he was told they were learning to be fit. All of this was excitement enough for Abebe.

Once a week, he had a day off. If they wanted, they could obtain a perm to leave the barracks. Sometimes he joined other bodyguards in excursions to the lake or to the cinema. The picture palace was a true marvel: flickering figures came alive in the darkness, so real they seemed to live inside you. In the films and newsreels, they saw the world for the first time: swashbuckling pirates and Egyptian temptresses, statesmen stepping from planes and huge dams under construction. But, exciting though it was to go to the cinema, it was not the real reason they enjoyed their days off. The best thing about being in the city was the way people stared at them. In their uniforms, Abebe felt as though they were the movie stars.

When they were on perm, bodyguards had to wear their uniforms, and they were given a severe warning about this. They must behave impeccably at all times, as though they were on the parade ground, and any brawling, drunkenness or unseemly conduct, they were told, would result in a dishonourable discharge. He soon understood why. Traversing the Mercato or riding on the bus in their pleated trousers and pressed jackets, they basked in admiration: men straightened respectfully and boys were wide eyed with awe. Girls, meanwhile, stole glances at them and, while Abebe heard the boasts of other bodyguards after their perms about how easily a certain young lady had fallen into their arms, he was always too shy to make advances himself. But this was what it meant to be a bodyguard. You made people proud. It was a responsibility as serious as defending the imperial palace.

In this way, several years passed, and then, in the summer of his twenty-first year, Abebe returned to his village to be married.

The bride's name was Yewibdar. He lifted her veil before the altar in the little church and didn't recognise the girl he used to see fetching water from the well. Her cheeks were soft and full, and her eyes shone with excitement.

She smiled at him demurely after the priest had given the blessings of Christ and Mariam, the Virgin, to their union.

Abebe wore his white guardsman's uniform, and there were many tears among the villagers who stood under parasols in the garden of the little church, tears of pride and joy. Abebe had entered the service of His Imperial Majesty. His father had recovered his strength at the news, which everybody agreed was not surprising as such a blessing was sufficient to bring about miracles.

Abebe had come back to the village with his uncle and his new friends from Addis, who caused a great stir with their brash city manners, talking loudly and eating in a leisurely, unconcerned way. After the ceremony, there was a lavish banquet. Yewibdar's father, proud that his daughter was marrying a bodyguard, had spared no expense. A healthy oxen was slaughtered and the choicest cuts were eaten by the men of the village, who enjoyed showing off in front of the city folk, slicing the raw meat with their long knives and flipping the choice, tender slivers directly into their mouths. The astrologer inspected the animal's entrails and predicted a healthy and fruitful union.

That night, Abebe lay with Yewibdar on a fresh straw mat and, early the following day, he departed for the imperial barracks.

16

On the empty terrain at Debre Zeit, a track meet was under way. The search was on to find athletes, those young men with the form and the will, the body and the mind. Niskanen had scheduled sessions twice a week on the rugged, austere plateau – except during the season of the long rains, when water sometimes fell from the skies in a solid mass, turning the whole area into a muddy lake. That day, however, the sun was shining.

The athletes were mainly guardsmen and some soldiers, all of them in shorts and vests. Some were doing press-ups; others were doing sit-ups, their hands behind their heads, swinging their elbows towards their feet. They performed the exercises as they had been shown, backs straight for the most part. Niskanen walked among them, pulling back shoulders and pushing down knees. Farther off, some apprentice athletes were running on the spot while others watched. A sandpit had been improvised and some were taking turns at the long jump. They approached with loping strides and threw themselves forward, landing with a tumble. A soldier raced forward with all his might carrying a tall pole. He halted in confusion in front of a high wooden bar roped between two posts. Another soldier followed, planted his pole in the ground and used it to lever himself up in the air, his legs pedalling furiously. He flew over the wooden bar in a graceful arc. A third soldier tried, but faltered at the peak of his jump. Soldier, pole and bar came crashing to the ground. Far away, a soldier hurled a javelin, sending it high in the sky. Niskanen watched it descend in a gentle arc and pierce the earth with a shudder.

A photographer was taking pictures that would appear in the Addis gazette and a journalist stood by his side, watching the activities with hawk-like pale brown eyes. Niskanen was pleased; it was a good time for the press to visit. It looked like a real track and field event, except that the athletes were all Ethiopians.

'They remind me of the African warriors I read about when I was a boy,' he ventured. 'We heard about the brave Zulus, how frightening they were with their animal skins and their spears ranged against the enemy.'

'It was not with spears that Emperor Menelik defeated the Italians at Adwa in 1896,' the journalist responded, 'but with guns he had purchased from the French. Perhaps he too had read about how the Zulus were massacred by the rifles of the Afrikaners.'

Niskanen had meant it as a tribute to the Ethiopians, but he realised he had been misunderstood.

'What I wanted to point out was that the athletes who took part in the Games in ancient Greece were soldiers too. Moreover,' he added, 'the Spartans and the Athenians fought in formation with spears and lances.'

The journalist's name was Fekrou Kidaneh, and he had been authorised by Tessema to write a pamphlet for the ministry to encourage participation in sports.

'Major Niskanen,' he said, 'may I ask you something?'

'Of course.'

'I would be honoured to be allowed to participate in your training programme. I have raised the matter with *Ato*. Tessema and he said he would have no objections if I were to study with you with a view to becoming an instructor. It is my belief that sport is going to be of great importance to my country.'

Kidaneh was slightly built, and by his hands Niskanen could tell that his bones were elegant but frail. If he practised any sport at all, it was most likely one where weight counted less than did coordination and strategy. He guessed him to be a tennis player.

'I'm glad to hear that you're interested in what we're doing. It is exciting, that's true. Important, I don't know. You can't achieve much without proper nutrition, for instance.'

He knew by now that he was easily swayed by the Ethiopians, with their subtle gift for flattery and tact. Why not? Having an assistant would be useful, and Kidaneh was obviously bright.

'Here,' he said. 'Let's see how you get on with this.'

He handed him the stopwatch.

Niskanen blew his whistle, waving his arms to call some of the athletes to him. An oval running track had been marked out in white paint. Niskanen picked out ten of the athletes and told them they were going to race 1,500 metres. The others ceased exercising and sat down at the side of the track to watch.

The athletes settled into their starting positions, lowering their heads, and Niskanen pointed his pistol towards the sky.

He fired the gun and the race began.

The runners sprang from the starting blocks, their elbows pumping. These were his best athletes. He had been concentrating his efforts on them for more than a year and he had managed to give them some elementary form, but he was surprised to find that they were more awkward now than before. It was as if they had become self-conscious, their spontaneous talent gone and, in its place, a clumsy repertoire of learned movement. They were like children who lose their ease of expression when taught to write. He would have to teach them to express themselves in the language of the athlete.

Soon, one of the runners had established a lead. Niskanen's gaze followed the group around the track. Their best athlete, Mamo Wolde, was in Korea, serving with the Second Battalion of the bodyguard, Ethiopia's contribution to the United Nations forces. A youngster named Negussie Roba showed promise in the sprints, but their hopes lay in the distance events. That meant Bashaye Felekeh and Wami Biratu.

As Wami passed the finish, Kidaneh squeezed the stopwatch and showed it to the major. Niskanen frowned, mentally comparing times as the panting runners gathered around him.

'Congratulations,' he announced. 'Well done, all of you. Now, I have an announcement to make.' He had saved the surprise for when the journalist was present. He addressed Wami sternly. 'You're coming with me to Sweden,' he announced.

'Yes, sir,' said Wami.

'We're going to run some tests on you there, to find out what you're made of!'

The Ethiopians glanced at one another and at the young journalist scribbling on his notepad.

Niskanen laughed. 'It's OK. There's nothing to worry about. They're biometric tests; we're going to measure your body.'

Both Wami and Bashaye would make good subjects, he told Kidaneh. They were promising athletes and they had been in the bodyguard long enough to be well nourished and fit. He had settled on Wami, however, because he was in his early twenties, younger than Bashaye. Negussie Roba was about the same age, but with different talents. Negussie was shaping up to be pretty quick. It would be interesting to compare the two, a sprinter and a distance runner. Plus, Negussie was showing an interest in the practical aspects of running. He would benefit from meeting some Swedish experts and seeing the facilities at Voladalen, where the best Scandinavian runners trained.

Niskanen had been honoured to be able to train there himself. It was Sweden's Olympus, he told Kidaneh.

On one wall of Lars Beglund's study was a nineteenth-century illustration depicting the Seven Ages of Man, from toddler to teenager to adult to stooped old man, life's bell curve. On another wall was a series of drawings of simian, Neanderthal and human skulls. Again, a bell curve, swelling and contracting. Niskanen pondered the drawings. Nature repeated the same forms in infinite ways, with infinite potentialities.

Through the glass partition wall Niskanen could see in the gym next door a wide rubber conveyor belt of a sort you might find in a factory. But this was a treadmill, electrically powered, and you set the speed so that you ran on the spot. It was a running machine, the first he had ever seen, and there was something chilling about it. It pitted the body not against a rival or even nature but against a machine: regulated, statistical, infallible. It suggested that the body too was a kind of machine. There were wires running from it to recording devices. With his electrocardiograms and the blood and urine samples in the refrigerator, Beglund was trying to uncover nature's design.

The conclusion of the biometric tests on the Ethiopians was unequivocal, he told Niskanen. 'Your Africans are perfectly well adapted to sporting competition,' he said.

'I'm glad to hear it,' said Niskanen.

'Indeed, they are perfectly fit.'

The Ethiopians had been following his training programme for more than five years, after all.

'There's nothing more to add?' he ventured.

'Nothing very important. There's a noticeable elongation of the tibia and a slight one of the other important leg bones, but it's not enough to be of any significance. It's within European population norms. Heart rates are good, on the low side in fact. Sugar uptake is excellent. There is one thing, however, that is rather unusual.'

Beglund opened the file on his desk and pointed to a chart. 'Look at this,' he said. 'It's quite surprising.'

The curve on the graph trailed gently downwards.

'I imagine it must be very hot in Ethiopia.'

'Sometimes. Depends on the season. Why?' asked Niskanen.

'It's the rate of dehydration. I've never come across such extreme cases before. I would have expected them to be accustomed to heat, of course, but the symptoms are quite marked. I calculated loss of water by the differences in body weight and it's very low, even over long periods, extremely so. These subjects are like camels.' He sat back, pleased at the way his measurements had revealed the invisible. 'They hardly sweat,' he continued. 'It's as if they are able to conserve water in their bodies the way camels retain water to be able to survive in the desert.'

'But there are no deserts in Ethiopia,' said Niskanen.

'Then we have another piece of the puzzle, that's all.'

'What do you mean?'

Beglund nodded at the cranial drawings. 'The human puzzle,' he said. 'Take these illustrations. They are sketched in detail, based on the measurements, but it's the work of artists. We don't really know why these skulls evolved the way they did. It's thought that language skills changed the shape of the jaw and encouraged development of the brain, for instance, but what about the effects of environment and diet on the body? We are just beginning to look at this area. Why do some people have particular aptitudes and not others? It is a fascinating question, but before we can even begin to answer it, we have to quantify. Your two subjects are most interesting, but they do not constitute a valid sample. I'd like to get my hands on some more of them.'

'Then you should come and visit us in Ethiopia some time,' said Niskanen.

17

Niskanen had moved from the Swedish compound to a villa in the suburbs of Addis. The house was more spacious than anything he was used to, and there was a maid and a gardener, but he was unable to fill it somehow. The furniture was locally made out of sturdy, dark wood: simple, uncomfortable chairs and a sofa. Sporting trophies and cups were neatly lined up on shelves, the only ornaments apart from an illuminated globe on the dining table – the vivid, glowing map of the world which had entranced him as a boy – and a pile of records by the gramophone.

He selected one of the discs and laid it on the turntable, then he took the tumblers he had filled with whisky and ice out to the terrace to join Tessema and Kidaneh.

They clinked glasses.

'So,' said Tessema, 'it appears that Africans are now ready for international competition.'

Niskanen leaned on the railing, taking in the fragrant tropical greenery and enjoying the trumpeter's easy phrasing of the old lullaby.

That morning, Kidaneh had untied the bundle of mail, sporting journals from abroad and correspondence with schools in rural areas wanting to send their promising athletes to the city. One of the letters was postmarked Switzerland. He had immediately turned the envelope over, staring for a long time at the five interlinked rings of the Olympic logo.

'Did you inform the palace?' Niskanen asked.

'I sent a note. But I expect His Majesty will want to see you – to thank you, personally.'

Ethiopia had been officially invited to participate in the next Olympics, to be held in Melbourne in 1956.

'It wasn't just me. Everyone has made a tremendous effort.'

'But it was your certification that made them accept our candidature,' said Tessema. 'We are in your debt, Major.'

'Oh, nonsense,' said Niskanen. 'It's satisfying to be of some use, that's all.'

Tessema's remark made Niskanen uncomfortable. Usually, Ethiopians never acknowledged anything that put them at a disadvantage. In this, even the jovial Tessema was just like the emperor. He hated any suggestion that his country was dependent on charity.

'Nevertheless,' he insisted, 'I'm sure His Majesty will want to reward you. It is only to be expected. You have performed an important service.'

'I really don't want any reward.'

'But you must accept the emperor's gratitude. It would be impolite to refuse.'

Niskanen thought about this.

'I am a Christian. It's our duty as Christians to do whatever we can to help those less fortunate than ourselves. That's the most important thing. That's what matters, not personal advantage or gain. It's doing one's duty that counts.'

Tessema looked at the sporting trophies neatly aligned on the shelf.

'They must have been surprised by the timings we submitted, don't you think?'

'The times speak for themselves,' said Niskanen. 'I think we can be satisfied with what we have achieved so far, but we've still got work to do.'

'It's OK,' said Tessema, 'we have more than a year of preparation ahead.'

Tessema had once remarked that Niskanen was always rushing, hurrying between the Ethio-Swedish Building College and the offices of the Red Cross in the Nursing School, fulfilling many responsibilities on top of his duties at the Ministry of Education. He said the major had no sense of fatality. He was always organising, always trying to get things moving, to raise funds for this or that. Then again, Tessema had joked, perhaps it was a good thing he left himself no time to dwell on the insurmountable obstacles before them!

'Now you are the one who is being optimistic,' said Niskanen. 'A year can go by extremely fast.'

'Perhaps,' said Tessema, 'but if I may say so, Major, you should take a break. Go to the countryside. You will see that it is very different, not like Addis at all. See the churches at Lalibela. They are unusual and indeed magnificent, carved out of the earth.'

'I'm sure you're right,' said Niskanen. He watched the eucalyptus trees swaying and rustling in the breeze. 'After all, it's my home now.'

The eucalyptus trees in the hills beyond the garden were tall and their peeling bark was silver like that of Scandinavian birches. If he observed the foliage closely, he could usually see some movement, some rustling of the leaves that indicated the presence of monkeys. The branches of the trees were full of them.

He had thought it strange at first that he was the only person who was amused by the monkeys, even though he was obliged to keep his windows closed at night because the monkeys were thieves and they would come in and take things from the house. He finally understood that this was why they were detested. As the years passed, although the monkeys still amused him – even on very hot nights when he would have liked to be able to open the windows fully – he had come to sympathise with the Ethiopians' sense of injustice.

Looking at the hills, he was struck by the realisation that, in seven years, he had seen little more of Ethiopia than the capital and the road to Debre Zeit, a lonely strip of asphalt traced across a treeless plateau.

'It must be so different from your own country. Don't you miss it?' asked Tessema.

'The winter, yes. I miss the snow.'

'I would like to see your country one day. It is hard for me to imagine a place where everything is always white, always covered in snow.'

Niskanen laughed. 'Not in the summer,' he said. 'In summer, the snow melts. It's hot, like in Ethiopia. It's green, like here, and the sun shines all day and all night.'

Tessema and Kidaneh exchanged looks of amazement.

'All night?'

'Yes, it's the Land of the Midnight Sun. In midsummer, the sun never sets. There is daylight all night long.'

'I cannot imagine,' said Tessema. Kidaneh shook his head.

'It's true!' Niskanen laughed. It had never occurred to him that his country could hold such wonder. His Ethiopian friends were at a loss for words.

Kidaneh had been examining the letter from the Olympic Committee, contemplating the famous logo.

'Do you know what these signify?' he asked. 'These five rings.'

Tessema shrugged.

'They are supposed to represent the five continents,' said Niskanen.

'Then I wonder which of the rings represents the continent of Africa,' said Kidaneh. 'The black ring at the centre, perhaps?'

There was no answer.

'If so, then how is it that no African nations have taken part in the games?'

'Until now,' said Tessema. 'Ethiopia will be the first, thanks to you, Major.'

Niskanen bowed his head politely. 'As I said, we have plenty of work to do.'

18

All that Abebe knew about the heats was that they were looking for guardsmen who could run fast. They were testing all the men, trying to find the fastest runners, perhaps for some kind of mission. He thought he might have a chance of winning, but he found there were guardsmen who could run much faster.

They had come in a truck out to the air force base at Debre Zeit, where they had been given shorts and running shoes – the first time he had worn such things – and told to line up on the track. Someone explained that they must run around the track, between the white lines painted to mark an oval circuit on the red earth, like a magical sign on the ground to circumscribe and channel their forces. The man introduced himself as Kidaneh and said he was a sports instructor. Abebe had never heard of such a title.

Abebe had run as fast as he was able. He had been told to run again while others were sent back to the changing rooms and now he was running a much longer race, twelve laps of the track, they were told, though he had lost count of how many times they had gone around. He was keeping his eyes on the leader; he knew only that he would have to run faster than Wami Biratu if he wanted to win.

In the barracks, they said that Wami had been abroad, to a laboratory where they had wired him to a machine to make him run faster. If he wanted to win he would have to run faster than Wami. But it wasn't easy. Every time Abebe caught up with him, Wami inched ahead without even looking around. Abebe, on the other hand, was getting tired. He noticed that he was panting harder than Wami, who seemed to be making hardly any effort at all. After a while, he realised he was falling behind.

Kidaneh was holding a stopwatch. Beside him was the major, the white soldier who gave them exercises in the barracks. The major's gaze was following Wami and the group of leaders around the track. There had been many of them at the start, but the laps had soon separated the best runners from the others; lap after lap, until they had run 5,000 metres. As Wami passed the line, Kidaneh squeezed the stopwatch and showed it to the major. The major frowned as the rest of the men came in and leaned on their knees, gasping for breath, or, like Abebe, collapsed on the ground clutching their aching thighs.

The major waited until the last remaining runners had passed the line before congratulating Wami. He told them their effort to finish the race was appreciated; winning wasn't everything, he said. Then he told the sweating bodyguards to go and get showered.

He turned to Abebe.

'Who is this?' he asked.

Kidaneh looked at his list. 'Abebe Bikila, private.'

Although he had yet to catch his breath, Abebe nodded.

He enjoyed training on the parade ground. He had learnt the names of the exercises and he was excited to find his body growing fitter, his stamina increasing too with the regular meals. Exercising was better than guard duty, where you had to stand perfectly still for hours, or cleaning out the barracks.

'Well, Private Bikila, I want you to do something for me. I want you to regulate your breathing.'

Kidaneh translated.

Niskanen held Abebe's chest, one hand on his back and one on his front. He breathed in and out slowly, deeply, in through the nose and then exhaling through the mouth.

'Like that. You must control your breathing.'

Without thinking, Abebe slowed his own breaths until he was in unison.

'Now, once more. Another lap. Yes. Go around again. Don't worry about speed. You don't have to run fast. Try to concentrate on your breathing...'

He repeated his demonstration of the right breathing tempo.

'OK?'

The major raised his arm and then brought it down to start the lap.

'He's not a sprinter,' he said to Kidaneh as he watched Abebe. 'Look at his hip carriage. He's a distance runner.'

A sprinter was an ungainly powerhouse, dangerous in his movements. You could feel the energy waiting to explode. With a sprinter, you could sense the nerves tensing with adrenalin, the muscles flexing. Abebe's torso was loose, his long legs reaching forward, pulling him effortlessly on. He held his elbows in tightly at his waist without having to be told.

He returned at a jog. This time he wasn't panting as before.

'Like this, sir,' he said.

'Good. Now we'll just have to build up your speed a little.'

They sent him off to get showered.

In the changing room, Wami was buttoning his uniform, full of himself after his win, watching Abebe.

'What tribe, Galla?' he shouted.

Abebe avoided Wami's stare, pretending he hadn't heard.

'I said which tribe are you, boy?'

Abebe timidly lifted his head, fearing he would be humiliated.

There was a long pause. At last, Wami spoke.

'You are good, but you will have to run faster if you want to catch up with us!'

Abebe nodded.

Wami and some of the others started to laugh. Their laughter ceased, however, as Niskanen and Kidaneh entered.

'You men had better be getting back for inspection,' Niskanen said.

The soldiers finished dressing hurriedly and left. Abebe was one of the last.

The major detained him and, once the others had left, asked him what they had been laughing about.

Abebe stared at Kidaneh uncertainly, but Kidaneh merely lifted his chin and looked away. Abebe didn't know whether he should answer. He didn't know how to tell a truth that was so shameful and so obvious.

'They are Amhar, sir. They laugh because I am Galla.'

Kidaneh translated.

'I see,' said the major.

He looked at the skinny young guardsman, his head bowed in shame.

'I'll tell you something,' said the major. 'I used to get the same treatment when I was a private.'

Abebe was surprised to hear that the white soldier had been a mere private. He assumed that if one was a major, it was because one's father and grandfather were majors too.

'Yes. My family came from Finland originally. Finland is a rugged country. The Finns are very poor and Swedes think they are superior to everyone in Scandinavia. They were always making fun of us.'

Abebe stared at Niskanen. He had always assumed that the major was a superior person, not because he was an officer so much as because he was white. It had never occurred to him that whites might be contemptuous of each other. Rivalry, jealousy and competition he would have expected, but *disdain*... This was new.

'People are the same everywhere. There's nothing you can do about it, except show them who's best out on the track.'

19

Mengistu Neway was seated behind his desk when Niskanen entered. The major was shocked that the newly promoted commander of the Imperial Bodyguard didn't rise and return his salute. It occurred to him, too, that Neway knew very well how to conduct himself and merely wanted to underline the fact he was now the major's superior.

'At ease, Major,' said General Mengistu, leaning back without a smile to study Niskanen. He wore the white uniform of the Guards, festooned with ribbons he had done nothing to earn.

Niskanen found Mengistu Neway disquieting. He had gone from lieutenant to general in record time, though Niskanen couldn't see what he had done to merit promotion. He didn't even strike him as the military sort. He had the features of an Egyptian; he always looked as though he were making some secret calculation. He had risen fast chiefly owing to privilege or political acumen, as far as Niskanen could make out.

Neway began by asking whether the arrangements for their departure for Melbourne were to Niskanen's satisfaction, but soon came to the point.

'It's extremely gratifying for all of us that Ethiopia has been welcomed by the Olympic family,' he said. 'Members of His Majesty's Imperial Bodyguard will be competing in the Games. That is good.'

He paused before he continued. Niskanen said nothing.

'I'll be frank. His Majesty is concerned about prestige abroad. He has asked me to ascertain Ethiopia's chances of winning a medal. It would be unfortunate if the outcome was, in any way, humiliating.'

'Wami Biratu shows a lot of promise. His times for the one thousand and five thousand metres compare with the best internationals. I'm convinced we have a good chance with him. Bashaye Felekeh is very talented too. A natural runner. And Mamo Wolde has given some encouraging performances in the past.'

Niskanen was genuinely confident. Wami and Mamo were in their early twenties, strong boys from the country with an aptitude for running.

'You are to be commended for what you have achieved so far, Major, but things will be different in Australia.'

'Mamo's not in peak form, not as yet. But he has the ability. I'm sure he'll acquit himself well.'

He admitted that Mamo had returned from serving in Korea only a few months ago, not enough time to get back in shape. 'On the other hand, serving with joint forces might give him an advantage. He'll be used to rubbing shoulders with people from different countries. He'll be less inhibited.'

General Mengistu appeared to be weighing the nuances in Niskanen's arguments.

'Most of our people don't even know about the Games,' he said, smiling at Niskanen. 'But you do understand their importance to His Majesty, don't you?'

'Naturally.'

'I just wanted to be sure,' he said.

Niskanen was uncomfortable.

'We'll do our best.'

'Here in Ethiopia, we are great admirers of you Scandinavians. Your kind of socialism is much debated in developing countries. Independence is essential to national development and the Scandinavians have found a third way.'

Niskanen didn't respond.

'We must do the same, but you must understand that ultimately we will have to do it without your help. Not just *your* help, but anyone's.'

This was fashionable talk in certain circles. Niskanen was wary of it and wanted to change the subject.

'How is your brother, by the way?' he asked. He had heard that Germame Neway, his former pupil at the Haile Selassie I Secondary School, had been awarded a grant by the emperor to attend university abroad.

'He graduated with honours from Columbia. He's at the Ministry of the Interior now, on a provincial posting for the moment.'

Mengistu Neway informed him that the subject of his brother's master's thesis was 'The Impact of White Settlement in Kenya'. He enunciated the words as though the thesis were a spell, able in itself to dissipate the shadows of colonialism.

He stood and smiled at Niskanen.

'My brother had a high regard for you, Major. He always says your classes were a respite, that you never looked down on us, not like the British.'

He came around the desk to shake Niskanen's hand.

'Anyway,' he said, 'On behalf of the Imperial Bodyguard, let me wish you the best of luck.'

20

Abebe had been given a pole with the red, orange and green flag and ordered to stand with the rest of the men in one of the two opposing lines that formed the guard of honour. They were going to welcome the bodyguards returning from Australia. Abebe had never seen so many flags before. It was a sunny day and there were flags everywhere, fluttering proudly in the breeze.

Mamo Wolde led the parade, marching with his chin high, and behind him came a dozen guardsmen wearing vests with their names written on the back. Abebe recognised some of the men. He had asked in the barracks why it was they were being given such a hero's welcome and had been told that they had honoured Ethiopia on the field of sporting competition.

Following behind them were Major Niskanen with the members of the Athletics Federation wearing blue blazers with the crest of the Lion of Judah on the breast pocket, and then the politicians in dark suits. The imperial band thumped and blasted behind with their drums and horns, and the noise had drawn people in their thousands to watch the parade as it wound its way towards the palace, where the athletes were to receive decorations from His Imperial Majesty.

Abebe recognised Wami Biratu and some of the other guardsmen he had competed with at Debre Zeit. He began to understand why it was so important to run those races. He had been content to participate; it was simply one of his duties as a bodyguard, he thought. Now he saw that there was more at stake. Running was more than a simple exercise, it was a competition. Moreover, it was evidently an important one.

Behind him, he could hear the comments of the city dwellers. The older people, who could remember the war of liberation, were surprised that athletes were being honoured in such a way. What were these sporting triumphs? they asked. What was so hard about running? they laughed. When *they* were youths, they had stood firm and fought the enemy! But younger men and boys, seeing the spectacle, said that when they grew up, they wanted to be athletes too. They all agreed, however, that Ethiopia's achievements should be celebrated. The world was changing, and the nation had to change with it.

Abebe saw the bodyguards marching past, heroes honouring Ethiopia on the field of sport, and he decided that he wanted to be one of them.

As soon as they returned to the barracks, Abebe asked the sergeant whether he could race like the athletes who went to Melbourne.

The sergeant had looked at him doubtfully. 'Now you want to run,' he said. 'You think you can be like them?' But he said that everyone would be given a chance and it would be up to Abebe to show his worth.

The national team hadn't won any medals at Melbourne, but they had acquitted themselves well. Niskanen stood on the parade ground and received the emperor's salute with a sense of achievement that surprised him; Ethiopia wasn't his country, after all, yet it was as if these people were his own, and their pride was his too.

Mamo had come in fourth in the 1,500 metres, beaten to the bronze medal by an Australian, Landy. It was an honourable showing for Ethiopia's first-ever participation, however, and if His Majesty was at all disappointed, he didn't show it. Wearing the serious, smiling countenance of a child playing his favourite game, he solemnly pinned medals on everyone in the team.

One thing was certain: the Games had demonstrated that Ethiopia was credible in track and field events. They had received invitations to participate in other international meetings, but travelling abroad was expensive and the opportunities would be limited. In the meantime, there was the next National Armed Forces Championship to prepare for. Even better, it seemed as though everyone in the bodyguard was now determined to beat Mamo. The competition could only be fruitful.

Meanwhile, Niskanen had been trying to analyse their weaknesses.

Once again, in Melbourne he had seen an athlete from the Third World beating a top competitor: this time it was in the marathon when Alain Mimoun beat Zatopek. Mimoun was running for France, but he was another colonial boy, an Algerian, a native of North Africa. He had the same bony frame as many of the Ethiopians, the same sturdy lightness. He suspected that Mimoun had grown up in a mountainous region, a terrain much like Ethiopia's. Most probably he was more accustomed to the dry Australian heat than Zatopek.

Was it climate, or nutrition, perhaps, or some other factor that made people what they were? Or was it something innate, something ancient and immutable, that made a good runner?

He had seen Mimoun duelling with Zatopek before, and each time the Algerian had to settle for silver while the Czech snatched gold right in front of him: first in the 10,000 in London, and then four years on in Helsinki, when Zatopek won both the 10,000 and then, a few days later, the 5,000; each time, Mimoun was just a few metres behind him. In Melbourne, the field was younger and their ages were beginning to tell. Neither of them took any medals in the distance events. Unexpectedly, Mimoun put down for the marathon at the last minute. He overtook Zatopek halfway and then beat a Slav and a young Finnish runner.

Despite the heat, despite his age, the Algerian had refused any assistance after he crossed the finish. He didn't collapse to the ground like the others after more than two hours of strenuous exertion. He must have been exhausted, utterly worn out as only a marathon can leave you, but nevertheless he waited for Zatopek, who arrived struggling in sixth place. Along with the entire stadium, Niskanen had stood up and applauded as the two old rivals embraced.

Melbourne had demonstrated to Niskanen that distance running was where the Ethiopians' strengths lay. Negussie Roba had reached the finals in the 100 and 200 metres, but the Americans and the British dominated those events. In the four years to come, he would be concentrating his efforts on the longer races. In Mamo and Wami, he had runners who might one day equal Zatopek and Mimoun in the 5,000 and 10,000 metres.

The marathon was another matter.

21

The heats were held on military bases around the country but they were open to anyone who wanted to emulate the athletes they heard about on the radio, not only the soldiers in the garrisons. Abebe donned his shorts and vest and jogged with the others along the wide avenue that led out of Addis from the guardhouse.

In heat after heat, he had run faster, though he had no idea of how fast he was running, whether he was doing well or not. His strategy was simple. He would stay with the leaders, whoever they were, and try to get ahead. Usually, it didn't require too much effort.

Each day, there were new faces on the starting line, faces he had never seen before, men from Tigray and Gojam. Each time, he was among the first to pass the finishing line. And yet, spurred by the other runners, pulled on by their determination to win, he began to find after a while that running was not as effortless as he had first thought. He had to strive harder to pass them. He slept deeply from tiredness and woke to find the muscles of his legs stiff. Each morning, however, when he looked at the bulletin boards, he saw his name again on the lists.

On the day of the finals of the Armed Forces Championship, even more people were lining the streets than when the athletes had returned from Melbourne. Abebe was down for the 10,000 metre race. He had been disappointed to be eliminated from the sprint races days before but he knew he could never hope to beat Negussie Roba. The instant the pistol fired, he was already behind, and there simply wasn't enough time to catch up. Negussie was younger than him, barely twenty years old, and he was undoubtedly the best sprinter in Ethiopia. Over the short distances, Abebe just couldn't summon the muscle power he needed.

That morning, he had been privileged to study Negussie from the trackside, admiring his sheer force as he won first the 100 and then the 200 metre race, powered by legs that sent him hurtling forward like a bull out of a stall.

'Think you can beat us?' laughed Wami Biratu as they limbered up for the first of the distance events.

Abebe looked at his feet, too shy to answer.

It was the first time he had been on the starting line with a real champion. Everybody knew that Wami Biratu had raced in Melbourne against the British. The other runners, too, cowered timidly.

'Watch out,' warned Wami. 'You boys are going to learn a thing or two.'

Wami and Bashaye were the oldest of the competitors, and they stretched their limbs proudly before the younger entrants from the provinces.

Bashaye must have been nearly forty years old. He was a veteran, a legendary soldier who had fought alongside his father against insurgents in the south when Abebe was just a child. Like Wami, he wasn't quick enough for sprints, but over the longer distances he was still able to beat the younger men. The runners talked about how he had come in twenty-fifth in the marathon in Melbourne, about halfway down the field, they said admiringly. He had run without faltering for two and a half hours. It was as if Bashaye and Wami had learned to pace their exertions like tireless cheetahs who must stalk all day for a kill.

Abebe didn't know whether it was respectful to seek to best his elders. The games of *Gena* he had played in the village were always with boys of his own age. Athletics was new, and the first rule seemed to be that everybody was equal in all respects but one.

Abebe couldn't help noticing that Mamo Wolde ignored their mockery. Abebe had been studying Mamo, and he was excited to be lining up alongside him. Mamo was the best runner in Ethiopia. He was also a real soldier. He had been in action in Korea. But he had come in fourth in Melbourne, so he had not received any medal at the Olympics, and this must have been troubling him. Mamo was going to want to assert himself, he would be determined to show what he was capable of. Abebe knew that Mamo was the one he would have to keep up with – if he could. They were both about the same age and, though they had never spoken to each other, he knew that they both came from the same province. He would have liked to enquire about Mamo's family – perhaps they had relations in common? – but the atmosphere in the new sports ground was far too tense.

A track had been marked out in white paint on the red dust and terraces of wooden scaffolding had been erected. Shaded by umbrellas, Niskanen and Tessema were watching the races. Behind them, farther up, stood the emperor and members of the royal family.

They raced around and around the track, two dozen runners, sweating and puffing hard. Luckily, there was a breeze, cooling them a little, but the sun was hot and it made Abebe's head swim. He tried to keep as close as he could to Mamo and soon lost count of the number of times they had passed in front of the major. Inevitably, Wami and Bashaye had had the same idea. They pounded the hard dirt track in a group until, after the fourteenth lap – what he found out later was 7 kilometres – Bashaye began to slow. But Mamo maintained his lead and pulled farther ahead, taking Wami with him.

Abebe couldn't keep up with them. He remained in third place, unable to force his legs to make any more effort.

Dejected, he watched the leaders pull away, feeling as if he were trapped in a dream. Struggling to advance, he allowed himself to be overtaken.

By the time they returned to the stadium, the cheering for Mamo had died down. The excitement was over.

Abebe had come in ninth.

The National Armed Forces Championship closed a few days later with a marathon. Abebe had run the 5,000 metres the previous day and come in sixth. He was improving at least.

There had been no heats for the marathon, and it seemed as if all the competitors in the championship were going to try to make the course. Thirty or more runners had massed behind the rope and they were now waiting almost casually for the race to start. It wasn't like the other races, it wasn't going to be won with a difference of seconds, and so there wasn't the same pressure.

Mamo was among the runners at the start. He approached Abebe and spoke to him in an accent that was familiar.

'I knew you were behind me the other day. You were running good. What happened? Did you get a cramp or something?'

'No, it wasn't that,' replied Abebe. Mamo hadn't introduced himself, nor had he begun their conversation by asking Abebe after his health and that of his family. It was as if the track had made them equals, intimates.

'You know if you get a cramp you just have to keep going. You must try to ignore it and after a while, if you're lucky, it will go away.'

'It wasn't cramp. It was my legs. They were getting heavy.' He didn't want to admit that his leg muscles had become as hard as iron. Lifting them by the end had become near to impossible.

'I know. You think you can hardly make them work. But you're still running. You look down and the ground's still going by beneath you. Your legs are working, even though it doesn't feel like it.'

'That is what happened,' said Abebe. 'Just like that.'

So Mamo had the same problems. He felt his legs getting harder too. He had to force himself on.

'Anyway, you put the pressure on me for a while there.'

Abebe was surprised.

'You were pacing me good! You shouldn't have given up!'

He wanted to thank Mamo for this information and ask him more, but the marathon was about to start.

'Next time, I will try not to give up,' he said.

'Let me give you some advice.'

Abebe nodded.

'Take it easy. Let them sort themselves out, stay near the front but don't push. Let the leaders get tired, let them believe you haven't got anything left in you. Then you accelerate.'

It sounded sensible enough, but it also occurred to Abebe that perhaps Mamo was trying to trick him. He was a Galla, it was true, he was one of Abebe's kind, but he had been a bodyguard for longer.

'But,' he asked, 'why are you telling me this?'

'Wami's so full of himself. He thinks he can win everything. Someone's got to show him. If not me, then you.'

And this is what Abebe did.

He resolved not to push himself too hard at the start. It was his first marathon, the first time he had run such a long race. He prayed that he would have enough stamina to keep up with the leaders and that there would be some strength left in him at the end. Halfway through the long jog through the countryside, after he had passed the turning point and was on his way back towards the capital, when he realised he was winning, Mamo's words had returned to him. He kept on pushing. He forced himself past the moment when his legs became heavy, and soon a kind of lightness came over him. He was as nimble as the wind, sweeping forwards.

Mamo had fallen back. Later, he would tell Abebe that the marathon wasn't his race, that he was better over the middle distances. Wami too was behind him, but much closer, Abebe knew, though he couldn't see him when he glanced back. He was almost three-quarters of the way through the race and his pace wasn't faltering. The marathon was his race, the one he was born to run.

When he returned to the track, the crowd cheered. They had been listening to the commentary on transistors and knew that the favourite, Wami, had been beaten by an outsider. They already knew his name.

'Abebe!' they shouted. 'Abebe Bikila!'

He passed the finish and quickly caught his breath.

'Congratulations,' said the major. Tessema shook his hand and the star of the St George football team slapped him on the back like a fellow sportsman.

Someone else said he had done well. He had brought honour to the bodyguard.

As he stood on the dais between the two other medallists and bowed to receive the medal from Tessema, he stole a glance at the emperor. It was the first time Abebe had ever felt the gaze of the King of Kings upon him, a scrutiny that filled him with burning humility.

He saluted Tessema and then turned and saluted His Majesty, as he had seen earlier victors do.

The emperor returned his salute.

The guardsman stood soldier-straight while the band played the national anthem, trying hard to hold back the pride and glory swirling inside him.

22

Niskanen had invited Ben and Tessema over to try his new sauna. He had bought an old iron stove in the Mercato to burn the wood and workmen from the Ministry of Building had constructed the cabin in his garden. The wood was not pine but a local wood, dark and dense, making it sombre inside. Even if one's bones never got as cold as they did at home, he was glad he would be able to warm away the stiffness in there during the Ethiopian winter, those few months when, because of the altitude, it was surprisingly damp and chilly.

He felt the sweat beading on his skin, the cleansing exfoliation. He was very pleased with the result of his efforts. Tessema, on the other hand, was near to fainting.

'Can't take it, eh?' Niskanen jibed.

'Your country is cold, so I can understand that you would like this heat.'

'You'll get used to it.'

'I am not so sure,' demurred Tessema.

'It relaxes the muscles,' explained Niskanen. 'If we were in Sweden then afterwards we could go out in the snow to cool off.'

'You Swedes are so pragmatic. You have even found a way to make use of snow.'

There was a pause as they basked in the heat, and Niskanen guessed that Tessema was trying to picture the snow, the coldness of it, and what it would be like to go from tropical heat to Arctic cold in a matter of minutes. He had realised that the Ethiopians could not imagine his world, as he could not have conceived of theirs.

Ben didn't seem to be enjoying the stifling heat much either, nor the silence it induced.

'What about this Cup of Nations?' he asked. 'What do you reckon of Ethiopia's chances? Think you'll beat the Egyptians?'

'Why do you ask this?' queried Tessema. 'Is the American Council going to start sponsoring our soccer team now?'

The new African Cup was an important tournament. Tessema had joined with the Egyptians and the Sudanese to approach FIFA for affiliation. Niskanen knew how proud he was that their league had been accepted.

'I just asked because maybe the South Africans would like to know,' said Ben.

'That is what I think too,' said Tessema. 'Well, you can tell them we are not going to Khartoum.'

Niskanen was surprised.

'Why not?' he asked.

'Because the South Africans are sending their national team.'

'So?'

Tessema hesitated, uncomfortable with what he was about to say.

'Selection for the South African national team is whites-only. For this reason, we will not be going to Khartoum. We are boycotting them...'

Niskanen recalled that the Axis powers had been boycotted from the London Games by the Olympic Committee, but it was the first time he had heard of a single country leading such an initiative.

'It's a great pity,' continued Tessema, his pace slowed by the heat. 'Our players were looking forward to it. Our people – all African peoples – adore soccer.'

'Hey, hey, hold on!' Ben's energy was undiminished by the condensation in the sauna. 'It's supposed to be the first all-Africa soccer tournament. How can you boycott the South Africans because they're white? You know what that is? That's colour prejudice!'

'And what are they doing?' Tessema retorted angrily. 'We won't play against them, but the reason is not because they are a team of white men. We would like nothing more than the chance to beat them on the football field. They are denying Negro people the chance to play on their team on grounds of colour. They are segregating them, denying them opportunity. That is what Negroes must contend with in South Africa, and in parts of your country too.'

Tessema stared reproachfully at Ben and the American muttered something about the Deep South being 'backward'.

'Here in Ethiopia, we were never a subjugated people, we were never enslaved. We were never humiliated, and so we shall never accept humiliation!'

'You know what it means if other countries follow your lead?' asked Ben.

'Yes, we do. His Imperial Majesty is fully aware of the implications. He is tired of the hypocrisy. He has given his approval to our initiative.'

Niskanen leaned forward and opened the heavy iron lid of the stove to poke the coals. Ben shook his head slowly.

'The South Africans are going to be pissed!' he said.

Tessema ignored him and, after a while, turned to Niskanen.

'It's getting hot in here,' he said. 'When are we to be allowed to step outside?'

'Not yet...'

23

Thirty runners were jogging steadily, spread out along the road to Debre Zeit, defiant human figures on the empty plain. A shepherd tending his goats gaped as the runners passed, surprised at this human commotion, at odds with the steady flow of the world. Niskanen was following in a jeep with Kidaneh, a pastor with his flock.

One by one the runners passed, then one of them stumbled and fell to the ground.

Abebe was at the rear and stopped to help his comrade.

'Don't worry about him,' shouted Kidaneh. 'We'll take care of him. You can't afford to lose any time.'

He gesticulated ahead and Abebe set off again while an assistant coach – since the Melbourne Games, anyone who couldn't run wanted to coach – jumped down from the jeep to help the fallen athlete.

Though he ran well, Abebe had not been able to repeat his victory at the next Armed Forces Championships, nor the year after that. Nonetheless, Niskanen had persevered. Abebe was modest and taciturn, qualities Niskanen appreciated, but winning the marathon had made him less rather than more confident.

It was typical of the Ethiopians. Niskanen had been conducting a series of trials, narrowing the field, testing capacities. He was soon going to have to make the selection and yet, despite all the training, there were worrying inconsistencies. Even the best runners aren't always at the peak of their form, but the Ethiopians tended to perform erratically. The hardest thing was to persuade them of their own abilities.

When they caught up with the group of runners, he found they had taken an unscheduled break at the halfway point and were sitting or sprawling on the ground by the road. They had misunderstood the instructions, said an assistant coach. Kidaneh laughed and suggested it was because they were spooked.

'Perhaps they've seen a spirit, you know, a ghost,' he suggested. 'For them, the spirits are everywhere!'

'Nonsense,' said Niskanen impatiently.

But Kidaneh grew serious and said it wasn't nonsense at all. If misfortune befell one of them, he explained, if they lost a race or pulled a muscle, they would not attribute it to their own doing, or to chance; they would blame others.

'Imagine you are running and you stumble on a rock that causes your ankle to twist. Whose fault is that? You would say that it was an accident: nature put the rock there; you didn't see it; your muscles weren't fully warmed up. For them, these coincidences are unlikely. In fact, as far as they're concerned, it would be naive to think that everything was the fault of coincidence. It's because of someone's actions; and if that someone is invisible, then it's either a spirit or someone who has invoked sorcery.'

Niskanen didn't believe in this superstitious mumbo-jumbo, of course. Yet he was aware that even someone as rational as Kidaneh thought there was something to it. 'I suppose so,' he said. 'But we can't afford to let it stop us.'

He turned his attention to the runners.

'All of you, up!'

Abebe had removed his training shoes and was massaging his feet.

'OK,' snapped Niskanen. 'This time, no stopping! Everybody back to camp. Let's go!'

He blew his whistle to signal that the pause was over and Kidaneh clicked his stopwatch as the runners set off. It was about eight kilometres back to the base. Niskanen gave them twenty-five minutes. Anything under would be good.

Abebe struggled to put his shoes back on. The group was leaving him behind. Finally, he stuffed the shoes in the pockets of his ample shorts and ran to catch them up. When he arrived back at the base, Niskanen had overtaken the runners in the jeep and was waiting at the entrance to the air force base with Kidaneh, who clicked his stopwatch and held it out for the major.

Niskanen noted the time in his log and, as he did, he realised that Abebe's feet were bare.

'What happened to your shoes?'

Abebe shook his head.

'No shoes, sir.' He produced the running shoes and held them out for Niskanen's inspection.

Perplexed, Niskanen waved him inside. 'Well done, anyway. Go and get showered.'

'Yes, sir.'

Niskanen gazed at the time he had noted, then he checked the stopwatch again.

'Twenty-two minutes,' he exclaimed to Kidaneh. He could scarcely believe it.

Niskanen and Kidaneh were together on the terrace of Niskanen's villa. Niskanen was perusing the log, something he did for long moments.

He had decided to make some comparison tests to see whether what had happened with Abebe was a fluke.

'It's incredible. Look at these times! He's faster without shoes!'

He turned the log around to show Kidaneh.

28th June. Thirty-two kilometres on road (without shoes): 1:45:00.

29th June. Rest.

30th June. Thirty-two kilometres on road (with shoes): 1:46:30.

Kidaneh glanced at the log and leant back.

'Why are you so surprised, Major?' he asked. 'Abebe never wore anything on his feet before he became a member of the Imperial Bodyguard and you gave him his first pair of training shoes. When I was a boy, I used to run thirty miles a day, from my father's railway station to school and back. None of us wore shoes.'

'But these times!'

Over a distance of 32 kilometres, Abebe was a minute and a half faster without shoes! That equalled two minutes over the full marathon distance. Yet Niskanen knew that what Kidaneh was implying was true: it might have nothing to do with the shoes. Still, two minutes could be enough to make a difference in a marathon.

They had narrowed the field down to fewer than a dozen athletes and they were going to have to make some difficult choices.

He stared at the log, hoping Abebe's times would decide for him.

1st July. Morning. 5 x 1,500m on road at five-minute intervals. 4:12; 4:18; 4:13; 4:14; 4:14. Afternoon. Forty-five minutes of light jogging over mixed terrain.

2nd July. Rapid straights alternated with slow bends.

3rd July. Rest.

4th July. Morning. Ninety minutes of mixed terrain: 300 metres uphill alternated with 300 metres of jogging on the flat. Afternoon. 3 x 1,500m: 4:13; 4:15; 4:15.

5th July. Morning. One hour of mixed terrain. Afternoon. One hour of jogging over hills around the lake. Sauna.

Niskanen had read in an interview with Zatopek how he felt 'exalted' by his style of training, the interval method of alternating bouts of fast and slow running. But he had read too about the Australian international Elliot, who favoured an 'emotional' style, running freely up and down dunes, through parks, in the wild. He had tried that with Abebe and the others, sending them out across rugged, hilly countryside, although he made sure Abebe ran barefoot only on the road, to avoid injuring his feet on the sharp rocks. The natural style seemed to fit and the inclines helped to build speed.

A typical day's training began with an hour or so of running over mixed terrain in the morning; 300 metres uphill alternated with 300 on the flat to recover. In the afternoon, he might put them through a classic series of heats, say four times 1,500 metres on the road with five-minute breaks in between.

Since there were no asphalt tracks in the country, Niskanen had measured out the distances on the road between Addis and Debre Zeit. For the marathon distance, he added another kilometre without telling anyone, just to be certain. Nearly every day, he, Kidaneh and the boys were out on the road and the surrounding hills. Training sessions always began with twenty minutes of stretching, and Niskanen liked to end the strenuous days with a sauna for everyone at his house to relax the muscles.

The results were better than he had dared to hope. Wagkira, a regular soldier from the provinces, was running marathon distances in less than two and a half hours. In Wagkira, he felt he had a contender for the toughest race of all.

He feared that he would have to choose between Wagkira and Abebe. With six weeks to go, he didn't want to have to give up on any of them.

7th July. 5,000 metres on road: 14:47:08.

'I told him I wanted him to do it in under fifteen minutes – and he did!'

He pointed at the last entry.

8th July. 36 kilometres on road: 2:00:45.

'I agree Abebe has speed, but we don't know if he has the stamina,' said Kidaneh. 'The marathon is a very difficult race, very uncertain. You yourself said we should concentrate on the five and ten thousand.'

Niskanen was pinning their hopes for the forthcoming Rome Games on the 10,000 metres, where he felt they had the best chance of winning a medal. They had Negussie for the sprints; he was their fastest runner, but the competition in the 100 and 200 metres heats would be fierce. Their chief hope was still Mamo Wolde. He had competed well in Melbourne and he had improved since then. He was in his late twenties, at his physical and technical peak. For the moment, they had found no younger runners who could outclass him, although they had high hopes for Said, a young Muslim. And then there were Wami and Bashaye: although they were getting on in age – they were both in their mid-thirties – their times were still consistently good.

'It's a shame we can't take them all,' mused Niskanen.

'You know that's not possible.'

The Ethiopian Olympics Committee had decided along with the National Sports Confederation to concentrate on cyclists rather than athletes. Tessema had gently reminded him that athletics was not the most popular sport in Ethiopia. He had explained that the government was building a new bicycle factory and since the cycling team had done well in Melbourne, it had been decided to put an extra effort into the cycling events. 'A medal there would be good for the factory's output,' he had pointed out. 'Besides,' he added, 'the

Italians are expecting to put on a strong show in the cycle races.'

Niskanen could understand that, for the ministry, the fitness of a people and its army was not a sufficiently important function of sport. There were also considerations of prestige and propaganda: a victory over the Italian cyclists would be invaluable.

'I know he won the armed forces marathon, but that was a fluke; he hasn't been able to repeat it,' said Kidaneh. 'And Abebe has no international experience, remember. Imagine him lining up with Americans or Soviets... You know what they're like.'

If Abebe showed any promise, the experienced American and Soviet athletes would do whatever they could to intimidate him. They would try to undermine him. It wouldn't be hard, Abebe was timid and deferential; moreover, he was an African, an outsider. As such, he already suffered unconsciously from what Niskanen had heard referred to as an inferiority complex.

'We could enter Wami for the marathon too, if you want.'

Niskanen knew that Kidaneh the aspiring politician had become involved in sport because he had understood that it was an area of development favoured by the emperor. But sport was as much a matter of strategy as anything else.

The Ethiopian delegation stood on the runway beside the Air Ethiopia aeroplane that had brought him to Addis more than a decade before. Niskanen was leading an African team to the Olympic Games for the second time, and he found himself imagining what it would be like to be waiting on the tarmac at Helsinki. He wondered what his fellow countrymen would think when they saw him parading around the track with the Ethiopian team, a white man marching behind an African flag with fourteen Ethiopians. It was an unexpected destiny, but then that was probably the best kind.

The Ethiopians were waiting with him, watching the aircraft taking on fuel. They wore new blazers with the Lion of Judah on the breast pocket and carried heavy army bags. Eagerness and apprehension burned on their faces. The younger ones were nervous at the prospect of boarding the aircraft for the first time, but Mamo and

Bashaye were explaining that there was nothing to fear. Negussie Roba told them about the time he flew to Sweden with Niskanen, spreading his arms to mimic the plane swooping down to land on snow. Wagkira listened doubtfully to Negussie. Even though he was thirty-seven years old, Niskanen had decided to take him with them. Wagkira shook his head sternly, telling the younger athletes there was nothing to fear, that Negussie was just boasting. Nevertheless, Said fell to the ground, praying to Allah for their safety.

Niskanen would have liked to have brought Abebe too. A month earlier he had run a marathon in 2:21:23, an average of three minutes, twenty-one seconds per kilometre. Ten days later, he had covered 32 kilometres in 1:42:36, an average of three minutes and ten seconds. But over the last few months Wagkira had more than once run marathons in two hours and twenty minutes – beating Zatopek's record of 2:23:03 in Helsinki. Niskanen wanted to give him the opportunity. It would be his only chance, after all. Four years from now, it would be Abebe's turn, and four years would give him time to reach the maturity you needed for a marathon.

Niskanen saw the jeep approaching fast, carrying Tessema and Kidaneh. It screeched to a halt beside them.

'There is a problem, Major,' said Tessema.

Neither of them spoke.

'Well?'

'Wami has had an accident. He has broken his ankle.'

'His ankle?' Niskanen was incredulous. 'How?'

Tessema and Kidaneh glanced at one another nervously, deciding who would answer.

'He was playing football,' said Tessema.

'Football!'

'Yes. He is in the infirmary. They have taken an X-ray.'

'But...'

Kidaneh shook his head slowly.

'The physician said there was no possibility that his ankle would heal in time.'

Niskanen looked at the aircraft and then at the group of runners waiting expectantly in their new blazers.

'Get Abebe. We're taking him with us.'

24

The aeroplane rolled forward, thundering and shaking until, just as it seemed the great hulk would break apart, it lifted like a crane from a lake, defying nature and sending a shiver through Abebe. He had seen planes crossing the skies before but now, strapped helplessly to the seat, he saw the ground receding, the people and the buildings becoming insignificant, the way God must see them. Soon he was lulled by the steady whine of the engines; he thought he saw rainbows in the spinning propeller blades and angels hiding in the clouds. When he looked around, Niskanen, Kidaneh and Tessema were gazing out of the portholes too, each deep in their thoughts.

The aircraft flew for many hours over mountains, deserts and rivers. At one point, far off in the distance, he saw rising from the rolling dunes of sand the geometric summits of the pyramids. He had learned at school that the Egyptians had come to Ethiopia, to Axum, where they left an obelisk to relate the great battles of their kings. Then Menelik I had come with the Ark containing the laws of God. From his divine viewpoint, high in the sky, Abebe marvelled at the herds of ibex flowing like quicksilver and turning sharply to avoid the shadow of the aircraft. They sprang forward, their bodies forever in flight, their legs seeming never to touch the ground. How puny and graceless humans were compared to these animals. In the sky, he was infinite and insignificant.

In no time they were sailing in the air over the sparkling blue sea. He was astonished to see ships passing below, ploughing slow, straight courses through the quiet immensity.

Suddenly, the aircraft began to fall, and panic seized him properly this time. The voice of the pilot crackled over the intercom to announce that they were beginning their descent for Rome. He was sure they were going to crash, and it was only the city appearing in ever greater detail which relieved him of these thoughts. He saw it unfurling, avenues leading to more avenues like the veins of a leaf, streets branching off from these, and in the streets, cars like beetles and people as busy as ants. And then he saw the shadow of the aircraft which flitted over the rooftops, coming alarmingly close, and then closer still, until the aircraft was reunited with it and – in the same instant – the earth.

The landing was bumpy. The aircraft bounced and hurtled on. But then it slowed and he began to relax, overcome by a new excitement. He was in another continent, a foreign land.

Stepping out of the cabin, Abebe paused at the top of the gangway and tasted the thick, dirty air.

Inside the airport terminal – a palace of glass that managed to be the largest yet also the lightest building he had ever seen – arriving athletes were being assailed by reporters and photographers. Abebe was stunned by the number of people, even more so by the loud, burbling noise they all made together. He and the others stood gaping in amazement at the throng of people: athletes, coaches and newsmen from all over the world.

Abebe had never seen so many white people together in one place. Many were blond, like the major, and for the first time it occurred to him that the major had a family, relatives who resembled him, men with broad cheekbones and bulky, powerful shoulders. Some of the white people were tall and blond haired like him while others were short and dark haired like the Greeks or Lebanese in Addis; they were as different from each other as Kenyans or Egyptians from Ethiopians.

He was surrounded, outnumbered, for the first time by white people, many of whom seemed as disoriented by it all as he was. He saw people with yellow faces too – a page of the school atlas come to life – and, as they stared at him, he saw puzzlement and surprise in their secretive eyes.

Newsmen roved among them in the gigantic building with

notebooks and cameras. One of the reporters, carrying a tape recorder and a microphone, approached a group of white athletes near by and asked them which country they were from.

'South Africa,' one of them replied.

Abebe turned to Kidaneh. 'There are white Africans?' he asked.

'Yes,' said Kidaneh. 'There are all kinds of Africans.'

Abruptly, the radio reporter turned and pointed his microphone at them.

Abebe recoiled instinctively as though from a snake.

'Hey, I only want to ask you a question. Which country are you from?'

Abebe shook his head in a panic.

'Ethiopia,' answered Niskanen. 'Not me. Them.'

'Which sports are you down for?'

'Track and field. We are entering our runners in the hundred and two hundred and eight hundred metres, the fifteen hundred and the five and ten thousand metres, and the marathon.'

'You have forgotten the cycling events,' said Tessema.

'Wait a minute. Ethiopia used to be called Abyssinia, yes?'

Kidaneh answered this time.

'That is correct.'

The reporter fiddled with a button on his tape recorder, watching the red needles flicker as he began speaking. 'How does it feel to be here in Rome as guests of the Italians, considering your country was recently under their domination?'

Niskanen was uneasy. He looked at Kidaneh, who leant towards the microphone.

'In Ethiopia, we are proud of our tradition of hospitality,' he answered, 'and we expect to be shown the same hospitality in return.'

The hotel was a tall, crumbling house in a narrow street, bigger than but just as dilapidated as any Abebe had ever seen in Addis. As they approached on foot, carrying their bags down the chasm of peeling brickwork festooned with washing, the Ethiopians – fourteen black men and one Nordic – were scrutinised from wrought-iron balconies by hundreds of pairs of dark, disdainful eyes.

That night, they sat down to dinner in the trattoria next door to the hotel. Abebe and the other athletes were confused when the plates of steaming spaghetti arrived. Abebe pulled out a strand with his fingers. It wriggled like a long, pale worm. He was waiting for it to cease struggling when he realised that the diners at the other tables were staring at him. He looked around for help. Kidaneh was pretending he hadn't noticed anything, but the major was smiling.

'That's not how they eat here!' said Kidaneh.

He ostentatiously picked up his fork and demonstrated how to eat the spaghetti, twirling it around until it formed a bundle.

Abebe copied him, surprised by the sour taste of cold metal in his mouth. He had never used a knife and fork. Like all Ethiopians, he ate with his fingers.

'You know, there is a saying,' quipped Niskanen. 'When in Rome, do as the Romans.'

He ate a forkful of spaghetti, noisily sucking up a long strand.

Abebe was gratified that he wasn't the only one who was having difficulty.

The next day, Niskanen took them to register for the Games. The Olympic village was like the airport terminal, a group of buildings that boldly and wilfully dwarfed their occupants. It was called a village, yet there was nothing about it that resembled Abebe's village. There were paved roads for the little cars and the trees had been planted in straight lines and trimmed so they stood like soldiers on inspection. The scale was gigantic, but people came and went, seemingly too busy to be bothered by the surrounding splendour.

The Ethiopians walked for a long while, seeing athletes everywhere exercising on the neatly cut grass between the buildings. Finally, they came to the one that Niskanen had been seeking, and he told them to wait outside while he went in to register everybody.

Abebe and the other athletes crouched in the shade of a tree.

They watched a woman stretching, wearing shorts that revealed long, graceful legs. Abebe had never seen a woman wearing shorts and it finally dawned on him that the only explanation could be that she was a competitor in the Games, a female athlete. The Ethiopians forgot their timidity and stared at her. They had heard about female athletes and they had occasionally glimpsed foreign women playing sports in the gardens of villas in Addis, but she was the first sportswoman they had ever seen. Not only this, she was African. They knew at once she wasn't from Ethiopia, however, and it was hard to believe that she was from Africa either. It was unimaginable to them that their sisters or mothers could devote themselves to such an activity, to leisure and competition.

She was performing the same exercises that Niskanen had taught them, bending over to touch her toes, swinging her arms and then squatting and stretching out her legs, first one and then the other, slowly and deliberately.

Finally, she drew herself up and, planting her fists on her hips, spoke to them defiantly.

'What's the problem? Ain't you boys ever seen legs before?'

Abebe and the others didn't respond. They were shocked to be addressed by her so directly, and the truth was that Abebe had never, except stealthily – between parted branches as they bathed or through the reed walls of a hut – seen the legs of a woman. Even his wife's legs he had only seen as an outline in the dark.

They continued to stare.

'I guess you ain't,' said the woman. 'Not like these anyway, huh?'

She resumed her exercises, trying to ignore their stares.

Finally, she was joined by her teammates: men and women. More than their easy camaraderie, there was something about their powerful physiques and the casual way they stood and touched one another which told Abebe they all came from the same place. Yet they were black and white. It didn't seem possible.

They soon noticed the Ethiopians, still crouching under the tree and staring, and one of the athletes, a man this time, called out to them.

'Where you boys from, anyway?'

Abebe exchanged glances with his teammates, too petrified to speak.

Thinking he hadn't been understood, the athlete pointed at himself and said, 'America.' Then he pointed at them.

'Which country?' he asked.

Abebe and the others looked at Mamo. He had fought in Korea with the United Nations. It was up to him to reply.

'Ethiopia,' said Mamo.

'Where's that at?' The American athlete turned to his teammates. 'Must be someplace in Africa. There're so many damned countries over there. Well, we're Americans! Pleased to meet you.'

'Please to meet,' replied Abebe. He understood that it was a polite greeting and he responded as he would in his own language, repeating the phrase with a rising note to suggest concern.

'Yeah, right. So, what are you all entering for, what sports?'

Abebe was puzzled. In Ethiopia, there would have followed a long, patient exchange of enquiries concerning the health of family members and relations, but the American athlete was asking about sporting disciplines as though this was enough to find a common ground. Through sport, it seemed, they could establish fraternity.

Mamo said he was competing in the 1,500 and the 5,000 and 10,000. Negussie told them he was a sprinter, he would be running in the 100 and 200 and the American laughed in a friendly way and said he would see him on the line.

Then he looked at Abebe.

'Which sport, which event?'

'Marathon,' said Abebe.

'The marathon? Hey, that's a tough one. You know what happened to the guy who won the first marathon, don't you?'

Abebe shook his head.

'Well, he won. But it just about took everything he had outta him. He dropped dead right on the finish line!'

He mimed a runner coming to an exhausted halt, lolling his head and letting his tongue hang out.

'Did too. Stone cold dead! His name was *Phi-dipperdees*. He was from Greece.'

'Mike!'

It was the woman interjecting in a tone that was amused but admonishing. 'Stop that! Leave the poor boy alone. You just trying to frighten him, you big bully! Anyway, he can't understand a word you saying. Least, I hope not.'

'I was just having some fun, Wilma!'

Her name was Wilma, Abebe noted.

She smiled compassionately at the Ethiopians, and he wondered whether this was because of the story Mike had told.

25

It was early morning and the air was still cool. Later, the heat would be suffocating. For Abebe, the heat in Rome was more oppressive than it ever was in Addis, and it was made even worse by the exhaust fumes from the cars, a brown haze that accumulated during the day, hanging in the air and obscuring the sun. But it was still too early for the small cars stuffed with families which revved and hooted, jostling for every inch of space, surrounded by buzzing swarms of scooters. The sun had not yet risen, the time Niskanen preferred to begin work. They were not training, however. Niskanen had borrowed one of the little cars and he was taking Abebe and Wagkira down to the south of the city where the marathon would be run.

The major wanted them to go over every step of the course before the race. He wanted them to be thoroughly prepared, he said, to know every contour, every stone. The circuit took them over roads that were banked deceptively and there were gradients that you didn't sense at first. They had already covered three-quarters of the 42-kilometre route, but on three mornings, 10 kilometres at a time. The marathon was just two days away now and they were going to cover the last leg. It would be their final practice. Tomorrow, they would rest, and the day after would be the day of the race.

They drove through the city with its wide squares and fountains to the Colosseum, the immense, circular arena in which, said the major, the Romans would feed Christians to the lions. The marathon was due to start and finish in the shadow of the Colosseum rather than in the Olympic Stadium; the route took them southwards out of the city along a cobbled road, the Via Appia, for just over 20 kilometres and back again.

They trundled along the old road, passing the catacombs, the underground warrens where Niskanen told them the Romans buried their dead. Abebe thought it reasonable for them to want their ancestors near by, but he couldn't help fearing they might want to intercede in the race. He kept his thoughts to himself, however, and tried to concentrate on the shiny black cobblestones.

Niskanen drove with his shoulders hunched over the wheel of the Fiat. He had a grave expression, and Abebe could guess what he was thinking. The Ethiopian athletes had fared less well than in Melbourne four years ago. Only Said had come through the early rounds in the 800 metres with what everybody said was a respectable time of one minute fifty, but he had been eliminated before the semi-finals. The 10,000 metres was taking place later that day, but Mamo had failed to qualify. As for Negussie, he hadn't even made the quarter-finals in the sprints. The major said the only consolation was that the Americans, too, had been defeated in what was usually their race. For the first time since the twenties, they hadn't won a single medal in the 100 metres. 'It just goes to show that no one is unbeatable,' he told everybody.

Abebe had watched the finals of the 100 metres in the giant stadium, bigger than any he had ever seen, packed with more people than he had ever seen in one place, for a race that lasted ten seconds. He had never experienced such excitement. The first, second and third places were taken by a German, an Australian and an Englishman. Right behind – so close you could barely distinguish them from the leaders – were three blacks: the Frenchman Saye – who was really from Cameroon – and the Americans. Niskanen told them that, in the sprints, what mattered was the initial explosion at the start and the last few seconds. Although you were already going flat out, you had to be able to call on a reserve of power, an extra burst you didn't know you had until, spurred by the competition, your muscles pumped even harder.

'But the race that poses the greatest challenge to a runner,' he said, 'is the marathon. Speed is required, of course. You have to run a mile in under five and a half minutes, then another mile in the same time – and then another, never faltering, never slowing down, for twenty-six miles. So you need stamina, but also determination and endurance. Then there's the problem of cramp.' If a leg muscle seizes, he told them, the only thing is to ignore the pain and keep running.

'But don't worry. You can do it, I'm sure.'

When Niskanen spoke again, it was to tell them that the favourites for the marathon were the Russian, Popov, and an Australian named Power. But it was Rhadi, a Moroccan, that he said they would have to watch out for. 'Remember, they'll be running in a block, all together. Make sure you keep up with them,' he said. 'You can't afford to fall behind because you might not be able to catch up. Nobody will want to push it too soon. But that means you won't know what they have, what their reserves are like.'

They halted at a wide crossroads near the spot where they had broken off the last time. In the middle of the empty piazza stood an obelisk, a tall stone needle pointed at the heavens.

'When you reach this point, you must begin to make your move.'

Abebe and Wagkira got out of the car and began their warm-up exercises, stretching their legs against a wall and lifting their knees to their chests. The sun was rising and the obelisk cast a long, elegant shadow.

Niskanen was contemplating the monument. 'Do you recognise it?' he asked them.

Abebe had seen a number of them in the Italian capital, but this was the tallest. It rose higher than any of the nearby buildings, which were set a respectful distance from it.

'Most of the others here are from Egypt, but this is from your country, from Axum. Mussolini had it brought here during the occupation.'

Niskanen said it was nearly 30 metres tall and Abebe wondered how it was that Ethiopians had built such a thing. He was astonished to hear how old it was. 'The Axumites became Christians about the same time as the Romans,' Niskanen told them. 'But this is older. It's from the first or second century after Christ.'

'The Romans not always Christian?' asked Wagkira.

'No,' answered Niskanen, 'they were pagans, they had many gods.'

Abebe admired the soaring straightness of the monument, an eerie symmetry tapering upwards to the heavens. The head, rounded like a helmet or the head of a snake, unsettled him; in his village, people still feared the power of snakes. There were strange markings on the sides but nothing they told could alleviate the shame and anger he suddenly felt at the thought of this monolith being carried off to Rome.

Niskanen spoke encouragingly to them. 'You'll be coming by here after about an hour and a half. This is the crucial stage of the race. This obelisk will be your signal. We're ten kilometres from the finish. When you reach this point, you must increase speed. From here on, you must give it everything you've got. I've been looking at the timings, and the runner you have to be concerned about is Rhadi.' He told them he was less worried about the Russian favourite than about the Moroccan. He remembered Alain Mimoun from Algeria running in Melbourne, and he had come to the conclusion that North Africans, like the East Africans, had an aptitude for endurance events. Rhadi had qualified for the 10,000 metres final, which was being held that afternoon, and his form was impressive.

'Don't let him get too close. If he's still with you when you pass through here, you must do everything you can to put some distance between you.'

Abebe and Wagkira both nodded eagerly. From here on, they understood, any action would be decisive. They had to win the race – for the glory of Ethiopia.

'I know you'll both try your best,' said Niskanen. 'Now, Abebe, what about your shoes?'

Abebe took off his shoes and held them out for the major's inspection. The black stones felt cold under his feet. They were polished and dense, so smooth he could slip easily over them.

He wriggled his toes. 'I run like this?' he asked.

Niskanen handed back the shoes. Abebe had been complaining about them: they were loose and uncomfortable. Perhaps it was the heat, or the trial runs on the uneven Roman cobbles, which was causing the soles to come unglued, but they would have to do for the time being.

'Put them back on. We'll get you a new pair later.'

He was confident that Abebe could race barefoot if need be but it wasn't worth risking an injury. Even if the course took them over cobbles and asphalt, one sharp stone could put him out of the race.

'We're not trying for any records today,' he said. 'I just want you to get to know the ground thoroughly. I want you to be one hundred per cent prepared.'

Abebe saw that he had taken out his stopwatch nonetheless.

That evening, Niskanen picked up a local newspaper in the lounge at the Olympic village. The Italian journal devoted page after page to trumpeting the national team's victory in the cycling competitions. The emperor was not going to be happy when he heard that the Italians had won most of the gold medals while the Ethiopian cyclists hadn't even qualified. Their only chance of a medal now was the marathon. Abebe and Wagkira were their last hopes.

Abebe found the major in the lounge reading the newspaper. It was where he went every evening with Tessema and Kidaneh, while the athletes talked outside their quarters in the hot night or watched replays of the competitions on the new invention, the television.

He was glad that the major was alone.

Niskanen invited him to sit down. He knew how reserved the boys were, and how shy. If Abebe had come to the lounge, there was an important reason, but he would still have to encourage him to speak.

'Is anything the matter?' he asked.

Abebe fidgeted, gathering his courage. The two weeks they had spent in Rome together had altered their relationship: they were no longer major and bodyguard, they were coach and runner. Abebe had felt emboldened enough to interrupt Niskanen. The race was just one day away and he wouldn't have another chance.

'I have a question, sir,' he said, lifting his eyes to see whether he had the major's attention but all the while keeping his forehead lowered in abasement. 'Is it true about the first marathon man? Is it true that after the race, he died?'

Niskanen knew at once what Abebe was talking about.

'Who told you that?' he asked, looking up from the newspaper.

Frightened now, but determined, Abebe looked up.

'The Americans told us.'

'Yes. It's true,' Niskanen said carefully. He knew that the Ethiopians were superstitious; they imagined connections he didn't see, reverberations and restless spirits invisible to him. 'But you mustn't worry. That was a very long time ago, in Greece. It wasn't really a race. He was a soldier, and he ran all the way to Athens to report that the Greeks had won a great victory; they had defeated the Persians at a place called Marathon. So it's called the marathon in commemoration, but that's all.'

'If I win, will I die?' queried Abebe.

Niskanen had told them about the combats that once took place in the great Colosseum, in the shadow of which the race would be held, fights to the death between the Roman emperors' fiercest gladiators.

'No, Abebe, nothing of the sort. You've run marathons before. You aren't going to die. Trust me. The marathon is a gruelling race, a hard race, and many of the runners will not finish...'

Niskanen thought of all the runners he had seen struggle past the line, collapsing. There was a look men had at the end of a marathon, a look of concentration, oblivion, of utter exhaustion that you never saw any other time.

'But nobody is going to die. Believe me. You're going to win!'

Abebe had run marathons before, it was true, but that was in Ethiopia. That afternoon, in the stadium, he had seen the victors in the 5,000 metres pass the finishing line and slump to the ground. They lay there with their chests pounding, unable to rise. They had made twelve laps of the track; the ones who hadn't fallen away exhausted, that is, the dozen or so who remained out of the forty-four who had started.

When they passed the finish, lights exploded as bright as the sun and the public had howled with savage glee.

26

It was late afternoon when the mass of runners grouped under the great arch. The Italian organising committee had decided that the most gruelling of sporting contests deserved a gladiatorial setting. Constantine's Arch, in the shadow of the Colosseum, was chosen as the starting and finishing point. But there had been confusion and delay in organising the race and the pressmen and spectators were sweltering, their impatience worsened by the September heat. The race was already due to start and all the stewards seemed to be shouting, pointing and blowing their whistles at once.

The runners too were growing anxious. Some of them were already perspiring, though they had yet to even begin to exert themselves. One of them stared down incredulously at Abebe's bare feet.

He nudged his neighbour. 'D'ya suppose they couldn't afford to buy him any shoes?' Then he looked up at the lean black athlete.

'Anyway, good luck, mate!' he said cheerfully.

Abebe nodded. He tried to seem unconcerned, and kept his eyes fixed on Wagkira in front of him, wearing the same green singlet with the yellow belt and red shorts. He continued to lift his knees in a manner he hoped would betray his training, but the truth was that he was deeply embarrassed.

'I'm from New Zealand,' said the runner. 'You?'

'Ethiopia.'

'Oh.'

They had gone to the Adidas stand in the Olympic village the day before but there were no shoes that fitted him. His big toes were too large and his outside toes too small. 'They're almost ingrown,' said the Adidas man. He was curious about Abebe's feet and said he had never seen anything like them: the soles and heels were as hard as corns! He told the major they had given away 1,500 pairs of shoes and they had hardly any left. Rafer Johnson, the black American who had carried their national flag in the opening parade, had taken six pairs alone! They couldn't find a pair of shoes anywhere that Abebe was comfortable with and finally the major had decided that, since there wouldn't be time to properly break in a new pair, Abebe would race barefoot.

Even though he was accustomed to heat, it was usually fresher in Addis and the heaviness was beginning to tell on him. He wasn't perturbed by the delay, however. While the other runners had been bolstering themselves psychologically, and were now coiled like springs, he waited, impressed to be part of the mêlée of athletes from thirty-seven countries. Simply to be among them was sufficient reward for him; it was glory and honour enough. The important thing in life was not winning, but taking part, the major had said, and he had seen the same words written on the giant scoreboard in the stadium during the opening parade. Still, the major had told him he could do it. He said that he was as fast as the best of them. And he had an advantage: surprise.

It was as if the race would never start. Photographers and pressmen mingled with the runners, asking last-minute questions and taking more photos. The press were still wandering among them when, without warning, a pistol shot rang out.

Abebe set off with the group that came bursting through the central vault of the triumphal arch, and immediately they had to make a wide detour as the stewards pushed a stalled car out of the way. The runners had yet to spread out; they advanced in a dense huddle followed by cars and scooters sounding their horns. Abebe was thrilled to hear the cheers of the spectators lining the route encouraging them all on indiscriminately, as though the triumph of one would be the triumph of everyone.

Gradually, the cacophony of whistles and klaxons faded. The spectators lining the route were fewer, spread apart now like the runners. As the distances between them increased, Abebe began to perceive the capacities of the other competitors. He could see their limbs pumping, hear their breathing. Ahead of him, he saw the leaders, the ones he would have to beat. Most of them were whites: Europeans, Soviets, Americans or runners from countries he didn't know. There was one who looked like an Egyptian and there was an Indian too. Somewhere behind him was Wagkira. As he had overtaken him, his older compatriot had given him an encouraging nod.

One by one, the runners passed under the vaults of a second arch, the Porta Ardeatina, leaving behind the fanfares of the city and emerging into the countryside, a landscape of gentle yellow-green hills. Abebe was one of the first dozen or so to pass; he knew he was doing well, and, unconsciously, he began to relax. He forgot Niskanen's advice. He wasn't racing any more, he was running. His heart stopped drumming – the pounding he always experienced at the start of a trial – and thumped evenly, regular as his shortened breaths. When the time came for the spurt, then he would run.

He was serene, his concerns lost in a cavernous, calming emptiness that always came as he ran. He measured his advance by the sun, by his shadow growing longer in the advancing dusk. He could smell wild sage and pink laurel, sweet and appetising to his heightened senses. It was always that way as he ran; first the emptiness, then, after a while, everything became sharper, better defined. In the twilight, he heard church bells ringing across the fields like the bells that rang over the highlands at home. Children sat on the verges at the side of the road, watching wide eyed.

Never be in a hurry, Niskanen had told him, and even if you are, never let any of the other runners know. The difficult thing, the trick, he said, was to move up without letting the others sense your haste, so it would seem to them as if it was *they* who were dropping back, rather than you overtaking. Keep a steady pace, move up gradually, then use your reserves for the final dash, for overtaking the leaders – that had been Niskanen's advice. It was OK when you were running against your comrades. For the first time, Abebe was racing against runners he didn't know, runners who weren't his friends, but enemies determined to beat everyone else and win.

It wasn't until after they passed the 10-kilometre mark and the distances between the runners had lengthened that he became aware that the strategy Niskanen had given him for the race was not a secret. He realised the other runners were all playing the same game, pretending to be slower than they really were, trying to hide their true potential and conserve their strength until they needed it.

So slowly had the gap closed that Abebe didn't even realise he had caught up with the runner ahead until, without even a glance behind him, his rival increased his efforts. It was barely perceptible, and it made no difference immediately to the distance between them, but it was enough for Abebe to know. The other runner was near his limit. Abebe could sense it. All he had to do was to keep going...

Gradually, he passed the runner, neither of them giving a hint of any extra exertion, moving as though each was in a different dream; the white athlete surrounded by green fields, Abebe on the empty plateau. Abebe didn't know who he was, for they wore only numbers. Niskanen had warned him that the runner he had to be wary of was Rhadi, wearing number twenty-six.

As he passed the 15-kilometre point, he grabbed a plastic cup from the stand and drank as he ran like the others. They had been running for nearly an hour and ahead of him he could see only three runners now: two whites in the lead and behind them a runner he didn't recognise. Soon, he had caught up with this runner. He looked like an Egyptian but he wasn't wearing number twenty-six either. Abebe was getting worried. He would have to have this number twenty-six in sight – not too close, for that would give him away – but close enough that when it was time to make the final burst, he would be able to catch him up. That would be the moment when he would begin to race, not simply run; then he would expend his remaining energy, exerting himself to the limit and beyond, defying the agony. But there was no sign of any twenty-six. Where could he be, this dangerous rival? Had he already passed him, perhaps, or was he far ahead somewhere?

Abebe saw the sweat darkening the vest of the runner in front. Pinned to his back was the number 185. Effortlessly, imperceptibly, Abebe increased his speed.

Effortlessly, the other runner did the same.

Something was wrong...

They were both gaining on the two leaders, the two white runners, but Abebe couldn't get past the runner who was wearing number 185, who remained defiantly ahead. Abebe had no choice but to watch his spindly brown legs lifting high and the heels of his new white Adidas shoes.

It was as though, by his very exertions, Abebe was the one pushing him on.

He pushed harder.

They passed the first white runner.

He pushed harder.

They passed the second white runner.

Now they were in the lead: the Egyptian – if that's what he was – wearing number 185, and Abebe.

That was when he felt the pain stinging under his ribs.

As they mounted a long incline, the stitch jabbed at his side, angering him with its unwanted, untimely reminder of his human frailty.

He willed himself on, his efforts to get ahead forgotten. Now he feared losing ground and being overtaken himself by one of the runners they had just passed.

Niskanen watched the sun setting over the ruins outside the marquee, willing Abebe on.

After the chaotic start – which had infuriated Niskanen but greatly amused Tessema and Kidaneh – they had gone to the tent to listen to the race commentary on a transistor that belonged to the Americans.

As well as officials and coaches, the marquee was crammed with athletes. They all wanted to take part, somehow, in one last race.

This really is a surprise. After holding the first two places for nearly an hour, the British entrant Kelly has dropped back along with the Belgian van den Driessche and it seems that the two Europeans have surrendered the lead to two unknown runners. A Moroccan, Rhadi, is in the lead with an Ethiopian hard on his heels. It's an astonishing sight, I must say: the

Ethiopian, Bikila Abebe, is racing barefoot! There's no more than a yard or two between them and that's how it has been for the last fifteen minutes. Rhadi was down as number twenty-six but for some reason he's wearing number one-eight-five, the same number he was wearing two days ago in the ten thousand metres. Because of the heat here in Rome today – it was well above thirty degrees earlier – the organisers decided to delay the start of the race but there's still plenty of time to go before they get back to the finish line under Constantine's Arch. Meanwhile, the New Zealander McGee is passing Kelly and it looks like he might be getting ready to mount a serious challenge to the two North Africans…

'Africans?' queried Mike, the American athlete. 'I thought Morocco was in France…'

Niskanen approached the table where Kidaneh was sitting with the American athletes.

McGee has plenty of experience on his card but we know very little about the other two. Rhadi came from nowhere to win the international cross-country championship earlier this year. Then, he was racing for France but now he's in the national colours of his native Morocco. Bikila, the African who's been right up there behind him for the last ten kilometres, hasn't taken part in international events before. He gave his occupation as… a private in the Imperial Bodyguard of His Majesty, Emperor Haile Selassie I. Well, the Negus can certainly be proud of his bodyguard today. Barefoot or not, he's managed to outpace some stiff competition.

The Americans had been listening intently. Wilma looked up from the radio and nodded approvingly.

'Looks like your boy is doing pretty good!' she said.

Niskanen and Tessema exchanged glances.

'Come on, Abebe! You can do it!' Niskanen yelled.

'Yeah,' said Mike. 'You heard what he said. Come on!'

Niskanen didn't understand what was holding Abebe back. Why hadn't he made a break? What was he waiting for?

God had heard his prayers.

The stitch went away as suddenly and mysteriously as it had come, without any change of posture on his part, and Abebe felt that nothing could stop him now, the way you feel after pain ends.

From his preparations with Niskanen, going over the route stage by stage, Abebe knew that after the twenty-fifth kilometre there was a descent. The course rose slowly upwards and then there was a downhill stretch. That meant his rival would have been making an extra effort and it was possible the other runner didn't know what was ahead.

He decided it would be the moment to make his move.

They hauled themselves uphill, their paces slowing. The major said the difference could be as much as one minute per kilometre on a gradient, from three minutes to four. As soon as they had passed the stand, Abebe increased his speed deliberately, taking advantage of the descent, a flagrant, defiant burst that took the other runner by surprise.

Whoever he was, the runner wearing 185 didn't react fast enough, and before he could do anything about it he was behind the barefoot runner in the green vest.

Abebe was worried now. He still had not seen number twenty-six, and instead of fading away, falling back like the others, the runner he had overtaken remained right behind him.

He had glimpsed the man's gaunt, brown face as he passed, not the face of a European but an Egyptian, or a Greek perhaps.

In any case, there was no one else ahead of them.

Abebe was in the lead.

It was night by the time he rounded the corner into the Piazza di Porta Capena and found himself once again in the square with the monument from Axum. The stele stood as erect as a soldier, defying its captors and calling on Abebe to avenge its humiliation.

He passed the monument with his rival still hard on his heels.

As they crossed the square, a lorry pulled out ahead of them with a generator and a powerful electric floodlight mounted on the back.

A brightness as fierce as the sun flooded Abebe's face, forcing him to lift his arm to shade his eyes. He turned his head in reaction to the sudden glare and saw again the face of the runner wearing number 185. It had to be Rhadi.

This was the Moroccan Niskanen had warned him about. There

was no one else.

Profiting from Abebe's momentary distraction, Rhadi drew up almost level with him. The relentless duel continued as Rhadi forced the pace, hard on Abebe's heels.

Realising he might be in danger of losing the lead, Abebe forged ahead. The race he had measured out in his mind, jogging the route and listening to Niskanen, was over. He was running a different race now, and he was on his own.

Neither of them took any refreshments as they passed the 35-kilometre mark. There were just a few metres between them; Abebe didn't want to lose his scant advantage and Rhadi was determined to stay on his heels.

Seven kilometres more to go.

Twenty more minutes to run.

Abebe would soon have to make his move...

All he could hear was the steady panting of the Moroccan behind him and the spongy footfalls of his running shoes.

Slowly, almost imperceptibly, the rhythm of the footfalls changed.

The moment had come. He was making his bid. But, instead of accelerating, Abebe realised, the other man was slowing down.

27

The night was still, an apprehensive quiet. In the darkness, one after another, flames flared in the distance.

A yellow Fiat came slowly down the narrow Via Appia, its headlights illuminating the soldiers stationed every 30 metres and holding aloft paraffin torches. As it passed each soldier, an arm extended from the window of the vehicle, an arm belonging to a technician carrying a blow lamp. One after the other as the little car advanced the torches burst into flame.

Niskanen and Kidaneh watched from the hillside in trepidation. They had left the Americans huddled around the radio in the marquee and hurried to the brow of a ridge that ran parallel to the Via Appia.

They scanned the old road, its black cobbles glistening in successive pools of light. When one of the torches failed to light, a man jumped from the slow-moving vehicle and, with a large spanner, adjusted the wick, lighting it with a Zippo and jumping back in the moving car.

Niskanen prayed that Abebe hadn't made his move too early. He feared that once he had the lead, Rhadi might trick him, holding back his pace to lull the novice runner into thinking that he was secure, and then making a sudden break. He wished he could somehow communicate this to his protégé, but there was nothing he could do. He had to hope that Abebe had developed enough competitive instincts to know that this would be the decisive moment.

In the quiet after the car had passed, they strained their ears until finally they heard the shuffling of feet in the distance, a whispering sound that grew steadily louder.

Niskanen shut his eyes and prayed.

Come on, Abebe! You can do it!

The shuffling grew distinct, the sound of footfalls on the stones, accompanied by regular expulsions of air, the sound of breathing. Just then, Abebe came into sight, with Rhadi at least 10 metres behind.

'Come on! Come on!' Niskanen shouted.

But there was no need. Niskanen knew what had happened. It was Abebe who had accelerated.

As soon as he had heard Rhadi slipping back, he had drawn on the last of his reserves to pull away.

'Come on, Abebe! You can do it!'

As Abebe passed the point where they were standing, Niskanen and Kidaneh began to run along the ridge, keeping level with him. They ran until they stumbled, bumping into spectators who had camped on the ridge for the finish. They could see the Moroccan runner behind him, still forcing the pace, pushing as hard as he could, but his efforts were to no avail. He was pushing so hard it seemed that he was propelling Abebe even farther ahead. For the last few kilometres, Abebe had been tirelessly increasing his lead.

But even if he was unable to catch up, Rhadi still hadn't slowed down. He was fighting desperately for second place ahead of McGee, the New Zealander.

Niskanen and Kidaneh tried to keep up. Even after two hours, Abebe had barely dropped off from his top speed. He was still running at over 300 metres per minute, running like the wind, untiring and immortal.

Finally, there were too many spectators blocking their way, and Niskanen descended to the road with Kidaneh hard on his heels, losing track of Abebe and Rhadi as they passed the ruins of a fort. They saw McGee pass, grinning with sheer delight, pain and fatigue forgotten, knowing that, even if it was in third place, he would be there on the podium. He was followed by the parade of official cars and motorcycles.

Their way was blocked by the stands that had been erected along the road so they ducked back from the roadside and cut across to the banks of a nearby hill to get a full view. Niskanen was looking for Wagkira, hoping that the thirty-seven-year-old would make it to the finish too.

Suddenly, there was a flash and more electric lights came on, illuminating Constantine's Arch ahead.

Niskanen and Kidaneh were still pushing their way through the crowds and up the hill as the cries grew louder and then detonated in a roar of shared triumph.

Abebe had won!

It wasn't until he saw the arch explode with light that Abebe realised they had reached the final few hundred metres.

The way ahead was lined by policemen linking arms to hold back the spectators. Rhadi attempted a final surge, but Abebe sensed him closing behind and glided forward. A motorcycle carrying a radio reporter approached him and he thought it was going to knock him over just as he passed under the arch and over the finishing line.

He heard the crowd howling the way they had before in the stadium. This time, though, they were clamouring for him.

The ambulance men rushed up, ready to cover him with blankets but – almost as if they were afraid – everybody kept their distance. Abebe had become more than human; he wouldn't stop. Nobody could tell whether he was going to keel over and collapse, but the fact of the matter was he couldn't stop his legs, couldn't stop running. He turned around and ran back under the arch, where he bent over and touched his toes three times to honour the god of sport, then raised his arms wide in the air and, looking up at the starry night, thanked his God.

When he looked down again, he saw – in the instant before he was blinded by a battery of flashbulbs – a gleeful, ecstatic sea of faces sharing in his victory.

Within minutes, he found he was being carried high on what seemed to be the shoulders of the world, transported like a new-crowned king by his fellow athletes.

***

Under the marquee, the American athletes were still gathered around the transistor, surrounded now by many other athletes and coaches, black and white.

What a race! What a victory! Under the Arch of Constantine – the very spot from which Mussolini's troops set off to conquer their country a quarter of a century ago – an Ethiopian has won the Olympic marathon!

The Americans let out whoops of delight.

For the last hour, for every step of the last twelve miles, Rhadi Ben Abdesselem has been no more than a few metres behind him, forcing him on. But Rhadi couldn't find the extra speed he needed to overtake the barefoot runner…

Mike grabbed Wilma and led her in a buck dance around the room.

At a time when throughout Africa nations are throwing off their colonial shackles, what could be a more meaningful victory than the victory of Abebe Bikila here today? And barefoot at that!

Mike stopped dancing and stared at Wilma for a moment before they all rushed out to lift the barefoot runner high on their shoulders.

Niskanen and Kidaneh finally reached the reporters crowding around Abebe.

'How long have you been running?'

'Have you won any other international competitions?'

'How does it feel to be the first African to win an Olympic gold medal?'

Abebe looked confused.

Niskanen grabbed him by the shoulders. He wanted to shake him, hug him, so he would comprehend what he had done.

'They want to know if you think you can run some more!' he said.

Abebe frowned and considered the question. Then he broke into a wide grin. 'Yes,' he said. 'I could run ten, maybe twenty more, I think.'

The reporters laughed.

'Tell us about yourself.'

Abebe was bewildered. He didn't understand the questions he was being asked. He couldn't even guess at the ramifications of his victory. He had never won an international event before. He looked at Niskanen pleadingly.

'What I say, Major?'

'Say whatever you want. Kidaneh will translate.' Kidaneh shook Abebe's hand and said something in Amharic.

'Can you give us your full name?'

'My name is Abebe. My father's name Bikila.'

'Where were you born?'

'Name of my village is Jirou.'

'Your age?'

'I don't know.'

'Huh? You don't know how old you are?'

'He's twenty-seven,' interjected Niskanen. 'He's been running for about four years now.'

'Not so old, not today. I feel young! I race again now!'

The reporters had their quote.

As they scribbled, an Italian official interrupted them, positioning himself between Abebe and the pressmen and gesticulating at his wristwatch. He mimed hanging a medal around his neck and waved his arms to signal that the press conference was over.

The ceremony took place at the foot of the Colosseum, under the floodlit arch. An official hung the gold medal around Abebe's neck as the Ethiopian national anthem was played haltingly by the Italian orchestra.

Abebe shook hands with Rhadi and then with McGee, who told him, 'You did it. Never mind the shoes.' He was the same runner who had stood beside him at the start. They had all done it. Even Wagkira, who he thought was their best hope, had made seventh place, an achievement for a thirty-seven-year-old that, when he finally had time to consider it, Niskanen found more incredible than Abebe's victory. At any rate, he had been right about one thing: Ethiopians were born to run distance races.

The emotion welled in Niskanen as he watched Abebe receiving his gold medal. He had never had children. When he and his wife had wanted a child, it didn't happen. It became something they didn't talk about, and then after a while, there was nothing more to talk about. Abebe was twenty years younger than him; Niskanen hadn't known him very long – less than four years – but he had coaxed him and encouraged him, he had seen him learn the techniques he had imparted and, sharing in the joy of Abebe's accomplishment, he basked for that instant in an unfamiliar, intoxicating sensation of fatherly pride.

28

Abebe squatted on the lawn in the Olympic village, enjoying a last look at all the athletes. He wore his gold medal over his tracksuit, proud of it as the generals in the bodyguard were of their military decorations.

He saw other athletes wearing their medals too and felt a privileged kinship with them, even though they would all soon be returning to places like America, Europe or the Soviet Union, to lives he couldn't begin to imagine. Whatever anyone said about the honour of taking part, he felt sorry for those without medals. He was sad for Mamo, who had come so close the last time. He would be going home with nothing. Rhadi, the Moroccan, had told Abebe after the ceremony that he didn't mind not taking first place because it was Abebe who won. His victory was a victory for them all, he said. He was a soldier too, a marksman in the infantry. He said the King of Morocco had promised to promote him anyway.

Abebe tried to fix in his memory the sunlight on the marble buildings and the athletes, poised and superb. The Olympians, he had heard them called. And he was one of them.

He didn't notice Wilma approaching.

'Hi!' she said.

He was used to rigorous formality with women and didn't know what to make of her friendly manner.

'Good afternoon,' he replied, getting up quickly.

'My name's Wilma. Wilma Rudolph.'

She extended her hand with masculine self-assurance.

'Abebe Bikila,' he said, shaking her hand.

'I've never met anyone from another country before. I mean someone like us, a Negro. Oh my God! You don't even speak English, do you?'

Smiling at him, she reached down the front of her tracksuit top and fished out a gold medal.

'I got some of those too, but I ain't got the nerve to wear them like you.'

'I must not do this?' asked Abebe. Medals, he assumed, were for wearing.

'No need to go apologising. You wear it any way you want. You got a right to be proud of it. First African an' all. They gonna be proud of you when you get home to Ethiopia, that's for sure. What's the first thing you gonna do?'

'I am bodyguard of His Imperial Majesty Haile Selassie. This what I do.'

'That's your job?'

'Yes,' affirmed Abebe. It was not a job, exactly, but he didn't know how else to describe it. It was an honour to be a member of the Imperial Bodyguard. Now they were saying he had brought a great honour to his country.

'I'd like to go to Africa someday. Is it integrated?'

'Integ–rated?'

'You don't know about integration?'

Wilma sat down, folding her long legs under her, a gesture of casual intimacy that Abebe had come to realise was unavoidable. She patted the ground beside her, inviting him to sit down.

'Integrated. You know, black and white folks living side by side together, going to all the same places, using the same facilities.'

'In Ethiopia, white people are our guests.'

'Oh,' said Wilma, surprised.

'Like Major Niskanen, Sports Officer. Our guest.'

'Your guests, huh? It sure ain't that way in Clarksville... That's where I'm from: Clarksville, Tennessee. They like to joke and say they got no race problem in Clarksville, and the reason why's 'cause it ain't integrated!'

She explained that the mayor of Clarksville had called her coach to congratulate him and promised them a ticker-tape parade. 'They gonna integrate the town for a day, just for the parade, when I get home. And there'll be a banquet, an integrated banquet. Can you beat that? And the day after, it'll go right back to being just like it was before.'

She paused, unfurling her legs and stretching them out straight, an exercise reflex.

'Maybe I'll come to Ethiopia one day,' she said wistfully. 'I'd like that. I never thought these legs'd ever carry me all the way to Rome. So who knows?'

She laughed and threw her head back. Abebe had been watching her unconsciously stroking her long legs.

'Maybe I come to America, one day,' said Abebe.

'You do that. Tell you what, if you come to Clarksville, you come and see me, right. You promise?'

Abebe nodded.

'That is, if your wife don't mind. You married?'

'Yes.'

'What's your wife's name?'

'Yewibdar.'

'Yewibdar? That sure is a funny name,' she blurted. 'Oh, I'm sorry. How did you meet?'

'She from village. Parents choose. Parents find bride.'

'That's how they do things in Ethiopia, the parents arrange everything?'

Abebe nodded.

'Where I come from, it's us that chooses. You know. You can marry whoever you want. If he asks you...'

She stopped speaking, saddened now.

'I wish my parents had arranged things for me,' she said. 'I got a little baby, you see, back home, only I ain't supposed to say nothin' because the baby ain't got a father, legally speaking. You won't tell anyone, will you?'

'No.'

'They told me not to talk about it with anyone.'

Abebe knew about love marriages from the Indian films they showed at the cinema in Addis. They always seemed to cause great unhappiness.

'I say nothing,' he said, smiling to reassure her. It surprised him that Americans, who appeared to lead such perfect athlete's lives, could have any failings, any secrets to hide. Even her triumph entailed a compromise for her.

'Well,' she said, rising. 'Be seein' ya, Abebe.'

They shook hands again.

29

Assailed by the chanting throng, the parade moved slowly down Churchill Avenue. The whole of Addis had turned out to acclaim the bodyguard who was being fêted that day as a national hero. Abebe had won a gold medal in the Olympic Games and the entire continent wanted to wash his bare feet. Even the alleyways and stalls of the Mercato were deserted. The crowds were singing a song written especially for him, describing how he had brought great honour to Ethiopia and to the *Negus Negasta*.

In many parts of the country, however, the news had been greeted with a shrug. Nobody could say what the Olympics were, for a start. Abebe had run 26 miles? It was nothing to run twice that in a day on an errand. He did it in just over two hours? What was the importance of time as long you completed your journey before night fell and the countryside became rife with *shifts*, the thieves who beat and robbed you and then left you to die? Yet the entire world had acknowledged him as the champion. So – this was indeed an unprecedented event: an Ethiopian, champion of the world!

Abebe was invited to receptions all over Addis as a guest of honour. At the Greek club, the president of the merchants' association presented him with an olive branch and told him it had been cut from the tree that had served to crown Spyridon Louys, winner of the first modern marathon in 1896. Writing in the newspaper, Kidaneh had pointed out that this was the same year that the Emperor Menelik II defeated the Italian invaders at Adwa, calling it an eloquent coincidence.

Everywhere he went, people stared at Abebe; they wanted simply to be near him, to touch him if they could. They wanted to hear how he had overtaken Kelly and van den Driessche and then duelled with Rhadi; how it was to stand on the podium, head and shoulders above the rest, and especially above the arrogant colonialists. Wherever he went, young men wanted to challenge him to a race. Women looked at him with unabashed interest; and the brazen ones who waited near the palace and who were always eager to help a guardsman spend his wages shrieked and rolled their hips as he passed.

Best of all, along the roads he saw boys running with numbers written on paper and pinned to their vests; boys barefoot as ever. Indeed, every youth in Addis was there that day to catch a glimpse of the fleet-footed bodyguard and marvel at his heroic feat.

The open-backed army lorry, freshly painted white, followed slowly behind the lions at the head of the parade. The five imperial beasts strained at their chains, causing the crowds to pull back as they prowled left and right. On the back of the lorry, Abebe was wearing his new corporal's uniform with his gold Olympic medal hanging around his neck. The medal glinted in the light like a magical charm as he waved to the crowds.

Behind him on the back of the lorry, wearing the white full-dress uniform of the Imperial Bodyguard, was General Mengistu and, alongside him, a number of senior army officers. Until then, they had viewed sporting activities as mere training, but the top brass had been convinced overnight of the benefits and they all now wanted to share in Abebe's achievement.

Behind them, standing in the royal carriage, his hand resting on the hilt of his sword, stood the emperor in full field marshal regalia: gold braiding, white gloves, plumed tricorne. Behind him stood Crown Prince Asfa. He too was wearing ceremonial garb, though it hung off the round-shouldered heir like a heavy cloak on a frightened bird. Beside him, seated, was a woman with the same piercing stare as Selassie: Princess Tenegneh, the emperor's daughter, wore a simple summer dress and a sunhat. Servants followed the carriage holding tall parasols or walked alongside waving palm fronds to keep the imperial entourage cool.

Niskanen rode behind the emperor's carriage on a second lorry with Tessema, who had been promoted to secretary-general of the National Olympic Committee. When he announced his new post, he said he was sorry that Niskanen was the only one who hadn't been given a new title.

They were surrounded by politicians who all wanted to bask in the glory of Abebe's triumph. The former Minister of the Pen, Aklilou, made a point of sticking to his side. Niskanen had heard that Aklilou was soon to be made prime minister. He had gone from the Ministry of the Pen to the Foreign Ministry, where Niskanen had made his acquaintance. Like all educated and travelled Amhars, he preferred everything foreign, from medicines to telephones, and he was always asking the major to bring him new gadgets from Sweden. Still, he had been the first to say he had believed all along in what the major was doing.

Like the generals, the politicians too wanted suddenly to endorse the nation's sports programme. Niskanen didn't mind; he was too busy savouring his achievement. He knew perfectly well what people thought when they saw him parading with the Ethiopians around the field in Rome; now they all wanted to know how he had done it, how he had discovered and moulded a champion. Newsmen had come from France, Britain and America, and he enjoyed recounting the training sessions for them and seeing their expressions of disbelief when he told them that Abebe had lost only 350 grams during the race – incredible considering that the temperature and humidity in Rome was greater than anything he was used to.

Niskanen said he reckoned Abebe could beat Zatopek's one-hour record. He played down Abebe's time in Rome of two hours fifteen minutes and sixteen seconds, a new world record, though he was immensely proud of the fact that Abebe had beaten the previous Olympic marathon record – set by Zatopek – by nearly eight minutes. 'If Abebe had known it was Rhadi behind him,' Niskanen told the reporters, 'he would have pulled away earlier and then I'm sure he would have shaved off another two minutes!'

Everyone marvelled at how he had run barefoot, and they were even more baffled when they asked about diet. Niskanen relished telling them that, like many Ethiopians, Abebe fasted two or three days of the week, not eating any solids until after sunset.

They all wanted to know Abebe's secret, but the truth was he had none; all he did was run – but he ran faster and for longer than anyone else. He was not yet thirty, approaching peak form for a distance runner, and the major said he was confident that Abebe was going to set more records in the future; he believed Abebe might even be able to better Zatopek's time over the 10,000! In fact, if it hadn't been scheduled so close to the marathon in Rome, he would have entered him for that too. Nevertheless, he didn't underestimate the competition: Rhadi's mistake, in his opinion, had been to run the 10,000 metres beforehand. Fatigue had probably cost him the marathon.

The parade wound its way slowly to the gates of the palace, where a banquet was to be held – a banquet, His Majesty had stipulated, such as neither Ethiopia nor the whole of Africa had ever seen. As the cortège reached the gates, Abebe lifted his medal, which flashed in the sunlight. For many, it was difficult to understand why there was such a fuss over such a meagre trophy. Where were the spoils of his victory? they wondered. They cheered nonetheless, grateful for the spectacle.

Turning around to wave to the crowd, Abebe saw the emperor receiving the adulation as his due, the trace of an uncharacteristic smile across his lips.

He noticed that General Neway was not smiling, however. It seemed to Abebe that he was scowling darkly at him.

Rows of seats had been arranged in the palace garden in front of a raised platform. Gradually, the seats filled with the dignitaries, soldiers in uniforms and politicians in their suits, and with the Rasses, who wore the lavishly embroidered formal *shammas* that they donned once or twice a year only, for the emperor's birthday or an important state occasion. On the platform, shaded by white parasols, Abebe and Niskanen stood to attention before the Negus.

A valet advanced carrying a purple velvet cushion on which were laid several medals, military decorations that the emperor intended to bestow on Niskanen and Abebe, thereby circumscribing any magic that might be contained in the Olympic medal. Turning to the major, he spoke with gentle warmth.

'Major Onni Niskanen, in recognition of the loyal services you have rendered to Ethiopia, both as Sports Officer of the Imperial Bodyguard and as director of the Physical Education department of the Ministry of Education and Fine Arts – where your efforts concerning the fitness of our young people are greatly valued – it is our honour to present you with the Imperial Order of Merit.'

The emperor took the medal from the velvet cushion and pinned it to Niskanen's chest. Then he stood back and saluted. Niskanen saluted back, staring straight ahead over the plumes of the emperor's tricorne.

Selassie then approached Abebe.

'Private Abebe Bikila, in respect of your great athletic achievement, a feat that has brought honour to our country and to the entire African continent, we hereby award you the Star of Ethiopia.'

The emperor lifted the decoration from the cushion and hung it around Abebe's neck, before taking two long strides back and saluting him.

Abebe returned the emperor's salute, his hand trembling. His awe of the emperor was greater than any emotion he had felt at winning. Then it was General Mengistu's turn to present Abebe with his corporal's stripe. Abebe returned his salute with all the military crispness he could muster, sensing all the while that he had somehow displeased his commander-in-chief.

It seemed that the ceremony was over, and the assembled Rasses and dignitaries, growing impatient under the blazing sun, were hoping that His Majesty would withdraw to the palace, their signal to rise and bow. But, exceptionally, the emperor appeared to have forgotten the protocol. Instead of turning to leave, he was scrutinising his Olympic laureate.

He fished in the pocket of his dark blue tunic and approached Abebe again.

'Corporal Abebe, you have honoured your country and the entire African continent,' he repeated.

There was a pause, and it was as if he didn't want the moment to end.

'On behalf of the Ethiopian people, we hereby bestow upon you this special tribute from the Imperial Treasury.'

He handed Abebe a small gift case and stepped back, saluting him once again before turning on his heels and marching evenly away.

In the barracks, Abebe took off his medals and hung them inside the door of his locker. He could hear the imperial band playing the national anthem outside for the fourth time. The dignitaries were enjoying a picnic, to which he was not invited. He wasn't hurt by this and didn't consider it a snub. He was a bodyguard, after all – even if he had been promoted to corporal. In any case, he was getting tired of all the speeches and the toasts. He couldn't wait for his leave to begin, so he could return to the village to see his wife and his son. His family were the ones to whom he most wanted to relate his victory. He couldn't wait to tell them about all he had seen, about the camaraderie and joy of the competition.

He opened the gift case that the emperor had given him and was stunned to see nestling inside a gold ring set with a single large diamond.

He closed the case and put it hastily back in his pocket, suddenly aware that he was being watched from the shadows by General Neway.

30

In a four-poster bed so large it made him seem like a child, Selassie was lying awake listening, as he did every morning, to the murmurs of the palace. He was in the habit of pre-dawn prayer and contemplation. It afforded lucidity, time to put in order the complaints and the conspiracies. In the darkness a cock crowed, silenced by the growl of a lion.

It was not yet dawn, but His Majesty propped himself up and pressed the button on the wall beside him. There was a distant rumble from the generator and electric lights buzzed on throughout the palace. With a series of precise movements, Selassie raised himself from the bed and waited in his nightshirt for the valet to enter with his dressing gown. He was more than sixty years old but he still stood ramrod straight, as though inspecting a parade, and from that moment until night, when he returned to his chambers, he would not allow his posture to relax for an instant. Imperial bearing was a signal of his inflexibility. If during the Hour of Judgements he had to uphold a capital sentence handed down by a regional court, or if he imposed a death sentence himself – as he had had to do nearly every day since he ascended to the throne thirty years before – it should be with fairness and consistency. If he flinched or stooped for an instant, it would be interpreted as a sign of weakness.

Outside, in the gardens, another deep growl came from one of the cats.

The gardens were still enveloped in the morning mist when the emperor emerged, alone and dressed in a dark suit, on the terrace at the rear of the palace to begin his daily walk.

As the emperor passed, a man slipped out from behind a tree, following him silently. The man, who wore an old *shamma* with his scarf drawn across his mouth, tiptoed closer and, after a moment, began to whisper. As was the custom, he spoke so quietly it was as though he were talking to himself.

'Neway,' he said.

Selassie walked ahead, giving no sign of acknowledgement until they came to the cages in which the imperial lions were pacing back and forth. There, he halted and instantly the man stopped too.

A keeper was waiting beside the cage with a sack. At the emperor's approach, the keeper pulled a leg of mutton from the sack and, bowing, held it out. Selassie threw the meat to the lions. He watched the beasts tearing at it and then he turned his head slightly and nodded, dismissing the informant. The man bowed low and withdrew, retreating backwards the way he had come without taking his eyes from the emperor. The servant with the sack handed His Majesty some more pieces of meat, and the emperor moved on to feed the panthers. The big black felines prowled loose, chained but not caged.

As he fed them, he was observed from behind a tree by another man. He was middle aged, and wore Western clothes. He waited for the emperor to recommence his walk, making sure that the first informant had receded beyond earshot, before stepping forward in the dim light. Just as the first had, he fell in step behind the emperor and began whispering.

Selassie listened without comment, his hands clasped behind his back. He came upon a flock of flamingos and smiled faintly at the sight of the timid pink birds scattering in panic. At his nod, the man fell silent in mid sentence. He halted and, with a bow, retreated backwards.

Neway.

Next – springing up as though from under the ground – came another informant: a hunchback, his face drawn and hollow eyed from lack of sleep. He too made his report in the same manner. He too whispered the name Neway.

The emperor walked on alone as the morning mist began to disperse and the first rays of sunlight struck the high branches of the trees. The Hour of the Informants was at an end. The day could now begin. Selassie's day was evenly and purposefully divided into Hours. The Hour of the Purse would follow, then the Hour of Judgements. He turned and headed slowly back the way he had come, uninterrupted this time, alone except for the restless beasts.

The two Rasses entered the Hall of Audience and bowed low, drawing back their left legs, bringing their shoulders to their knees and lowering their heads until their brows touched the thick wine-dark carpet.

Slowly, they raised themselves before the Negus. They exchanged anxious glances before one of them stepped forward to speak.

'Germame Neway has been taking bribes and using them to build schools! He has been turning fallow land over to peasants. Next he will want to expel the landowners! He will finish by confiscating imperial property.'

The second Ras stepped forward.

'This is how he repays His Most Venerable Majesty for sending him to university in America. He brings back Marxism!'

The emperor studied the Rasses, gauging their fear and considering the nature of the threat. Their white linen *shammas* were creased from the long journey. He knew that it wasn't their concern with the danger of the Soviet creed which had caused them to come all the way from their province. They were there because they were afraid of losing their privileges.

It puzzled him more that Germame Neway should be so high minded. Did he not realise what privileges he enjoyed? He could have a comfortable life, but instead he was agitating for reform; he was willing to sacrifice his career for a few peasants. The emperor was saddened as much as he was angry. The Italians had massacred those of his generation whom he was relying on to implement change and he had been faced with no alternative but to recruit new blood for the task of modernising Ethiopia. He sent them to be educated abroad, and they came back with their heads full of ideas. Giving land to the peasants, indeed! They had not seen the Soviet leaders in *their* palaces, as he had.

He thanked the Rasses and instructed them to return to their province.

'We are well aware of the situation,' he said.

General Mengistu was seated behind the desk in his office in the imperial garrison. Opposite him sat his brother, Germame. The hotels of Addis were crawling with informers, people who wanted to earn the emperor's favour with a titbit of information or a scrap of rumour. Inside the garrison, right under His Majesty's nose, was the safest place to meet.

The provincial governor leaned over the desk and, looking over his shoulder, said quietly but urgently that the time was right. 'The Negus will be in Brazil. The army and the police won't try to stop us. With the tyrant out of the country, they will hide. We must strike!'

Mengistu Neway leaned back. His mouth tightened. He said nothing. Germame looked over his shoulder once more before continuing. 'We've been waiting a long time for this moment! You are the commander of the bodyguard, the men will obey you. And Prince Asfa will accept our offer. He won't have a choice!'

The general nodded slowly.

In the last few years – ever since his favourite, the young Prince Makonnen, was killed in a car crash – the emperor often seemed to go out of his way to show disregard for Prince Asfa; he was forced to bow like a commoner, his forehead in the dust, if he wanted to address his father at court. He would quickly rally to their cause.

'What about the runner?' asked Germame Neway. 'Have you been able to indoctrinate him?'

'What would be the point? He is like all of them, he believes he owes his entire wretched existence to the emperor. To take Abebe into our confidence wouldn't be worth the risk. His family could be starving and he still wouldn't unlock the granary unless the Negus ordered it.'

It was for this reason they needed Prince Asfa: to legitimise the revolution in the eyes of a people stubbornly loyal to the Solomonic dynasty.

'But he has become the idol of the Mercato,' said Germame. 'We need him to secure the support of the people.'

General Mengistu snorted.

'You can leave Corporal Bikila to me,' he said.

General Mengistu ordered the sergeant to unlock the armoury and hand out rifles to a small company of bodyguards. He had ensured that Abebe was one of them.

They had been woken in the middle of the night and told to dress quickly. In the armoury, the sergeant distributed clips of ammunition. He ordered them to load and make ready.

Within a short time, the general had roused Crown Prince Asfa, who emerged from the palace in his nightgown and climbed into the back of a jeep. He sat between two guardsmen, his head bowed. General Mengistu took a seat on the bench opposite, his hands folded on the rifle that lay across his lap, his finger on the trigger.

Abebe could see them from the lorry that followed with the rest of the guardsmen. He knew at once that something was wrong: the crown prince wasn't dressed properly and he never once looked up, but kept his head lowered before the general as if in supplication while they drove along the dark avenues. They had been given clips that contained live ammunition. For most of their duties, they used only blanks.

The guardsmen in the lorry with Abebe were quiet. They had an important mission to fulfil, General Mengistu had told them in the armoury, a historic mission. The hour of liberty had come for the Ethiopian people, he said. Then he reminded them that it was their duty to obey orders, and that the penalty for refusing an order was death.

Mamo was among the bodyguards selected for the mission, and Abebe wanted to ask him whether he knew what was going on. But when he looked at him, Mamo shook his head, indicating that he should remain silent.

From the route they were taking, Abebe realised they were on their way to the radio station. He had become a frequent visitor to the little studio in the bungalow with the tall antenna on the roof. He had recounted his victory again and again on the radio over the last three months. He didn't mind at all. It seemed that no one in Ethiopia was bored with hearing about it.

As soon as they arrived, the general jumped down and ordered them to secure the building. He told some of the guardsmen to spread out and cover the entrance and said the rest should follow him. They entered and found the bungalow empty except for some technicians dozing on the sofas in the reception area. Mengistu woke them and ordered them to work.

Abebe was made to stand guard in the control cabin while the general marched Prince Asfa into the studio. He handed a piece of paper to the prince and told him to read it.

As he scanned the text, the prince's face grew pale.

General Mengistu nodded at the technician and said something to the prince. His words came through the speakers in the cabin. 'Now we will find out if you have the courage to act, or if your father was right about you all along. He calls you a fool and a coward. Now is your chance to show him.'

Through the glass partition, Abebe saw Prince Asfa turn towards the microphone and swallow.

'In the last years, stagnancy has reigned in Ethiopia,' he said, reading from the paper. 'Disappointment and discontent have spread among peasants, merchants, office workers, in the army and the police, among students, through every class of society.'

Prince Asfa looked around helplessly. To one side of him, the barrel of a rifle was pointing at his ear; on his other side, General Mengistu grinned with malevolent satisfaction. Abebe was stunned: the crown prince was betraying his father the emperor by speaking these words.

He looked down and continued to read:

'No progress is being made in any quarter because a handful of dignitaries have set themselves on a course of egoism and nepotism instead of working for the good of the whole community. The people of Ethiopia have waited patiently to be delivered from oppression, poverty and ignorance and now the time has come to put an end to three thousand years of injustice.'

General Mengistu nodded slowly and the guardsman with the rifle shoved the barrel closer to the prince's ear.

'To remedy this,' the prince said, reading slowly, 'a government of the people has been formed.'

He gulped.

'With myself, Crown Prince Asfa Wossen, at its head.'

Abebe realised with horror what was happening. With His Majesty out of the country, General Mengistu was trying to seize power. He was using the crown prince to do it. But he knew the Negus would do everything to hold on to his throne, even if it meant sacrificing his son. His fury at such a betrayal would be unbounded. He remembered the sermons of the priest in the village: *Whosoever challenges the King of Kings shall face the wrath of the Father, the Son, the Holy Spirit, the three hundred and eighteen fathers of Nicaea, the curse of Arius, and perpetual damnation!*

While the crown prince was speaking on the radio, all around the capital, in the villas hidden away behind high walls and leafy gardens, notables were being woken from their sleep; rifle muzzles poked through mosquito nets and prodded at flabby bellies through crisp linen *shammas*. Guardsmen disturbed the Rasses at their morning ablutions. The elderly aristocrats looked up into the stern faces of the young men and understood that the coup had come. Without the emperor to protect them, they were at the mercy of the insurgents. In one of the bedrooms, however, the guardsmen found no one. The Ras they had come to arrest had gone. After searching under the bed and in the wardrobe, and then throughout the villa, they left.

Quietly, Ras Kassa slipped out from behind a curtain and picked up the telephone.

That same night, in the great dining hall of the palace, a banquet was being held. The conspirators had chosen to act knowing that most of the Rasses and the important functionaries in the capital would be there. It would be easy to detain them while the arrest squads rounded up the rest.

General Mengistu burst into the great hall, knocking a white-gloved lackey out of the way, followed by Abebe and the guardsmen.

He ordered them to surround the guests.

They spread out around the room, one behind each diner, uneasy to be in the presence of the country's aristocracy, the dignitaries and the members of the Crown Council, some of whom had dangerous reputations. Abebe recognised Makonen, the informant who always had the ear of the emperor. He seemed to recognise the barefoot runner and his stony, fearless expression told Abebe that, even if they were only carrying out Mengistu's orders, they were guilty of treason. Abebe, the hero of Ethiopia, was now its enemy. He had heard the prince declare that he had usurped his father, and outside the great hall Mengistu had warned them that their allegiance was to the new Negus, but Abebe knew he was now part of the insurrection, and the penalty for treason was hanging. He tried to hold his rifle steady.

General Mengistu was enjoying the moment.

'Look at them,' he said. 'A feudal aristocracy feasting while the poor sleep with empty bellies.'

The ageing, dignified Empress Menem sat at the head of the long table. To her left was the young Princess Tenegneh, wearing a black gown that sparkled in the candlelight. Twenty more guests were seated at the table, almost all elderly men and women, impeccable in their manners and dress. They wore traditional *shammas* embroidered with gold thread. They were dining from a porcelain service and the table was set with silver cutlery and crystal glasses. There was more food on the table than Abebe had ever seen, even for the most lavish of weddings.

'You are under arrest. All of you. You will follow me.'

General Mengistu spoke with calm and authority, but it was clear that he had not foreseen the reactions of the diners.

Instead of cowering in terror at the guns, they barely flinched. They kept their eyes on Empress Menem, waiting for her reaction.

Mengistu was unprepared for what happened next. The empress simply ignored the intruders. She didn't even acknowledge them; it was the way she rode in the imperial Rolls-Royce, staring straight ahead. He repeated that they were under arrest. Still nobody moved. Abebe looked at Mamo, wondering what it meant. But he had his rifle trained on one of the diners and it scared Abebe to see he didn't dare to look up.

After a moment, the princess recommenced eating. Slowly, others at the table did the same. One of them even resumed his conversation, speaking in French.

'Vraiment, c'est trop! Ça manque totalement de... '

Abebe saw that the General had no power over them, not even with his rifle. Whatever the empress instructed, they would do. If they had to die right there, they wouldn't hesitate to die for her.

General Mengistu gave a signal and several of the guardsmen cocked their rifles.

Abebe nervously did as his comrades and pulled back the firing pin. In the lorry on the way back from the radio station, Mamo had whispered to him that if shooting broke out, they would be finished. Now he saw that Mamo had his eyes fixed on General Mengistu. He knew in that instant that Mamo was going to shoot his commander-in-chief.

Without looking around, Princess Tenegneh indicated to the maître d'hôtel to serve the next course. Then she spoke calmly to her guests. 'After dinner, we shall be under arrest,' she said.

The empress nodded in accord and the princess turned to the rebel general.

'Very well,' he said. 'It will be your last banquet.'

He ordered the sergeant to keep them covered and then he turned to the diners.

In his best French, he spat out the words.

'Bon appétit.'

31

The emperor stared out of a window as big as a wall in the salon of the hotel suite, contemplating the gleaming towers of the brand new Brazilian capital. Seven skyscrapers erected in the middle of nothing, a gesture of defiance to a generous but capricious nature that could feed millions one year and leave them to starve the next, impeding development. He envied the Brazilians their resources and admired their independence. That is what he had come to discuss – an alliance of non-aligned nations – that, and coffee. Brazilian exports were ruining the market for Ethiopian coffee. Ethiopian development was falling behind.

Aklilou had been listening on the telephone, and now he replaced the receiver and prepared to speak.

'There has been a communication from the British embassy. The rebellion has come.'

'The Neway brothers.'

Aklilou nodded in confirmation. 'Germame and the general. The Imperial Bodyguard is with them. They have arrested the empress, Princess Tenegneh and the ministers. According to the British, the army is still loyal to His Majesty.'

'What about my son?'

'Apparently, he has made a broadcast in support of the rebels.'

The emperor said nothing for a moment. His eldest son was ambitious but weak, and he cursed his own negligence. There was a time when he would not eat unless all of his entourage was still alive after the first course. He was growing old.

'Make the arrangements,' he ordered. 'We shall leave at once.'

More than forty years had passed since he himself had plotted to seize power. As a young man, Ras Tafari conspired with his cousin to overthrow the weak and dissolute Emperor Lij Yasu. His cousin ascended to the throne, becoming the Empress Zauditu, and Tafari waited, ruling from the shadows until, on her death, he became the Negus. He changed his name to Haile Selassie, meaning Hail the Trinity. It took five years to track down Lij Yasu and arrest him. He was kept in the palace dungeon, in chains of gold as befitted his rank, until his death fourteen years later.

Such a pathetic end would not be his, Selassie vowed. King of Kings, Elect of God, Conquering Lion of Judah, he would confront the rebels and crush them.

In the great hall of the Haile Selassie I University, Germame Neway, flanked by several armed guardsmen, faced the room full of students.

He held up a piece of dry, stale bread.

'This,' he said jubilantly, 'this is what we fed the Rasses and the ministers today, so that they will know what our people live on!'

He turned the shred of *injera* around slowly, so they could appreciate the poetic justice. They had turned the world upside down; the privileged were forced to eat the rations of a peasant.

'You must help us to succeed!'

After being searched three times, Niskanen was finally allowed in to General Mengistu's office in the imperial garrison. It was a disturbing sign: the new regime was paranoid. Inside, they were not alone. An armed guard was stationed against one wall.

He had worn civilian clothes to cross the capital, though it turned out the streets were deserted. It was the first time he had ventured out since he had heard Prince Asfa's broadcast the day before, and there was a disconcerting silence around the city. The revolt was no popular uprising, he surmised, but a plot fomented by an elite with a few hundred men, perhaps a few thousand at best.

Early on, a warning had gone around the foreign communities to stay off the streets; in any case, there was nowhere to go: the airport was closed and there were no trains leaving for the port at Djibouti. By midday, the telephone exchange had shut down and Ethiopia was isolated. Niskanen spent the first night in the cellar of his house, knowing that if the shelling began he would be safer there. From the radio, he had learned that Ethiopia's new masters were none other than Mengistu Neway and his brother Germame.

As a precaution, he had decided not to wear his uniform, and he now felt at a disadvantage before the general. Mengistu Neway was the new ruler of the country. Even though the radio broadcasts had reassured foreigners they would be safe and their assets would not be confiscated, he was wary.

'Hello, Major,' Mengistu said. 'You took a great risk coming here. The streets are not safe.'

He sounded tired but he had a victorious lustre in his eyes. He was exhilarated, driven by a dangerous combination of glory, fear and ideology. 'What can I do for you?' he asked.

'Where is Abebe?'

'He is with us now.'

'What do you mean he's with you? Is he safe?'

'I mean that Ethiopia's barefoot runner, the hero of our people, has decided to give the revolution his full support. Corporal Abebe believes wholeheartedly in our cause. Right now, he is among the men guarding the arrested Rasses.'

'What choice does he have but to support you? He's under your command. He doesn't even know what the word revolution means.'

'And you, Major? Do you know what our revolution means?'

'I am a Swedish subject. It's not my—'

'Be careful, Major,' interrupted the general, 'I could have you arrested as a foreign spy!'

'My country has a policy of neutrality,' Niskanen reminded him flatly. 'It's not my place to comment on domestic politics.' Still, he couldn't leave it at that. Mengistu wouldn't want to risk upsetting the international community by detaining foreigners – Ethiopia depended on them too much for that – and he didn't like being threatened. 'I have to say that *your* revolution, as you call it, doesn't stand a chance. The army is waiting for His Majesty to return. When he does, you'll be finished.'

'You Swedes believe you are not like the colonialists, with your stoic sort of socialism and your practical Christianity. You think our people can be improved by education. Perhaps you are right that they need education, but forgive me if I consider your attitude condescending, simply a milder form of imperialism. Anyway, you are wrong, Major. The army is going to come to the conclusion that what we want is best for the country. After all, when did they last have a pay rise? We will succeed because the people are with us.'

'What did you tell me once? The people have always been there, you said. On the way here, I saw nobody. The streets were deserted. They're all in hiding.'

'There is no need to worry, Major. When they hear that Abebe Bikila has joined our cause, they will rally to us. When they hear of his courage and sacrifice on behalf of the new Ethiopian people's republic, then they will rise up.'

At the airfield outside Addis, three tanks swung their turrets towards the Air Ethiopia DC-9 as it taxied to a halt. They raised their cannons, aiming directly at the fuselage. The aircraft carrying the members of the imperial delegation returning from Brazil had been given permission to land by the officer in charge, who immediately notified army headquarters of His Majesty's return. A welcome had already been prepared.

Inside the aircraft, Selassie waited by the door. Through a porthole, Aklilou was anxiously scanning the tarmac, looking for a sign of the rebels' presence.

Finally, he signalled with a nod that they were ready and, placing himself in front of His Majesty, prepared to step from the aeroplane. If there were any snipers lurking, he would serve as a human shield.

As the steward pulled down the lever, however, Aklilou felt a hand on his shoulder. Selassie gently drew him aside. What was the use of being emperor if you couldn't trust your own countrymen?

The Negus stepped from the plane, his demeanour stern, like an angry, reproachful father, his back straighter than ever. He didn't flinch as he stepped out, but hesitated for a moment before descending the steps, smelling the air. Beyond the familiar freshness of eucalyptus there was no trace of smoke, no acrid odour of burning flesh. It was a good sign. There had been no shelling, no rioting, no shops or homes set alight. The people had not joined the revolution.

He approached the first of the tanks and stood defiantly before it. After a while, there was a murmur of radio communication inside the tank; abruptly, the turret opened and a soldier emerged. The soldier saluted and, without showing any emotion, Selassie saluted back.

32

Abebe could hear shells bursting in the gardens of the palace and the panicked cries of the wild cats. That morning, they had been woken by far-off bursts of machine-gun fire and the distant thunder of explosions somewhere in the city. He thought at first it might be the rebels, but now there could be no doubt. The artillery was trained on them. The army was approaching the palace and someone said the emperor himself was leading the assault.

There was the smell of powder and smoke and a terrible noise filled the hallways: the revving of a tank advancing, changing gears and then rumbling forward, crushing fences and walls. Cooks and courtiers spilled outside, running every which way in panic. The imperial lions strained at their leashes. If the lions died, it would mean the end of the kingdom. Abebe wondered what chance the animals had against the shells.

He was inside the Green Chamber with five other guardsmen, guarding the arrested dignitaries. They had been brought out of the cells, still wearing their finery from the banquet, and up to the royal chambers without being told why. There was no need. From the sounds of battle outside they must have guessed. Neway's coup was collapsing and the army was fighting to regain control of the palace.

One of them, an elderly Ras, had been watching Abebe.

'You are the Galla who won the medal,' he said.

Abebe nodded.

'This is how you repay His Majesty. Your people are dogs! You are no better than a jackal!'

He spat at the herdsman's son.

Abebe lifted the barrel of his rifle and waved it at the old Ras. The sounds of gunfire were coming closer. He could hear a commotion outside the door and wondered whether the army had reached them.

Just then, General Mengistu burst into the Green Chamber, followed by more guardsmen.

'Over there!' he barked. 'The men! All of you! Against the wall. You women, get away!'

Defying him, the Rasses moved closer together, standing in front of the women.

Angrily, Mengistu grabbed one of the Rasses and flung him towards the far wall. Herded and shoved by the guardsmen, the other Rasses joined him. The women were separated from the men now and they cowered together, whimpering – all except Empress Menem and Princess Tenegneh. The empress stood impassively, a look of contempt on her face. The princess glared defiantly at General Mengistu.

'You will hang for this!' she promised.

Mengistu snorted and then began to laugh, bitter, unfinished laughter that trailed to silence.

Earlier, the princess had whispered to Abebe, telling him that he wasn't responsible, and that if he helped them, she would see to it that he was pardoned. But even if he wanted to help her, it was too late now.

The general turned to his men and, in a calm, determined voice, ordered them to shoot the prisoners.

Abebe looked at the other guardsmen uncertainly.

They cocked their rifles and aimed at the Rasses lined against the wall.

Abebe's rifle was trained on the old Ras who had insulted him. He had never used it to kill anyone. He had always imagined such a moment might come, heroically, in a battle against an enemy of his country.

'*I said shoot them!*'

The Rasses stared beyond the guardsmen, as though to look at their executioners would be to concede their legitimacy. They drew themselves up, tall and proud, preparing to die. But no shots came, only the booming vibration of another explosion outside.

'I see your revolution has won neither the hearts nor the minds of your troops, General,' said one of the Rasses contemptuously.

Exasperated, General Mengistu fired at the Ras.

The old Ras crumpled and fell groaning to the ground. Blood streamed from under him.

In slow succession, some of the guardsmen fired their rifles too. One after another, the Rasses dropped like marionettes. The floor was covered with heaps of bloodstained white *shammas*, and the wives started to shriek.

When the shots abated, just six Rasses remained standing, spared at random.

Mengistu Neway turned his rifle on Abebe.

'Shoot them!'

Abebe lifted his rifle and pointed the barrel at one of the old Rasses.

'Galla dog!' spat the Ras.

'Shoot them! What are you waiting for? Or so help me I will shoot you!'

Abebe's finger tightened on the trigger. He knew the safety catch was still on and he knew that General Mengistu would soon realise it too. He thought his legs were going to buckle under him. He couldn't fire at the Rasses, even if it meant that Mengistu would probably shoot him. To fire on them would be to betray the emperor, to betray his father, his village, his oath as a guardsman.

He was about to lower his rifle when, suddenly, there was a volley of gunfire. General Mengistu had started shooting the remaining dignitaries.

He glared at Abebe. 'Look what you have done,' he said.

At this, some of the other guardsmen began shooting too, firing repeatedly this time, relishing the pleas of the dying for mercy.

Abebe lowered his rifle.

He saw the empress and the princess watching the killings impassively, as though it didn't matter, as though they could never be defeated by this murderous act alone.

Just then, an explosion shattered the windows and black smoke filled the room.

General Mengistu surveyed what he had done, transfixed by the last act of his revolution, before leaving hurriedly. He was trailed by the guardsmen, panicked now and without a commander. Only women remained in the Green Chamber: the empress, her daughter and the others weeping for husbands, uncles and cousins, their white linen robes stained with blood. One of the guardsmen seized Abebe and pulled him from the room.

They ran from the palace, dodging the smoke and the army patrols until they reached the Entoto hills beyond the city.

Silver eucalyptus trees shimmered in the moonlight, but their slender trunks and high foliage offered little cover. All around, the guardsmen could hear shouts, cries and intermittent shooting.

Abebe huddled against a tree and waited.

He was still wide awake, hollow eyed and shivering with fear, as the day broke.

At the same moment, down Churchill Avenue, the Emperor's Rolls-Royce drove slowly towards the palace. As it passed, His Majesty's loyal subjects dropped to their knees and battered their heads against the ground. None dared to lift his brow from the dust. Their lives belonged to the emperor. He could drive over them, crushing them, if he chose.

Selassie had sent a double – one of several courtiers who stood in for him at boring state functions – to accompany the men who stormed the palace the day before. He was only now arriving at the devastated imperial residence.

That afternoon, on one of the lawns of the avenue, His Majesty addressed the people.

'We are disposed to offer amnesty to all those who would care to recognise their mistakes,' he said.

But the people had seen the bodies dangling from the trees in the Mercato, the bullet-ridden corpse of Colonel Gebayu in his khaki uniform and those of others who had been foolish enough to join the rebellion.

Throughout the city wafted a stench of powder and carrion. The army had been given orders to account for every one of the missing guardsmen, alive or dead.

The emperor stood alongside his son, a son who had betrayed him, shown weakness and incompetence, and said that the crown prince had been manipulated by others. His Majesty did not identify these others, however, for he couldn't bring himself to say that they were the very ones upon whom he had been counting to bring progress to Ethiopia, the ones he had picked out and sent to study abroad and then given posts in which they could have made reforms gradually, fairly, without upsetting the nobility.

For without the nobility, what was Ethiopia?

Abebe walked with his hands tied behind his back, followed by three soldiers.

The soldiers were waving their arms and whistling as they shoved him along the street, kicking his ankles and jeering. They were walking him through the capital to the guardhouse, enjoying the surprised looks of the people.

'That's right,' they shouted. 'It's the barefoot runner!'

He was still barefoot, but he wasn't going to be doing any more running, they laughed!

They passed the bodies hanging from the trees.

The soldiers belonged to the imperial army; their rough khaki was ragged compared to the gabardine worn by the guardsmen and they spoke the idiom of the Mercato, vulgar and loud. They had found Abebe asleep in the morning chill, exhausted with fear. They had recognised him at once as the hero of Ethiopia. Now he was their prisoner.

One of the soldiers fired his rifle in the direction of Abebe's bare feet, and the little puff of sand caused them all to laugh in derision.

At last, they came to the jail, where Abebe was flung into a cell full of captive bodyguards. General Mengistu was one of them.

He looked at Abebe in disgust, then turned away.

Abebe saw that the other side of his face was badly swollen, purple and bleeding, the skin flayed, and that one eye was completely white.

33

All around, wreckage was being cleared away. Dusty labourers, men and boys, had formed a line and were passing from hand to hand charred rocks and pieces of still-smouldering wood. Another line comprised of women conveyed red bricks from the piles by the kiln. As he crossed the palace grounds, Niskanen watched this ragged horde performing their ceaseless toil. It seemed so natural, their misery so endless, passing things forever from hand to hand. The workers looked half starved and the women in the other line were probably their wives and daughters. For them, it was fortuitous that the palace needed repairs.

He had brought with him a letter from the Olympic Committee, one of hundreds he had received since news spread that Abebe Bikila was facing execution for his part in the failed coup. Sporting federations, political organisations in Africa and even civil liberties groups in the United States had written expressing concern. But the letter from the International Olympic Committee was the one he thought would carry the most weight. It was an invitation for Abebe via the Ethiopian Athletics Federation to attend the premiere of a film of the Rome Games.

He entered the gardens to find Selassie, his shoulders rounded, his gaze lowered, contemplating the imperial lions. They sprawled motionless on the ground.

Approaching cautiously – he had never been able to get used to their supposed tameness and feared that one day they would decide he was an interloper in their world, in Africa – Niskanen saw that the great beasts were silent. They weren't making their habitual rumblings. He couldn't hear the deep purr of their breathing. They lay utterly still.

He finally realised why.

'There is no need to be scared. They have been poisoned.'

Niskanen assumed at first that this had been a last, vengeful act on the part of the rebels. Then he understood that it was not the rebels who were responsible.

'They betrayed me,' said Selassie. 'Instead of defending the throne, they allowed the traitors to enter.'

Niskanen looked at the dead lions and wondered what weight the letter from the Olympic Committee could have against three thousand years of imperial tradition. However much he wanted to be part of the international community, Selassie, like his people, was bound by feudal ties. These obligations had prevented the masses from rising against him; they were more important than prestige abroad.

'What can we do for you, Major?'

Niskanen decided not to mention the letter.

'I expect His Highness knows why I have come,' he said.

'You are here to plead for the life of Corporal Abebe Bikila.'

'It is my hope... ' He paused. 'And the hope of others in the international community,' he added, 'that His Imperial Majesty will find it in his heart to show clemency.'

Selassie turned to Niskanen, his regard suddenly as sharp as steel.

'You would have me show mercy to the traitors? If we pardon them, what will the others think, those who are watching and waiting?'

'I understand, Your Majesty. I was only concerned with Abebe.'

'They are still there, the greedy sympathisers who think they will be better off. Our ambassador to your country, for example; he even had the nerve to toast the rebels! He raised a glass of champagne. What would this cowardly person think if he heard that His Imperial Majesty had pardoned those who tried to steal his throne? He would think he might be able to succeed one day. He would plot another coup, and we would be too busy trying to please the international community to notice. We intend to provide a demonstration of what his fate will be if he ever returns here, a lesson for all the rebels.'

'But Abebe wasn't involved. He wasn't one of those wanting to usurp His Majesty's crown. They forced him to do it. He was hiding out in the hills because he feared for his life.'

'It was not reform the rebels wanted. Ethiopia is already a socialist monarchy, like your country. No matter what they say. It was power they wanted.'

Niskanen looked at the lines of labourers in rags and farther away, by the kilns, he could see their homes, a few tattered tents.

'Power for themselves. Germame and Mengistu Neway wanted power. Oh, they were calling for progress and justice. We too want progress and justice, but these things are slow in coming.'

He turned back to look again at the dead lions.

'They were guilty of treason. The punishment for treason is death.'

Niskanen stood in the aisle of St George's Cathedral and crossed himself, his head lowered. Discreetly, he took a seat in one of the wooden pews. He looked up and saw a brightly painted figure of the Virgin and Child. Before the altar, the *Abuna* was burning incense. But the old priest soon disappeared into the vestry, pretending not to notice the presence of strangers.

The Coptic church was lurid and colourful; all was mystery and sentiment, more so than in a Catholic church. A thousand candles burned, a thousand prayers to a thousand saints. Higher up, he found the simple solace he was seeking in the greying wooden vaults of the roof and the murky glass of the windows.

He leaned forward and prayed.

In the silence, he sensed someone watching him from behind. Slowly, he became aware of how stiff his shoulders were, how tense from clinging to hope. Turning around, he saw that he was being watched from the rear of the cathedral by Helen.

The wife of the American consul nodded and smiled at him with a gentle expression of sympathy.

Finally, he stood and turned to leave. She stood too, and waited as he approached her.

They had known each other for over a decade now. They met regularly at charity affairs, Red Cross functions, even sometimes at sporting events when Ben was obliged to attend. He had seen her face lose its bloom but acquire strength. There was no disenchantment yet.

He greeted her with a slight bow, opening the heavy wooden door for her, and they stepped from the darkness into bright sunlight.

She told him how she had been chaperoning a women's delegation from the United Nations around town when the coup began. They had barricaded themselves in the Hotel Ghion as shots rang out and shattered the windows. They all feared they would be taken hostage.

She said she had heard about Abebe.

'I've been coming here every day since we found out,' said Helen. 'I've been praying for him. I was hoping that I would see you, Major. I know I could have called. I wanted to call but I knew you must be busy. He does have a chance, doesn't he?'

'Yes, of course he does.'

That was a good way to put it, the best that could be said for now. Niskanen had tried all the diplomatic channels he could think of but it was Red Cross policy not to interfere in state affairs and the Swedish ambassador had wrung his hands. They all said there was nothing anyone could do. The emperor was the final, the only, court of appeal, and nobody wanted to intervene. He suspected the truth was they thought Abebe was guilty.

'I wanted to tell you that we're all praying for him,' she said, giving Niskanen a supportive smile. 'My husband's been in touch with Washington.'

'Please tell him I'm most grateful.'

'And if there's anything I can do... I thought we could maybe organise a petition.'

When Helen had told Ben about the idea of a petition to save Abebe, he had laughed. This isn't a popularity contest, he scoffed. Selassie isn't kidding. Niskanen was comforted by the suggestion, however. 'That's very good of you,' he said. 'Perhaps it might help.'

He didn't know what more to say.

She took his hand and held it tightly.

'Well,' she stammered, 'I'd better be going.'

Niskanen watched her descend the steps. He wanted to call her back, to talk about the petition, about how lonely he sometimes was in Addis. He was distracted by the door of the cathedral opening again.

The *Abuna* stepped from the dark.

'Good afternoon, Major,' he said. The *Abuna* was the archbishop of the Ethiopian church, the most important cleric in the land.

'I understand you have sought to plead with His Majesty on behalf of Abebe Bikila,' he said.

'I'm sure he wasn't involved. Abebe is a simple man, the son of a shepherd. He knows nothing about politics.'

'Be that as it may, I'm afraid he was involved, Major. There are witnesses to the massacre. They murdered fourteen nobles, some of the most respected members of the court.'

'If he did shoot anyone, he was acting under Mengistu's orders.'

'Whoever gave the order is not important.'

'This is not Christian justice!' exploded Niskanen.

The *Abuna* didn't try to correct him. He said simply, 'The emperor rules by the grace of God. He is our link with tradition, and with God. His decision will be just and merciful.'

Niskanen regretted his outburst. 'I'm sorry. It's not my place.'

'Your anger is understandable.'

'There's one thing I would like to ask. I would like to see Abebe. Can you help me visit the prison?'

'That may be possible, but if I can arrange it, you must promise not to raise his hopes unduly. His fate is in God's hands now.'

He paused, and Niskanen nodded.

Then the *Abuna* reminded him that many of the victims were members of the royal family. 'The wound is deep, Major.'

Two weeks passed before Niskanen received word that the *Abuna* had interceded with the emperor on his behalf. He had been granted permission to visit Abebe in the palace dungeon.

The smell made him choke. The walls ran with vomit and excrement, the air stank of disease and fear. If anything confirmed the feudal nature of the regime, it was the palace jail. The prison belonged to a medieval African state, a terrifying and squalid one, with iron rings embedded in the dark stones. Niskanen was led to an empty, gloomy cell where, after a long wait, Abebe was brought in.

The first thing he registered was that Abebe had lost weight. His already slender body was 10 kilos lighter at least. His features were drawn and empty; the warders probably hadn't fed him. The way they undoubtedly saw it, he was going to die anyway. To Niskanen, it was nothing less than barbaric.

As soon as the warder closed the door, Abebe bounded towards the major and fell at his knees.

'I did not kill, Major,' he pleaded. 'I disobey order. No shoot. General Mengistu, he knows.'

'I believe you, Abebe,' said Niskanen. 'I know you didn't do what they say. You had no choice. I know.'

He helped Abebe up and noticed bruising on his legs. At first he thought it was from the chains he was wearing, but Abebe stood unsteadily and Niskanen guessed that the soldiers had beaten him.

'A date has been set for the trial,' he said. 'We're hoping that His Highness will accept the American request for international observers.'

'I am innocent,' protested Abebe. 'God knows this. God will help me.'

Niskanen was silent. He was convinced that Mengistu had used Abebe for cover, that he was innocent, but the truth didn't matter. He didn't want to tell Abebe that it was going to be a military trial, a court martial, and that the verdict had already been decided.

He held Abebe's shoulder and squeezed it softly. It was bony and weak. 'We're going to have to get you back in shape. You're not getting enough exercise in here.'

'I don't think I run very far,' joked Abebe. 'Not today.'

Then he showed the major his feet. The red weals from the whipping had blistered. For days, he had been unable to stand because of the pain.

'We're lucky,' said Niskanen, inspecting Abebe's wounds. 'It doesn't look as if there's any infection. But they ought to be bandaged. Try to keep them clean, keep them off the floor. I'll see if I can get a doctor to come in here and see to you.'

Abebe said he couldn't do much training for the moment, anyway. The cell was small, too low even to stand up properly, let alone exercise, and there were seven of them in there.

Niskanen was angry. Beating prisoners was illegal, it was savage. He thought about making an official complaint. After all, no self-respecting army should tolerate such lack of discipline. Then he realised what had happened: Abebe had been tortured deliberately. It wasn't victimisation by the soldiers. Someone was trying to extract a confession.

'Don't worry,' he reassured Abebe. 'It doesn't look serious, it's nothing that's going to stop you running.'

Abebe smiled.

'We've been getting offers from around the world, by the way. Everyone wants to race you.'

He had transmitted the letters to the Ministry of Education, pointing out that Abebe would make an excellent ambassador for Ethiopia's achievements, and asking what reply he should give. But he had received no answer.

Niskanen wanted to tell Abebe he was the greatest runner in the world, that nobody could beat his marathon record; and how proud he was to have trained an Olympic gold medallist.

'Trust me,' he said. 'I'm going to see to it that they all get the chance.'

That evening, Niskanen decided to go to the Hotel Ghion. He didn't think of himself as a drinking man – he didn't like to lose control – but he needed to restore his faith. He hadn't been able to lie to Abebe, as he had intended, even just to cheer him up. He was haunted by the spectre of the barefoot runner, thin, hurt and frightened. His death would be pointless, and it had occurred to Niskanen that if he had never won the marathon, he would probably not now be facing execution.

In the hotel bar he was grateful for the distraction of the clientele: businessmen, diplomats and their secretaries and staff meeting with locals. The foreigners had returned since the coup attempt, unruffled, it seemed. For them, it was business as usual. He ordered a whisky and soda and sipped it, nursing the glass in both hands as though it contained a reprieve. As he felt the whisky glowing inside him, he began to be convinced that even if the emperor didn't pardon him, he might give Abebe a prison sentence instead of executing him. Selassie was preoccupied with his reputation abroad. That would count for something, surely.

Then he remembered the imperial lions and he knew that the emperor's pride was greater than all other considerations.

Dejected, he was downing the last of his glass when he saw Ben approaching.

'Hey, Major Niskanen! Don't see you around here very often.'

'Just thought I'd drop by,' said Niskanen.

'Must be pretty hard for you. You're quite attached to him, I expect.'

He knew that people thought him a loner, a misfit. The truth was he hadn't noticed how fond he had become of all of them.

'I met your wife the other day,' Niskanen said. 'She was very kind.'

'She told me.'

'In the cathedral. She was alone.'

'She goes there all the time.'

'Perhaps you should be keeping her company.'

'My wife is a very religious woman.'

Their relationship was not his business but the whisky had gone to Niskanen's head. He could say whatever came into his mind; and he wanted to say how inhuman the country was, how backward and cruel its ways. Remembering where he was, he suddenly sobered. The hotel bar was full of informers.

'Sorry,' said Niskanen. 'It's none of my business.'

'That's OK. Tell you what, you can buy me a drink.'

Ben climbed on to a stool alongside him and Niskanen called to the bartender for two more whisky-sodas.

'It's hard for her to be on these postings. It wasn't at first, but it's been a long time. After a while, you get out of sync with the rest, with everything back home. You're a foreigner everywhere.'

'I know. It's reached the point where I don't think I could ever go back.'

'It might be different if we had kids,' said Ben.

He waited as the bartender set down their drinks. 'But, hey, I didn't come here to talk about my wife,' he said, taking a large sip from his glass.

'I guess you don't know,' he went on. 'They brought the trial forward. Mengistu was court-martialled today. Military court: no jury, no public, no appeal.'

'Did he say anything?'

'About Abebe, no. Nothing. Apparently he didn't show even the faintest hint of humility, no inclination whatsoever to obtain his distinguished majesty's pardon. I guess he knew he wasn't going to get a break whatever he said. He talked revolution and when the sentence was announced he said he hoped that spilling his blood would help the tree of liberty and justice to grow in Ethiopia. They're going to hang him tomorrow – with the other guardsmen.'

That night, Selassie sat for long hours in contemplation on his throne in the Hall of Audience. The Englishman, Spencer, was there, waiting in the shadows to one side. Before the throne stood three Hindu astrologers. They had come to announce to His Majesty the results of their calculations.

The Indians put their palms together in front of their lowered faces and bowed slowly.

'Well?' queried Selassie.

One of the soothsayers spoke up. There was no point in hiding the truth that was written in the stars.

'His Majesty's house shall be empty,' he said.

The astrologers looked at one another, nodding in accord.

Selassie tensed. He stared at them angrily, then waved them away.

The three Hindus bowed and withdrew. As soon as they had gone, Spencer stepped forward.

'And you?' enquired Selassie. 'What does your science tell you?'

Spencer said he had come reluctantly to the same conclusion. 'My feeling is they are right.'

Selassie dismissed the imperial adviser in turn and sat alone in silence.

It was almost dawn when the *Abuna* came to the palace to make his report. Mengistu had not repented, he told the emperor, and therefore he deserved to be shown no mercy.

'His blasphemy towards the holy mother church and his defiance of His Imperial Majesty was unpardonable.'

When the revolt had erupted, the *Abuna* had immediately excommunicated the rebels. This more than anything else had deprived them of the support of the devout populace and the hungry though nonetheless devout and loyal army.

In the cell, Abebe and the other guards had watched in shocked silence as General Mengistu read Marx while the *Abuna* prayed for his immortal soul. The superstitious gibberish of the Church exasperated him, he told them after the archbishop departed. It was part of the arsenal of repression. He was going to die a modern death, he said defiantly, a death given meaning by ideology!

He surely knew that whether he repented or not, he had no hope of a reprieve. Mengistu had told them that, as a young guardsman, he had been given the job of executioner: he was the one who had hung the so-called traitors who liberated the country from the Italians while His Majesty was absent, under the protection of the British. He was the one who had driven the lorry away, leaving the patriots dangling from nooses. The emperor had given him a promotion to reward him for his loyalty. He scoffed and said it was cowardice, not loyalty, which had prevented him from acting; the tyrant had no qualms about killing anyone who might be a threat to him. 'I only regret I didn't agree when my brother said we should assassinate him. Now my brother is dead.'

The guardsmen were shocked. They listened to Mengistu railing against the emperor, calling him a despot, an autocrat, words they didn't know but which lacked all respect. The general had even decided at one point that he would begin their indoctrination, and he had started to translate from his book, but the words – capitalism, communism, alienation – made no sense to them. Land reform was the only thing they understood. They had all known grievances over land in their villages. So he said he would begin with that.

Selassie calls his regime 'state socialist', he explained, but Ethiopia is a monarchy. All the land in the kingdom belongs to H.I.M. The emperor lends it or rents it to the Rasses, who sub-let it to the peasantry. He receives a tax on all crops calculated according to the fertility of the land. Even in a bad year when harvests are meagre the tax is still due. He possesses vast estates in Harrar and Kalia, and several concessions are state monopolies, including the gold mines. One third of gold production goes directly into the imperial coffers. His Majesty complains that these incomes barely cover the expenses of the court and the Imperial Bodyguard, said Mengistu sarcastically. Then, of course, there are all the foreign trips.

Abebe was uncomfortable hearing this. He was proud of his uniform and he knew now that the bodyguards ate well compared to the soldiers in the army.

Mengistu's brother Germame was an administrator; he had studied the imperial accounts. The imperial family, the priesthood, local governors and senior functionaries and military officers controlled the best lands and made huge profits. Mengistu called them a feudal caste. He said Ethiopia's problem was not colonialism, but feudalism.

'The empress keeps a chest of gold under her bed,' he revealed. 'She is a shrewd businesswoman. As well as owning apartment blocks, she has shares in many of the new companies in Addis – businesses that can only operate with royal warrants. This is how they intend to modernise Ethiopia, by plundering even the few derisory examples of progress.'

He said the ruling class wanted modernisation without change, and that was impossible. Whether they hung him or not, a change was going to come. One day, the Ethiopians would be rid of the oppressor!

Abebe was surprised to learn that the emperor had raised the Neway brothers from modest origins. He had even paid the bill for Mengistu's wedding – and the bodyguards, when they heard this, were certain he was going to hang. But the more he thought about it, the more Abebe was perplexed by Mengistu's acts. As commander-in-chief of the Imperial Bodyguard, he had privileges, honour and wealth. Were these not enough? Either his greed and ingratitude knew no bounds, Abebe reasoned, or else what he said about the emperor was true.

Mengistu gazed up out of the small, barred window, waiting for the first glint of light. The others were silent. 'If you are going to hang,' Mengistu had told them, 'you ought at least to have some idea of the reason why.'

But Abebe didn't really believe that Mengistu wanted anything other than power and wealth for himself. In any case, it didn't matter. They were not dying for an ideal, like him. If they were going to die, it was because they had failed to defend the throne, they had failed the King of Kings, and there could be no greater shame.

Led by a captain, some soldiers entered the cell. The time had come.

Dawn was breaking and Mengistu closed his book and blew out the candle. He raised himself slowly, his body stiff. At the military academy, he had been taught not to reveal weakness, and he demonstrated the result of his learning now. He stared at the open door and the captain nodded, indicating that the time had come.

In the corridor, more guardsmen were being brought out of the cells. The soldiers went about unlocking the chains that attached them to the walls of their cells and then chaining the prisoners together.

'Rebels,' scoffed the army captain. 'You are all going to die!'

The guardsmen stared at the floor in silence. After a moment, Abebe lifted his head to see Mengistu looking at him. On Mengistu's face was an expression of satisfaction.

'I am happy for you, Abebe,' said the general softly. 'You did not have the courage to kill for the revolution. Nevertheless, you shall have the privilege of dying for it.'

The captain laughed.

'Not him,' he said, pointing at Abebe.

Mengistu flinched.

The captain grinned. 'His Majesty has granted the runner a pardon.'

***

That morning, though it was a little later than usual, after the sun had risen, Selassie took his walk in the gardens. He had given orders that he was not to be interrupted and he walked alone through the grounds, listening to the sounds of the new day: the cocks crowing, the roll of drums, the wooden trap creaking and the faint snapping of necks as the bodies dropped from the gallows.

Selassie had hung conspirators before. There would be others one day and he would be obliged to hang them too.

In the Main Square, given only sidelong glances by the multitudes who didn't want to be mistaken for sympathisers, the bodies of General Mengistu and six imperial bodyguards dangled from a gibbet. By midday, it was known throughout Addis that the barefoot runner, the hero of Ethiopia, was not among the hanged guardsmen.

This was taken to mean that Abebe Bikila must have been loyal to His Imperial Majesty throughout, otherwise he too would surely have been swinging in the air, his feet pointing lifelessly at the earth.

Niskanen woke with a start, damp with sweat, and realised he was sprawled on the bed still wearing his clothes. His temples throbbed and his forehead ached. The sun was up, but he couldn't think what day it was, the same or the next. He panicked, sensing someone's presence.

He raised himself up groggily and tried to focus.

It was Helen.

Through the door, he saw that she was looking at the photos on the mantelpiece in the living room. She wore a twinset that accentuated her soft curves, and the way the hem of her skirt hugged her taut calf muscles intrigued him suddenly. He was glad he had put away the photo of himself and the German soldiers. She was studying a photo of Niskanen when he was a young man. He was smiling broadly in the photo because he had just won a cross-country skiing event, the proudest moment of his life – until then.

That was when he remembered Abebe...

At the same instant, Helen noticed that the bedroom door was open and that Niskanen was there.

'I'm sorry,' she stammered. 'I came to tell you the news and the front door was open so I let myself in. I thought I would find you up by now.'

He squinted uncomprehendingly at her. Then he realised he must have passed out on the bed after drinking almost an entire bottle of Ben's bourbon, a desperate resort when his prayers had begun to seem futile.

'No, it's OK,' he said, sitting up. 'I always leave it open.'

He saw that she was blushing; she must have sensed him watching her. 'I'm sorry,' he said, wanting to put her at ease. 'I didn't know what else there was. Sometimes, the whisky helps.'

'You don't know! Oh. Then I can be the one to tell you. He was granted a reprieve! They didn't hang him! Abebe's alive.'

She sat down on the edge of the bed and took his hand.

'Our prayers were answered, Onni. The emperor decided to pardon him! He's free!'

He saw the reflection of his relief in her smile. Looking into her eyes, he laughed suddenly, overcome by unexpected joy. He wanted to kiss her, if only to see how it might feel to share this emotion with her, and he guessed she must have known, because she let go of his hand and stood up again.

'He's waiting for you.'

Kidaneh was already waiting at the barracks when Niskanen arrived with Helen. The army had taken control of the Imperial Garrison and, nervously, Niskanen presented himself to an army captain. The soldier stared at him mistrustfully, and at last told him to wait on the parade ground before he disappeared inside the barracks and returned with a key.

He opened an old wooden door in the side of the palace that evidently led to the dungeons, and Abebe was pushed out into the daylight by someone inside. His ankles were still shackled and he ran awkwardly across the parade ground and threw himself at Niskanen's feet. Pressing his forehead to the earth, he began to sob with relief.

Despite his joy, Niskanen was embarrassed by Abebe's display. He and Abebe were not equals, but Abebe wasn't beholden to him. He had been powerless to save him.

The major helped him up and signalled sternly at the captain to remove the chains from his feet.

'It's not me you must thank,' he said as the captain unlocked the iron shackles. 'We should be grateful to the Lord, and to His Highness,' he added.

He was a friend of Ethiopia, but he had learned that Ethiopia, rightly enough, recognised no debt to him, for to do so would be to accept subservience, to accept colonisation by him. If Abebe was alive, it was because His Majesty had wanted it so. They were merely trainer and champion; they owed their achievement to one another. But Abebe owed his life to the emperor.

He hugged the tearful Abebe. Then he bent down to examine the weals on his soles. They had almost completely healed and there was no sign of infection.

He caressed his feet, nodding with satisfaction.

Abebe was going to run again.

34

Two nurses lifted Abebe from his bed and lowered him into the pool.

The male nurses in the hospital were muscular types who hoisted his weight easily. He had seen burly athletes at the Games and the nurses said pumping iron made them as strong as oxen. They said they were fans of his and talked about lifting weights and body-building. He hoped their secret would work for him. But each day, as they lowered him into the water, they scrutinised him with a consideration that turned to sadness. Abebe knew they were looking for a response, some sign that sensation was returning to his limbs, but it had been months now and there was still nothing. He could feel the water only as it came up around his waist and lapped at his stomach. His legs seemed to no longer be a part of him, the legs that had carried him to the heights of Olympus, as one of the nurses had said, shaking his head.

Over the months, Abebe had seen the same white walls, the same white gowns, the same faces with the same kindly, patient expressions, but behind their masks he detected resignation, as if they knew, as he did, that a higher court, a higher power, would decide whether there was to be a reprieve, and there was nothing anyone could do but wait and, until such time, endure the sentence.

Perhaps that remission was going to come today with the visit of His Majesty. Despite what the physicians said, only the *Negus Negasta* had the jurisdiction to return vitality and strength to his legs, and Abebe feared that this was not his purpose.

Still, despite this conviction, Abebe accomplished what was

asked of him, the way he once diligently followed Niskanen's instructions. After all, the major's science had enabled him to become a champion, so there was no telling what other miracles it might accomplish, and His Imperial Majesty had no hesitation in equipping the army with the latest modern weaponry, so even the King of Kings put his faith in this sorcery.

Unquestioningly, Abebe surrendered his weight to the water in the pool, surprised as ever at how it held him up, at how his legs floated uselessly to the surface. If he leaned forward, they would trail in the water behind him, and if he tilted his head back, his torso would slowly rise and his legs would drift up to the surface, where they floated like the empty trousers of a rag doll.

At first, he had been afraid of the water, an unfamiliar and treacherous element, but the nurses had told him there was no need to worry, even if he couldn't swim; the water was heavily salted and it would support his weight. There were railings to hold on to and all around the pool men and women were bobbing in the water. Slowly his arms had become stronger, and after a while he could let go of the railing at the side and swim – if that was what it was – moving in a circle in the water. He couldn't see the point, but then he didn't understand at first why Niskanen made them run uphill, and so he accepted the nurses' instructions without question.

The doctors said the vertebra at the base of his spine had been jolted out of place; they said the nerves had been torn by the force of the impact and that with time and plenty of re-education they would knit back together. They said there was every reason to be optimistic. They didn't seem to understand that if such a misfortune as losing the use of his legs had come upon him, it could only be through the will of an enemy, a powerful enemy, someone he had deeply wronged.

He wondered whether it was someone he had eclipsed, a fellow athlete who had lost face, but he couldn't think of who that might be and he couldn't imagine any of the guardsmen desiring such a terrible vengeance. No, he was sure it wasn't any athlete; everything he knew of sporting competition had been joy and camaraderie. Rhadi and the New Zealander had stood in exaltation on the podium alongside him; runners had shaken his hand and carried him high on their shoulders. That was one of the best things about sport: nobody begrudged your victory, as long as it was honest.

He had reflected on the mystery during the months in the hospital, and for a while he suspected it might be the restless spirit of Mengistu seeking vengeance. It had occurred to Abebe that the rebel general may have blamed him for the failure of the coup, and that, after his death, resentment and frustration had transformed him into an evil, vengeful spirit. Sometimes an elder in the village worried about being plagued by a *zar* but in the city people laughed about such superstitions and Abebe didn't really believe it any longer; if you asked him, he would have said that ghosts didn't exist. Yet he had no doubt that magic was involved. Magic – and retribution. To lose the use of his legs was a punishment for something he had done.

Could it really have been the disgruntled spirit of one of the Neway brothers or a member of their family seeking revenge? This was certainly a possibility, even if Mengistu had appeared serene at the end. When Abebe spoke about this to Rita, the nurse, she made her *tsk, tsk* sound and told him to stop his foolishness.

'We don't believe in that sort of thing here,' she said, but he could see that she thought it might be the case.

But Abebe feared most – indeed, he was convinced – that the person who had brought about his misfortune was His Majesty, and that the emperor was on his way to see him now not to pardon him or to give him back his ability to walk and even run, but to gloat, to enjoy the spectacle of his ungrateful subject's pitiful condition.

He remembered the prison cell, the weeks of waiting, the hunger quelled only by the certainty that he was going to die. He had pleaded, in his mind, for leniency, but he knew there was no possibility. In the cell with Mengistu he had had plenty of time to contemplate his fate, and he was ready to go to the gallows without protest, turning his face to the ground as should any loyal subject of His Majesty who was guilty of treason. For even if he had not pulled the trigger, even if he had taken no part voluntarily in the plot, he had failed in his duty to defend the royal palace and protect the imperial family. He did not deserve the emperor's clemency, no matter how many gold medals he won. He had disgraced the uniform of the Imperial Bodyguard. By rights, he should already be dead.

Yet His Majesty had spared him...

As he performed the exercises he had been shown, twisting his torso and hoping along with the nurses that there would be a sudden, miraculous twinge of sensation in his legs, he remembered the first time he had been alone in the presence of His Imperial Highness.

It can only have been a few weeks at the most after his release from the dungeon before he received the summons of His Imperial Majesty. He had come with trepidation to the Hall of Audience, a part of the palace to which he had never before been admitted. There were layers of dark, dusty carpets and heavy curtains that preserved secrets and whispers in their velvet folds; on the wall was a tapestry depicting a fierce St George slaying the dragon.

Abebe performed the customary reverence, uncertain of whether he was still a guardsman or a prisoner whose execution had merely been postponed. Pressing his forehead into the thick carpet before the throne, his eyes shut tight, he couldn't see what was going on around him, but he heard the courtiers who had escorted him turn and leave, dismissed by His Majesty. He could sense the imperial presence, the gaze of the Lion of Judah bearing down on him, as well as the disdainful regard of the Minister of the Pen.

Outside, he heard doors closing along the corridor, followed by a long silence.

Finally, after an unbearable wait, the emperor had spoken.

'You may rise, Corporal.'

It was the first time His Imperial Majesty had addressed him and Abebe trembled at the sound of his voice, hard and nasal, and tense with rage. He stood to attention. He was glad he had been allowed to wear his uniform, hoping it might give him some protection, that it might reassure the emperor of his loyalty.

In the presence of His Imperial Majesty, all his instincts, every fibre of his being, told him to avert his gaze. So it had always been, since the very first time on inspection in the parade ground. Even then, though he forced himself to focus on the horizon as he had been told, he had not been able to avoid stealing a glimpse of the King of Kings. Now that he was actually in the imperial presence, however, he kept his eyes fixed on the floor while the emperor's words pierced him, sharp as the blade of a sword.

'We could hang you! We should feed you to the lions! You have dared to defy us; you, a Galla!'

His Majesty had paused, choked by an anger so fierce it seemed it would set ablaze everyone in the room.

'We have given you everything: your position, your very existence – and you have betrayed us! Did you want power for yourself? Is that it? Did you think you would be able to give jobs to your family? Did your victory in the race go to your head? Did it make you insane?'

The emperor paced back and forth, and Abebe sensed H.I.M. pausing to look at him.

He heard a contemptuous snort.

'We have decided not to kill you,' the emperor had said finally.

Abebe had been too frightened to register any immediate relief at these words. Without hesitation, he would have stretched out his neck for the executioner to sever his head from his body if His Majesty had ordered. But, surprisingly, the emperor's tone had changed.

'You are the one they want now. You are the one they admire in the Mercato. You are like a god to them now. They have heard of your deed and they are amazed. You have beaten all the whites, all the colonialists, and you are their hero.'

He turned away and sat on the throne.

'I suppose we should be grateful that you are too simple to understand what this means,' he said. 'Well, hear this: as long as you run, Ethiopia shall not fall! As long as you run, as long as you win medals, we shall rule!'

The emperor's voice hardened again.

'But if you should fail...' His Majesty had intoned ominously.

Abebe looked at his legs floating in the water.

In that moment in the throne room, he had been grateful only that his life had been spared – unaware that it had been taken from him, to be kept by the emperor like a talisman.

35

The dining room at Tore's villa was lit by candlelight, in part because no one in the foreign residential district could predict when there would be a power failure, but also, Niskanen knew, because the fragile flames reminded Tore and Anna of the candles that flickered in the houses of their homeland, warding off the long winter night. Niskanen had come to see that the hold of the Church in Scandinavia was no greater than it was in Ethiopia. There, people feared the spirits of the forests and their hopes burned in candles. In Ethiopia, though they had worshipped Christ for a thousand years more, they still feared ethereal, invisible snakes and put their faith in lofty trees that guarded their hamlets.

Once they had been seated, Tore's wife Anna instructed the butler to serve the soup. The Swedes were careful to uphold traditions, even more so in a distant tropical land where everything was held together by invisible allegiances and might at any time be overturned by unruly passions, where the sun dried everything to dust and the rains, when they came, turned it all to mud. The men wore dinner jackets and the women off-the-shoulder gowns with, around their necks, the sparkling, rough-cut gems in heavy silver settings that they bought from dealers deep in the alleyways of the Mercato.

Venturing into the thronging market, where every intersection resembled every other and every dark, turbaned face stared out menacingly from a different age, was for the women of the international settlement a thrilling dare. They outrivalled each other in purchasing handicrafts and bargaining for precious stones panned from the river beds in the southern provinces. Dinner parties were the occasions on which to display their finds, and Niskanen was careful to compliment the hostess on her jewellery.

He had asked Kidaneh to accompany him, as he often did. Ben and his wife Helen were there, and another guest, a stranger to their group who was not wearing a dinner jacket like the other men. The man had a rugged, burned, heavy-browed face and he apologised for his attire, a khaki hunter's jacket covered in pockets, joking that he hadn't been able to find a laundromat in the Afar, the desert region east of the highlands that was one of the most inhospitable places on earth. In any case, he admitted, after a few sips of one of Tore's vodkatinis, he was uncomfortable with formality. He couldn't stand the dinners at the National Geographical Institute that he was obliged to attend whenever he was in Washington.

As the main course was being served, Ben addressed their visitor.

'So, tell us, Professor, is the American Council going to get its money's worth?'

'You mean, did we dig up anything new?'

Professor Coon was evidently used to the insinuation that his activities – which he told them consisted of scrubbing at the earth with a toothbrush, sifting every stone on a dry river bed – were of only marginal usefulness.

'We found skeletal remains that might prove to be important. Plenty of interesting skulls, plenty. But not the Missing Link, if that's what you're wondering. No, that's still missing, I'm afraid.'

He tucked into his meat and chewed heartily, grinning at Ben the diplomat.

'But you expect to find it here in Africa,' continued Anna, a dutiful hostess keeping the conversation going.

'It seems pretty certain that the human race evolved from around here, either in the Afar triangle or to the south, in the Rift Valley somewhere,' said the professor.

'Evolved?' queried Niskanen. 'You mean evolved... from apes?'

'Probably.'

The professor looked around at the diners. He lowered his cutlery before he continued.

'How much do we know about the human race?' he asked. 'Does

anybody even know how many races there are?'

Niskanen didn't answer. He was uneasy about where the professor was leading them.

'I guess I'd have to say there are three races,' declared Ben. 'White... I mean Caucasian; Asiatic and... ' He looked at Kidaneh, who was eating his peas with deliberate care, pushing the fork against the flat of his knife to gather them on the tines. '...black.'

It was evidently the response that the professor had been anticipating.

'I'm sorry, you're wrong,' he said with satisfaction. 'There is only one race, the human race. Officially, that is.'

He related how, in 1949, the UN Economic and Social Council decided on a programme of disseminating the scientific facts, 'such as they are', designed to remove what is generally known as racial prejudice. The UNESCO statement on race, as it was called, said that scientists had reached a general agreement that mankind was one; that all men belonged to the same species, *Homo sapiens*. And within this single human species, variation was defined not by type, but by 'populations', which differed in the frequency of one or more genes. 'The total number of human genes is huge, but the number of genes whose varying frequency defines a population is relatively small,' said the professor.

'In other words,' said Helen, 'the likenesses among us are far greater than the differences.'

'Exactly,' affirmed Professor Coon. 'Sometimes you get a concentration of genes or physical traits within one population, but the significance of these concentrations is open to interpretation. I guess you could say that prejudice, like beauty, is in the eye of the beholder. What I'm doing is looking for bone fragments that will tell us how we came to be divided into Caucasian, Mongoloid and Negroid populations. I'm trying to make some sense of the puzzle. I believe, for example, that the Negroid population of Africa could be further classified as Congoid in the north and Xhosian in the south. There are mysteries aplenty: where do we put the Australoid population in the Great Chain of Being?'

No answer was forthcoming. The dinner guests looked at one another and then at the professor.

But Niskanen had heard the phrase before. A Great Chain of Being, with one of those populations at the head, pulling the rest along; a hierarchy of humanity, with one group, and one person, at its summit.

'A reason for classifying humanity,' he said, 'would be if you thought that physical differences are linked to differences in ability. This is what the Nazis believed.'

'I get this all the time,' responded the professor. 'Look, the basic task of anthropology is to measure and then catalogue the variations. The question is: how do you explain the variations? Are we all the same, and are the differences between us merely cultural? Or are they much deeper; so deep that we can never really coexist or compete on the same level?'

'And what is your view, Professor?' asked Tore.

'I'm a Darwinian,' replied Professor Coon. 'I believe we all do as best we can with what's available to us.'

Ben interjected. 'The major here,' he said, indicating Niskanen, 'reckons the disadvantages faced by our African friends can be overcome by rigorous scientific training.'

'Yes,' agreed the professor. 'A lot of people are wondering how he did it. I mean, barefoot like that.' He turned to Niskanen. 'Very low dehydration: three hundred and fifty grams, I read in the newspapers. Did you put something in his drink?'

'As a matter of fact, we gave him glucose,' admitted Niskanen. 'But that didn't have an effect on water loss.'

'Glucose?'

'In Sweden there have been studies about the way the body metabolises sugars. Glucose is taken up almost instantly. We put glucose in the bottles.'

'I see,' said the professor. 'Very clever, Major.'

Kidaneh replaced his cutlery on his half-cleared plate. He had been listening carefully to the conversation, and now he spoke up.

'Because we are African, you must find a reason. You cannot simply accept that we can run as fast as you. There must be an explanation, some exceptional circumstance that only your science can explain, because if we are the same as you, as the United Nations insist, that means the only difference between us is the opportunity to run, to develop; an opportunity we have always been denied.'

An awkward silence followed.

Happily, the dessert arrived, and Niskanen hoped no one would point out anything contradictory or colonialist in the fact that it was served by Anna's two Ethiopian maids. He was too preoccupied with this thought, and with the ironic possibility that the Missing Link might be buried under Ethiopian soil, to notice Helen looking at him with something that seemed to be – he decided later, when he pictured her expression to himself – admiration.

36

The Athletics Federation was located in a new concrete building, one of the many modern blocks in Addis recently constructed by Tore's company. The federation had been given two rooms, the first of which was crowded with desks and an over-full filing cabinet, and hummed with activity. Three students, volunteers in fresh white shirts, were working at the desks, engaged as junior clerks to deal with the flood of letters requesting Abebe's attendance at championship events or wanting to know how to train for sporting success.

The letters came from all over the world, but especially from all over Africa. More than just how he had done it, everyone wanted to know how they could do it! Abebe had become their inspiration; people wrote saying they had no shoes but they would run too, children sent drawings of runners. Tessema had instructed that all the letters should be answered diligently. When a reply was solicited by one of the shoeless children, he made sure that Abebe wrote 'the important thing is to take part' and signed his name. There was a pile of such letters waiting to be posted.

When Niskanen arrived, the clerks stood and saluted as usual, then they looked at each other eagerly before one of them announced there was someone waiting in the president's office to see the major, a foreigner.

'He said his name was Mr Dassler. He has come about shoes.'

'Shoes?'

The faces of the Ethiopians beamed with delight.

'Yes, sir. Athletic shoes.'

'What did you say his name was?'

'*Ato*. Dassler.'

'Very well,' said Niskanen. 'Better not keep him waiting.'

Several months passed before Abebe was strong enough to resume training. He began with leisurely runs, increasing his distance gradually without worrying about speed. He soon acquired company as he jogged along Churchill Avenue. Within a week he was being chased by an ever-growing crowd of children.

He tried to ignore them, but the children were thrilled to see the barefoot runner on his morning jog. They had discovered his route from the garrison out into the countryside and back, and every day their numbers grew. He was annoyed at first because they seemed to be making fun of him. They imitated his gait, mimicking the way he held his elbows tightly to his waist, swinging them just enough and no more. Now and then they would call out – 'Abebe Bikila, the barefoot runner!' – and one of them would dart in, swift as an ibex, to touch the hem of his shorts. Mamo laughed and told him that throughout the country unshod urchins such as these were pretending to be the hero of Ethiopia, imagining that they were the one who had made their parents rich.

Mamo said he understood Abebe's dilemma. 'It's as if you no longer belong to yourself,' he said. 'You are a part of everyone's destiny now.'

Finally, a little exasperated by the unceasing attention, he switched his training sessions to Debre Zeit. On the empty plateau he was able to concentrate at last.

He knew the routines by heart now and didn't need Niskanen to accompany him. Kidaneh was working for the United Nations' new African agency in Addis, so he wasn't around to check the times any more. Negussie Roba had taken over the stopwatch and he announced that he was going to become a coach one day too. 'Africa needs trainers as well as runners,' he declared. 'Perhaps more so,' the major had remarked.

Mamo ran with him, pushing him on. He too had been spared the gallows. Good runners, apparently, were hard to find.

Normally, they ran together without saying much, a special sort of silence, a shared contemplation, hearing each other's respiration, knowing when it came to speed and effort what the other was thinking. One day, however, while they ran, Abebe talked with Mamo about what had happened in the palace.

When they were in the room with the general and the hostages, Abebe had been convinced that Mamo was going to turn his rifle on Mengistu.

'If I had, maybe we wouldn't be alive now,' said Mamo.

It was a point Abebe had not considered. In the palace, he had not been worried about survival so much as duty.

'Why did he do it, do you think? Was it because he wanted power for himself?'

'Perhaps this was so. He was ambitious. Maybe the promotions went to his head. Or maybe it was the books he read. I don't know.'

'He kept saying that history would be his judge. He said we were ignorant because we didn't know history.'

'He was right about that.'

'What do you mean?'

'We are Oromo people,' Mamo said. 'We are less than animals to them.'

Mamo shot a glance at him and then looked over his shoulder, even though they were quite alone on the road.

'When Menelik conquered our lands and enslaved us, he cut off the right arms of the men and the left breasts of the women. That was the end of us; not even a hundred years ago, and we know nothing of it. In any case, what good would arrows have been against the guns he got from the Europeans. Mengistu said we were less than a colonised people, we no longer even existed.'

'You believe him?'

'It's true. The only thing we know about is His Majesty Haile Selassie I. We know nothing else. I have been to the library. There is nothing, only the *Kebre Negast*, the Book of Kings, and Mengistu said it was cobbled together by priests five hundred years ago; he said it wasn't true, it was just stories about King Solomon and the Queen of Sheba invented to hold the empire in place.'

Abebe was shocked. 'You mustn't say this,' he warned. 'We will be in trouble.'

'I know. But perhaps there will come a time…'

They ran on in silence for several kilometres, and it seemed to Abebe that their footfalls, which were usually out of step because of Mamo's shorter stride, were more so than ever that day. Yet he was unable to dismiss what Mamo had said. Mamo had fought in Korea and competed with the first Ethiopian Olympic team. Though their ages were the same, his greater experience made him like an elder to Abebe, and they were, finally, of the same tribe, they were both Gallas. There was this grain of truth in Mamo's words, at least.

Abebe was glad to see the major arriving; it relieved him to be able to get back to the business of running.

They followed the major's instructions to the letter, but it somehow felt better when he was with them. He was sensitive to their physical state, driving them harder when he could, easing off when they were tired. It was better than any fixed plan.

In the jeep alongside the major was the foreigner, a trim figure in a khaki suit. He was a blond man too, and though he was older than Niskanen he had the same compact, muscular body. Abebe guessed he must also have been an athlete. The major seemed to have much to share with the man, and while Abebe didn't understand what they were saying, he knew they were talking about athletic triumphs because he recognised the names of Zatopek and Kölehmainen. They must have been talking, as the major always did, of their heroism and endurance, of the victories they won and the victories that were snatched from them by injuries or fatigue or inadequate preparation, as the major called it.

'This is Mr Dassler,' said Niskanen. 'He has come from Germany.'

They shook hands and the German congratulated Abebe on his 'stunning' Olympic victory.

'Mr Dassler has brought something for you, Abebe. Take your shoes off.'

Abebe unlaced his shoes as the foreigner laid a silver case on the ground. He opened it and inside was a pair of brand-new running shoes. Kneeling before the barefoot runner as though before royalty, he reverently placed one of the shoes on Abebe's foot. Abebe was uncomfortable with this gesture. Despite telling himself it was normal – one of the customs of the sporting world to which he had been admitted – he couldn't believe that this man, who was older than him, and white, would abase himself in such a way. It was like the man from France who called himself a sportswriter, who had brought him a pair of spiked running shoes and insisted on training alongside him.

He saw that the German was staring up at him expectantly. Abebe flexed his toes and smiled. He was indifferent to the shoes, but he wanted to please.

The German's hopeful expression turned to one of satisfaction, as he continued to genuflect before the Olympic champion.

Later that day, as they sat in the officers' mess drinking coffee, the German shared his thoughts with the major.

'We realise you are accomplishing miracles out here with these black boys, Major, and we would like to do whatever we can to help. Bikila's development as an athlete is of enormous importance to us. There must be many good runners here, yah? Of course, we can't offer you financial assistance as their status as amateurs would be compromised, but I want you to know we're ready to do everything we can to help you. Whatever your requirements, you just let us know. Shoes, equipment, whatever you need.'

The sportsman-turned-entrepreneur sipped from his coffee cup and Niskanen did the same.

'Mmm. This coffee really is very good indeed!'

He looked at his surroundings in surprise.

'They grow it here, you know,' offered Niskanen.

In the year that followed his victory in Rome, Abebe became a regular visitor at the major's house. He perused the magazines the major received by post from around the world, studying the photos of athletes, and tried to read the books about sport that the major kept on his shelves, pondering the lists of names and the tables of times that shortened by seconds each year. Apart from his collection of jazz records, these were the only things to which the major seemed to attach any value. It struck Abebe that there was no sign in the house of any idleness, no luxuries or indulgences. He found it strange that an important person would not pamper himself as would an Ethiopian Ras. It was a difference between Europeans and themselves.

He found it even more inexplicable that there was no woman in the house, apart from the maid, and even she did not live there. But he concluded finally that the major was simply too busy. He began his days early; and in this respect he was like an Ethiopian, except, rather than praying in church, he preferred a game of tennis with Kidaneh or Tore. After rushing between the Athletics Federation, the Ministry of Education and the offices of the Red Cross, if he didn't have a fund-raising dinner to attend, he liked to spend his evenings in one of the many nightclubs in Addis, listening to local musicians playing the music of American jazzmen, which he said they did superbly well and with their own style. Sometimes, he invited Abebe along. They were always treated to the best seats in the house and it never failed to amuse the major to see Abebe overcome with shyness as, inevitably, he received an ovation from the patrons – usually, local businessmen and UN officials – whenever the owner swung the spotlight on them.

Mostly, he and the major talked about sport and jazz music. The major knew a lot about both and there seemed to be so much to learn. But, one evening, after the sauna that always ended a good day's training, Abebe asked a question about life in the West which, this time, seemed to make the major uncomfortable.

It had always puzzled Abebe how you picked the girl you wanted to marry.

'Sounds easy, doesn't it?' said Niskanen. 'You just choose, you fall in love, except sometimes the choices you make turn out not to be the right ones.'

Abebe was surprised at this possibility. 'How so?'

'What happens if the girl you marry decides, after a time, that she doesn't really want you?' Niskanen asked.

'But you choose,' Abebe insisted.

'Yes, you choose, but if the choices turn out to be wrong, then what?' asked Niskanen.

Abebe had imagined it would be liberating to be able to make for yourself the choices that governed your life: what work you did; whom you would marry. It had never occurred to him that the freedom to choose one's destiny might bring complications, that with the possibilities came dangers absent from a life ordained such as his.

Niskanen told Abebe about his marriage, about the pretty nurse who had taken care of him in the infirmary, whom he had courted and wed.

'We were young and we were in love. It was very romantic.'

Romantic love was something Abebe knew from the cinema in Addis. He had sat for hours entranced by the music and dancing that always accompanied this strange, problematic affliction. In the Indian films, love was passionate but often tragic; in the American ones, it was lighthearted and ended with a kiss. He understood the stories in the films from Bombay – he had known of lovers who eloped to avoid their parents' marriage choices – but he puzzled at the secret of the Americans' success. Everything seemed to work out for them, and any obstacles were usually of their own rather than their parents' making.

'You ask her to marry you?'

'Yes.'

'And then?'

'Then, well, it just wasn't right any more. That's why I came here, partly. Marriage is something you have to work at, you know. Like everything else.'

Niskanen couldn't believe what he saw as he stepped down from the jeep with Tessema. He was unable even to reach the door of the building that housed the Athletics Federation for all the cartons being unloaded from the rear of a lorry.

'What's going on? What is all this?'

Kidaneh was supervising the clerks carrying in box after box.

'Shoes,' he said.

'What?'

'Running shoes. From our friend, Mr Dassler.'

Kidaneh nodded and turned one of the cartons around to show him the green clover-leaf logo. The logo was the same as the one on the striped running shoes the German had brought for Abebe.

'There are four more lorries on the way from the port,' he said. 'Can you believe it? Enough pairs for every high school student in Ethiopia!'

They made their way inside the office. Boxes full of running shoes were stacked everywhere.

'Look at all these shoes,' exclaimed Kidaneh. 'Do they think we lack only shoes to be able to catch up with them?'

The offices of the Athletics Federation were cluttered with boxes full of running shoes and tracksuits.

A chubby, bearded man was waiting inside. He stood as they entered and, with what Niskanen recognised as perfect British formality, introduced himself as the leader of the African National Congress. Niskanen had seen it before in the Kenyans and the South Africans: the educated ones were more British than the British. It was one of the things he had come to appreciate about the Ethiopians: never having been colonised, their manners were their own.

The man, who was South African, said his name was Nelson Mandela.

'It's a great pleasure to meet you,' said Tessema.

On the way over, Tessema had told Niskanen that the South African lawyer had called the federation to ask for a meeting. Niskanen had heard of Mandela and knew about his reputation as a campaigner on behalf of his people because of the Sharpeville massacre, when police opened fire on locals demonstrating against the new Apartheid laws and killed over a hundred people.

He told Mandela he was surprised by the visit. 'What can we do for you?' he asked.

'I am glad to meet you at last, to be able to thank you for your initiative regarding the boycott of the Cup of Nations. Thanks to Ethiopia's actions, we realised at the ANC that sport could be an important weapon in our struggle.'

'We are honoured,' said Tessema, but then he added that the resolution had not come from the Athletics Federation. 'You must thank His Imperial Majesty. He was the one who took the decision.'

Mandela reflected on this before he spoke.

'As things stand, it looks as though South Africa is not going to be invited to take part in the next Olympic Games in Tokyo. But we have no influence over the decisions of the Olympic Committee. If South Africa is allowed to compete, there will be nothing we can do. If that happens, if the apartheid regime is invited to participate, we hope that we will be able to count on you to lead another boycott, but one of the Olympics this time. Because of your success with Abebe Bikila, others will follow.'

Niskanen was taken aback. The idea of declining an Olympic place for political reasons was beyond his imagination. In any case, he had no business, he reminded himself, getting involved in Ethiopian politics, let alone African politics. It was one of the principles of the Red Cross, it was what allowed them to function, and besides, it was not in his nature, it was not something he was comfortable with. Politics was a shifting terrain with only treacherous ideological markings.

Tessema, who was more of a politician, said he was sympathetic, but there was really nothing he could do.

'We are merely sportsmen, you understand.'

Mandela pressed them none the less. 'The apartheid regime in my country will do everything to avoid a boycott. Sport is very important for their international prestige. But the idea of black and white people competing alongside one another is anathema to them.'

'I will speak with His Imperial Majesty,' promised Tessema. 'That is all I can say to you. I must repeat, such decisions are not ours to make.'

Mandela sighed heavily.

'Your emperor is a strange fellow. He says he believes in progress, in justice, yet he is an autocrat. I am fighting to bring about socialist change in my country, yet he has helped me: he provided me with a diplomatic passport to attend the conference. He knows that change is coming in Africa. It has already come for the colonialists. But I think he is unsure of what these changes might mean for him.'

'Perhaps you are right,' said Tessema. 'My field is sports, you understand.'

'I think so.'

'The Athletics Federation is independent of the government, as I said. But you can rest assured that we will try to act in the best interests of Ethiopian sport, and of African sport in general.'

'Thank you,' said Mandela. 'That is what I wanted to hear.'

Mandela stood and shook Tessema's hand, then turned to Niskanen.

'There's one thing I'd still like to know,' he said. 'How did you do it?'

37

Niskanen drove through Addis, pressing the horn repeatedly in annoyance at the endless obstructions. There were more and more cars in the streets of the capital but nobody seemed to have agreed on a highway code; and, to make matters worse, construction work was going on all over in the characteristic spirit of eager confusion that he had somehow forgotten.

Two years had passed. He had been away from Addis – away from home – for months at a time, organising Red Cross operations in Nepal to help Tibetan refugees. His experiences in Ethiopia had given him an extra skill: they said he was just the person to pull things together where there was little hope and lots to do. They said he was good out in the field. He liked to think that his real quality was patience; he knew not to expect everything to happen right away, the way people often did when they first came out, but not to give up either when you realised how great the odds were against you, how much inertia and fatalism there was, how death was a familiar, constant presence.

He had been enchanted by the beauty of the Himalayas, but the resignation of the Tibetan Buddhists depressed him. Their villages and temples had been burned, they had been driven from their lands by the Chinese, yet they accepted this with calm. It was different from the kind of resignation he had become accustomed to in Ethiopia. If drought came, the Copts accepted it as God's will but their anger was great nonetheless and they asked themselves what they had done to deserve such a fate. Conversely, there was the possibility of pleasing God, and this meant they would strive, at least. Niskanen knew the spark was there and that, if you blew gently on it, you could get results. But you had to trim the flame, otherwise it burned brightly as misdirected zeal and everything ended up only half finished.

Carts and lorries loaded down with building materials advanced slowly through the mayhem. Everywhere, he saw wooden scaffolding rising, fresh bricks being passed by the long chains of women and children in rags, and walls rising up from the mud. In the months he had been away this time, new hotels had opened with wiring still dangling from the walls and elevators that didn't work. The shacks and shanties had multiplied as fast as the Swedish-built office blocks, the Chinese restaurants and American-style bars.

A banner had been strung across Churchill Avenue: *'Ethiopia welcomes leaders of Independent African States'*.

Niskanen halted to allow a nomad to drive his train of frightened goats across the avenue. As he waited, he noticed that workers were building a high wall along one side. The wall was being erected to hide from view the tin shacks and hovels that lined the route to the palace.

In the years since Niskanen had first come here, things had changed in Addis. The emperor no longer rode about his capital in the mornings on horseback; he travelled in a Cadillac, a gift from the Americans. The city had become chaotic, its citizens a desperate rabble, and the slums were growing as more and more hungry peasants arrived from the countryside. Building walls to hide them from sight was not the answer.

He finally arrived at Abebe's house and found his wife at the stove as usual. The modern house with all its utilities that Abebe had been given, located in a leafy new suburb of Addis, was not going to change her life, apparently; a refrigerator or a gas cooker made no difference to Yewibdar. She was standing over the pot, incongruous in her white *shamma* amid all the mod cons. The new baby, whose name was Dawit, slept in a fold of cloth slung on her back.

'Hello, Major,' she said, turning to face him but without looking up. The white shawl she wore over her head, far from hiding it, accentuated her fine-boned beauty. Yewibdar greeted Niskanen shyly as always. The gentleness and trust he saw in the eyes of many Ethiopian women never failed to charm Niskanen; it brought out his best instincts, although European men were not all like him, he knew. For some, it made these women easy game.

He told her he hoped she was in good health, and her child and her family also, and she replied that, happily, this was the case. Then she enquired about his family, and he replied, as he always did, that she and Abebe were his family! As he knew it would, his casual bending of etiquette – or perhaps the sentiment – made her blush.

Abebe was seated in a large armchair in the lounge, concentrating on a pamphlet he was reading. Beside him on the table was the gramophone that Niskanen had lent him and next to it an English-language Linguaphone course.

'Hello, Major. How are you?'

'Very well, thank you,' said the major. 'How are you getting along with that?'

'I am doing very well, thank you.'

'That's good. It'll come in handy in Boston.'

Abebe had never heard of Boston. 'Where is Boston?' he asked.

'In the United States. I've entered you for the Boston marathon.'

He had come to tell Abebe that, with the 1964 Olympics just a year away, he wanted him to face an international challenge. The races he had been running in Ethiopia and Africa were too easy for him. Niskanen suspected that Abebe had become a kind of fetish. He didn't know whether it was from respect or fear, but it was as if nobody in Africa really wanted to steal his glory by beating him – not yet anyway. Nobody wanted his record, his burden; and he wasn't facing the kind of challenges he needed.

Niskanen had kept him out of international events, but it was time to change that. He explained that the Boston marathon, the oldest city marathon, was the one where he would face the most experienced field. 'It will be the ideal opportunity to see what the competition will be like in Tokyo.'

'Anything you say.'

Abebe stood over the threshold of the escalator, amazed at the stairs that descended by themselves; he came back up the other side laden with shopping bags.

He had never seen so many things to buy, so much more than in Rome. He peered in shop windows, gaping at the dummies in their thick clothes and the profusion of goods, and it made him ashamed. Not knowing what many of the things were for, he felt helpless. He wanted to claim them for his people, bring them home and show everybody how they worked. Their escalator was not functioning and the modern world was receding out of their reach.

It was cold in Boston, and he emerged from one shop wearing a heavy wool coat and a new bow tie.

Afterwards, Niskanen and Kidaneh took him to a restaurant. They sat in a booth by a window and studied the menus the waitress had brought. Abebe was still wearing his coat and bow tie. He was pleased to find that the menu had vivid colour pictures of the dishes, although he still couldn't identify what they were.

The waitress returned promptly for their order and Niskanen asked what he wanted.

Abebe looked at the waitress, then at the menu.

'There is so much…' he whispered to Kidaneh.

The waitress glared impatiently at the two black men.

'Maybe I better come back in a while,' she said to Niskanen. 'When your friends have figured out how to read the menu.'

'It's OK. My friends can read,' retorted Niskanen.

'Yeah, well, what about the other one, what's he having?'

'I will have a cup of coffee,' said Kidaneh.

He closed his menu, placed it on the table and turned to look out of the window.

'Bring us three cups of coffee, please,' said Niskanen. 'And three portions of apple pie.'

The waitress went away and there was silence for a moment.

'So we are in America now,' said Kidaneh.

'I'm sorry,' said Niskanen.

'What are you apologising for? This is not your country.'

'No, but I feel… I feel guilty.'

'If this woman doesn't want to serve me coffee then she is an ignorant woman.'

'I didn't think it would be like this here in the northern states.'

'Why does she not want to serve us?' asked Abebe.

'Because we are black,' said Kidaneh.

It was rare that he spoke to Abebe directly, and rarely about anything other than running. Abebe knew that he considered him an inferior: Kidaneh's father was a stationmaster, a railway official; Abebe's father was a shepherd. But the waitress had treated them both with the same contempt, and this had forced him to acknowledge a bond.

'In America, we have no existence,' he said. 'We are like shadows to them.'

Abebe looked at Niskanen.

'Don't worry, it won't make any difference to the outcome of the race. On the track, everyone is equal.'

The waitress brought the cups of coffee and the plates of apple pie. She set the coffee down without a word and, as she was distributing the pies, Kidaneh sniffed at his cup.

'This is undrinkable!'

'Pardon me?' asked the waitress.

'It is worse than the water that runs in the drains of Addis!'

'Huh?'

'I think he's used to a different brand,' said Niskanen.

'We always serve the same brand. We've never had any complaints.'

'Coffee comes from my country,' said Kidaneh. 'That is where the coffee bean first grew. My ancestors roasted it and then ground it to make coffee. The coffee they drank made them feel like kings. If you do not have that coffee here, I'm sorry for you.'

'This is all we have,' said the waitress and, confused to be apologising to him, she hurriedly set down the last slice of apple pie.

Abebe copied Niskanen, slicing and spearing the pie with a fork.

'Now,' said Niskanen, chewing heartily to change the subject, 'let's concentrate on the race. It's going to be a large field...'

Abebe was disappointed to hear that Rhadi wouldn't be competing. He would have liked to race against him once again.

'There'll be plenty of Americans for you to worry about.'

Afterwards, they took a taxi. Abebe sat in the back with the shopping bags on his knees staring out at the wintry landscape. The bare trees looked forlorn in the dazzling sunshine and steam rose from manhole covers in the street as if from the bowels of the earth.

He felt the cold in his bones, a chill he had never known before. In Ethiopia, even though it was cold at night, there was always the fierce sun in the afternoons to remind you that the world had not died.

Winter in North America; Niskanen said it was like that for months until spring came. He explained how the seasons were different. Rain might fall at any time, not just during the wet seasons!

Abebe was glad to have his warm overcoat, just like the ones the Americans wore.

38

The ballroom had been specially redecorated for the banquet. Long tables had been set out, covered in scarlet cloth trimmed with ermine and laid with antique silver and porcelain. Heaps of game, fish, fruit, cheese and sweetmeats were laid on them exactly like the paintings of royal banquets in eighteenth-century Europe. All the guests were men, some wearing suits, some in military uniforms, some wearing the skins of leopards. Behind every second guest stood a valet in white gloves and a tail coat.

Selassie sat silently, alone at the centre of the high table; the king of presidents, the patriarch of African unity. The heads of the independent African nations had come together under his auspices: them, their secretarial staff, interpreters and the press. It was a happy day for all, especially the umbrella sellers. His Majesty had greeted Nkrumah personally at the airport: the pan-Africanist who opened the way for African independence and the progressive monarch walking side by side towards a resplendent post-colonial future.

The emperor rose to make the toast. He wore his field marshal's uniform with the eight rows of decorations and the Star of Ethiopia. He was flanked on his left by the prime minister, Aklilou, and the other ministers, and on his right by the tall Ras Kassa, standing at a respectful distance, and the senior Rasses in their ceremonial *shammas* embroidered in gold.

The conversation died away as the King of Kings surveyed the assembly.

He lifted a glass, his eyes twinkling in the candlelight – an unhabitual gleam of emotion – and the trumpeters in the galleries sounded a fanfare.

The assembled guests lifted their crystal goblets in response.

'To unity!' said Selassie.

'Unity!'

'To independence!'

'Independence!'

'To development!'

'Development!'

The emperor took a deep breath.

'It is axiomatic,' he began, 'that development in any country must proceed simultaneously in all areas of its life. As a country advances economically, equivalent progress must be made in the creation of more highly developed social and political institutions as well. Any attempt to retard advancement in any single area will inevitably retard the development of the whole and will create serious distortions in the overall fabric of the nation. This principle we have always recognised, and in our actions we have been guided by it.'

The emperor looked at the Rasses.

'The emphasis we give to development stems from our determination to eliminate ignorance and to prepare our people for the changes which Ethiopia's emergence into the modern world will bring them.'

Selassie's speech was long and meticulous. He was careful to ensure that everyone present was mentioned and he was eloquent and forceful about the ideals they shared. Afterwards, the only complaint from the delegates was that he had said everything they wanted to say, and they had no option now but to get down to business!

When at last the emperor concluded, the guests stood and applauded while girls in traditional dresses standing along the balcony showered the assembled diners with petals.

A voice could be heard, that of Miriam Makeba, singing a Zulu song with operatic clarity.

At that moment in Boston, a white runner crossed the finishing line of the annual Boston marathon, followed by another white runner, and then a third.

Abebe was nowhere in sight.

The house was dark and silent when he returned. He removed the heavy coat and slipped off his shoes before going into the bedroom. Dawit was sleeping. He was glad the little boy wouldn't know of his father's shame. Yewibdar was asleep too. He kissed her gently. He would have to tell her about his failure tomorrow. Removing his bow tie and unbuttoning his white shirt, he silently reassured her that nothing would change, though he didn't really know whether that was so.

He carefully folded the coat and put it away in a drawer.

Niskanen had told him after the race that sometimes you get a cramp like that and there's nothing you can do, but Abebe knew the major was disappointed. He had consoled him, rubbing his calf and telling him not to worry, that he would be on top form by the time they got to Tokyo, but Abebe knew he was concerned.

He had concentrated when the pain started, striving to focus on something else, the way the major had always said. He thought of his favourite song about the island in the sun, but the cold had dispelled Belafonte's voice and the pain had returned, nagging him for miles. All he was able to think about was the stinging muscle in his calf.

The next morning, when they awoke and Yewibdar asked how it had gone for him in America, Abebe avoided talking about his defeat. He dismissed it, saying it wasn't important; there would be other races, he affirmed. Instead, he told Yewibdar of all the things he had seen in America: the mechanical miracles, the wondrous comforts, the multitudes of cars and the treasures in the shops.

'Now I understand what His Majesty wants. He wants Ethiopia to be modern, like America,' he said.

Abebe wondered whether it would come in time for him, or for his children, or for their children, perhaps. And he wondered whether, by losing the race in Boston, he had delayed it even further.

39

Dusk was falling, a frustratingly quick fading of the light. That was a thing Niskanen still missed: the way in Scandinavia the sun never quite came up in winter. He recalled the orange glow in the sky as it traced its low arc, the twilight that seemed unending and the days that were achingly short.

He was out on the veranda, the log he had been perusing open on his lap. Kidaneh was sitting in an armchair near by, reading the United Nations gazette. Though he was now working full time for the UN, he seemed unable to forgo the excitement of the track.

'Well?' he enquired.

Niskanen had been remembering the cross-country races he had taken part in, remembering what it was like to lose, to be unable to summon the extra ounce of strength needed to push past the leaders.

'I still don't know what happened,' he said. 'His times here are as good as they were four years ago.'

'He wasn't used to the climate. The cold gave him a cramp. The others were used to it, and they were after him.'

Kidaneh reiterated that they didn't have the element of surprise working for them. 'He was marked,' he said. 'From the start, he was the one they were out to beat.'

'I suppose you're right. They were pacing themselves against him. It's ironic, really. Unwittingly, he helped them to win.'

'Did you talk to him about this?'

'No.'

'Don't you think he ought to be prepared? It's going to be even tougher for him in Tokyo.'

'At least it'll be warmer, but not as hot as it was in Rome. That will help. I've been wondering if we should do some training in a milder climate.'

'It might be an idea,' said Kidaneh.

He returned to his newspaper.

'Right,' said Niskanen. He returned to his log. There was little more they could accomplish in the months that remained before the Tokyo Games. Abebe's times were good, exceptional even; he was certainly up to international level, but most of his track experience had been with his comrades. He didn't know the tricks of international competition. Niskanen wondered now whether he had made a mistake. It might have been better if Abebe had competed more often abroad, it would have kept him up with the best runners. Perhaps he had been too proud, perhaps he hadn't wanted to risk a defeat that would tarnish the image of the barefoot runner, though this was precisely what had happened in Boston. Niskanen told himself he had been preoccupied with his responsibilities at the Red Cross, and Negussie Roba, whom he had put in charge of Abebe's training, was in awe of Abebe. He didn't have enough authority, enough perspective. In any case, he had instructed Negussie to concentrate on finding and developing younger talents, and the junior coach had concentrated on this with great zeal. There had been no one to push Abebe. For the Ethiopians, there was something miraculous about his victory. His glory was so great, his victory so prodigious, no one dared to try to steal it.

Perhaps Rome had been a fluke due to the heat or the confusion over Rhadi's number. In a race, it didn't take much to throw you off, especially in an unfamiliar situation. And once you fell back, it was hard to catch up.

'Listen to this,' said Kidaneh, sitting up and shaking the newspaper. '"Nelson Mandela has gone on trial in South Africa, accused of high treason. The African National Congress was outlawed during his visit to Addis Ababa last year and on his return he was arrested and charged with being the leader of a banned organisation. If found guilty, he faces life imprisonment or execution."'

Kidaneh stopped reading and looked up at Niskanen.

'I don't see how His Imperial Majesty could refuse the request of a condemned man.'

40

Abebe was running evenly and economically along the road to Debre Zeit, a course he covered several times a week. He did 5 or 10, sometimes 15 kilometres, and every few weeks, when Niskanen thought he was in good form, he would run 30 kilometres or even a full marathon, 42 kilometres. It was impossible to predict what would happen regarding South Africa. The Olympic Committee hadn't yet decided whether to issue an invitation to the country of apartheid. Meanwhile, they were preparing for the Games.

The tarmac unfurled like a long, straight ribbon across the barren terrain. Niskanen said the rocky landscape devoid of trees was like the Apollo photos of the moon. The emptiness helped Abebe to concentrate. It mirrored the solitude that came upon you as you ran; not desolation or loneliness, but a calming, supreme remoteness. Abebe was rarely alone, however. For the longer runs he was joined by Mamo or the others. There were always youngsters who wanted to run alongside him, to measure themselves against him, or copy his style. Abebe didn't mind, as long as they didn't ask him too many questions.

Niskanen was following behind, as he had been doing more often lately, checking Abebe's times, 'just to be sure'. The speedometer in the jeep was broken, but Niskanen would have known instinctively if Abebe slowed. He was carried forward on his long feet and thin legs at what he later found out was a record speed. He was covering a mile every five minutes; his pace hadn't slowed for more than an hour.

Abebe hadn't faltered, hadn't sensed even a hint of fatigue. Since the race in Boston, he hadn't experienced any more cramps. He was careful to warm up thoroughly, as the major had insisted. 'You have to be a little more careful,' he had warned. 'You're not as young as you were, your body isn't so supple.' Was this the first hint that he could not run for ever? The cramp he had experienced in Boston was just bad luck, the major said, and Abebe hoped he was right. He tried not to think about it too often, not because of the disappointment, but because he worried that dwelling on it would cause the evil spirit to return.

Suddenly, he felt a sharp stab and clutched at his side. He knew immediately it wasn't a cramp. You didn't get cramp under your ribs, he thought. It was what the major called a stitch.

He was almost relieved. He had a stitch, but one more painful than any he had ever experienced before.

The pain wouldn't go away. Instead, it grew worse and began to spread, no longer concentrated in one place. It radiated outwards, as though something in him were about to explode.

Doubling up, he stumbled over, clutching at his side, and collapsed on the road as the jeep carrying the major screeched to a halt.

Five hours later, Niskanen came out of the room in the clinic at the air force base and closed the door softly behind him. Tessema jumped up from the bench when he saw him.

Niskanen shook his head. 'Appendicitis,' he said. 'They're preparing to operate.'

'Then it was lucky you were there. He might have bled to death.'

Through the window, Niskanen saw the car he had sent for Abebe's wife Yewibdar arrive, and he went out to reassure her that everything was going to be all right.

The Russian doctors were going to make her husband better, he said. He explained that they were going to remove his appendix, but he could see it made no sense to her. She wept and touched his sleeve.

They returned inside to wait with Tessema, who spoke to

Yewibdar in Amharic, raising his eyes to the heavens, lolling his head and smiling. There was no reason to wait, but Niskanen didn't know what else to do. He didn't have anywhere else to go.

The doctor had been firm, almost pleased in that way doctors have; Olympic champions had to obey the same rules of nature as other mortals. There wasn't much hope of Abebe running the marathon in Tokyo, he had declared. It would be impossible for anyone to recover from an appendectomy in such a short time. 'No running for him for a while,' he had said.

Presently, Tessema broke the silence. He voiced what Niskanen had been thinking.

'We will have to concentrate on Mamo,' he said.

As he waited on the bench in the palace corridor, Niskanen sensed that the atmosphere had changed. The huddles of dignitaries embroiled in their plotting and whispering had gone. Had they been posted elsewhere, Niskanen wondered, or were they all in jail? There was an uneasy silence around him now. Officials went about their business with wary deliberation, as though it was not what really mattered.

The three successive doors to the Hall of Audience opened and closed – as if by magic, it always seemed to Niskanen – and once again he was in the presence of the emperor.

Selassie had his back to him, but turned as the last pair of doors closed. He came forward and shook the major's hand warmly.

'We have heard the news about Abebe. It is most regrettable. How is he faring?'

'The doctors removed his appendix and they say there were no complications so he should be back on his feet quite soon. He's recuperating in the infirmary at Debre Zeit. The nurses are making a big fuss of him, I hear.'

'Do we know when, exactly, he will be back on his feet?'

'Not in time for Tokyo, Your Majesty, I'm sorry to say.'

'That is a great pity.'

Selassie's mouth tightened. The usually inscrutable monarch didn't try to hide his thoughts for once. Niskanen saw not just disappointment but consternation on the emperor's face.

'We still have reason to be confident,' he said, trying to assuage the monarch's fears. 'We have new blood like Demissis for the marathon. He has plenty of talent and he's been coming along fine. He's not the only one. There are several promising younger athletes like Bezabeth. And I'm sure Mamo will show us what he is capable of this time.'

But Selassie was not listening.

'Mamo Wolde has not won any medals. He has been twice to the Games and he has won nothing. He has tasted failure and he can't get the taste out of his mouth.'

'I think this time he will be sufficiently motivated.'

'You are a man of faith, Major. Even if your methods are scientific, you have faith. Moreover, you have been able to instil this faith in them. We have been impressed by this.'

The emperor had not mentioned the boycott, which, if it happened, would mean that nobody was going to Tokyo, and Niskanen was unsure of how to raise the matter. He was not a politician, he was a sports instructor; as far as he was concerned, sport was separate from – and above – politics. Nevertheless, he was ready to say he supported the emperor's position if he decided to withdraw.

'May I enquire about the attitude of the imperial government to the presence, eventually, of South Africa at the Games?'

'You wish to know if we are prepared to lead a boycott, I take it? That is what everyone is asking.'

The view among his fellow Swedes was that apartheid was abhorrent: creating a separate category of citizenship for blacks was institutionalised racial discrimination; it was what the Nazis had done with the Jews. At the Red Cross, people were saying the townships in South Africa were like concentration camps.

When the emperor spoke, his voice had become steely and rasping again. 'Until the philosophy that holds one race superior and another inferior is finally and permanently discredited, and everywhere abandoned, there will be war,' he said.

Niskanen had heard Selassie's speech to the United Nations the year before, supporting the anti-colonialist struggles of the peoples of Mozambique and Angola. He was familiar with the theme.

'Ethiopia will not permit African people to be insulted, we will not tolerate injustice,' said His Majesty, fixing Niskanen with his intransigent stare. 'Therefore, we have let it be known that should South Africa be invited to participate, Ethiopia will be unable to attend.'

Then the emperor's tone softened. 'We are confident, however, that the members of the committee will see the prejudice to Olympic ideals that the system in South Africa represents, and that they will act accordingly.'

Niskanen nodded. 'One sincerely hopes this will be so,' he said.

'Therefore,' concluded the emperor, 'we must prepare for competition – as we would for battle!'

'Indeed, Your Highness.'

'With or without Corporal Bikila.'

Afterwards, with the log open on his lap and a stopwatch in his hand, following Mamo this time in the jeep on the road to Debre Zeit, Niskanen recounted the meeting to Tessema. He had the impression that the emperor had flinched as he uttered the name of his Olympic champion, as though the guardsman had some power over him, was a chink in the imperial armour.

'I suspect that His Highness would very much like another gold medal,' said Niskanen.

'Naturally,' Tessema replied. 'The emperor is a greedy man.' He laughed. 'He already has all the gold in Ethiopia. The mines belong to the imperial family, you know! But that's not enough.'

He trailed off, conscious of his uncharacteristic and dangerously unpatriotic remarks.

'Perhaps you are right. But I doubt he would let his hunger for Olympic medals take precedence over his leadership of the Organisation of African Unity. He won't compromise if doing so will reduce his political standing.'

41

Ignoring the pain, Abebe gradually heaved himself up and got out of bed. He felt the bandages straining at his midriff as he moved to the window, and hoped the stitches wouldn't burst. Looking out at the dusty field below, he saw Mamo entering the base at a jog. He appeared to have been exerting himself and Abebe wondered whether he had enough of what the major called stamina. Then he saw the major arriving in a jeep behind Mamo and he knew at once he was not content. The major always tried to encourage them, but he was never really able to hide his feelings, especially when it came to running. Abebe knew how seriously Niskanen took athletics, and he knew the major was right. He wanted to tell Mamo not to give up.

Later that day, Mamo came by to see him but didn't mention his time until Abebe asked about it.

He had covered 13 miles, a semi-marathon, in one hour fifteen. They both knew this was too slow. Eight years had passed since Mamo had come close to a medal in Melbourne. He was about the same age as Abebe, and would soon be turning thirty-five. There would be many younger, faster men wanting a crack at the 5,000 and 10,000 metre titles. That left the marathon, and the marathon was never really Mamo's race.

'Major Niskanen said we're going to be doing some uphill running next week,' Mamo said hopefully. 'To build up speed.'

'That's good,' said Abebe.

That night, Abebe was unable to sleep.

Finally, he got up from the bed and, suppressing the pain, pulled on his tracksuit.

Passing in the corridor, Niskanen noticed that the door to Abebe's room was ajar. He entered and found the room empty.

He stood puzzling in the darkness for a moment, and then he heard the sound of faint, uneven footfalls outside. He went to the window and peered down at the parade ground.

Abebe was running around the moonlit track.

He was running barefoot. Niskanen supposed he had not been able to find any shoes. He was running at about half his usual speed; his shoulders were tight and with one hand he was clutching at his bandaged side.

Niskanen sat on the empty bed and listened.

Gradually, the quiet shuffle of Abebe's footfalls became more regular, more steady.

A week later, Niskanen took Abebe to the infirmary to have the bandages removed.

The doctor unwound the dressing cautiously and probed at the flesh around Abebe's appendix scar.

'Shouldn't be any problems. I don't think they left anything in there.'

He prodded Abebe again to be certain.

'How do you feel?' he asked.

'I feel well, Doctor.'

'I think he will be able to run again some day,' joked the doctor.

Abebe and Niskanen grinned at each other.

It was Niskanen's turn to host a cocktail party at his villa, and he was pleased to be able to announce that it was also a send-off celebration. He had heard from Kidaneh at the United Nations that the members of the Olympic Committee had voted in camera not to issue an invitation to the South Africans. The threat of a boycott had been enough. Niskanen was in a jubilant mood: his best runner was back on his feet and they would soon be leaving for Tokyo.

While Helen, Tore and his wife Anna were listening to Stan Kenton with Kidaneh, Niskanen was out on the veranda drinking whisky with Ben. Now that the doctors had said it was OK for Abebe to run, he was confident. He told Ben the doctors had been right when they said it was a miracle.

'Twice in the last four days he's run times that proportionally were better than Rome!' he enthused.

'But he hasn't run a whole twenty-six miles,' said Ben.

Although Abebe had been running longer distances every day, it was true that he had not run a full marathon since the operation.

'I made sure we kept the distances down, no more than fifteen miles. I didn't want to run the risk. He might as well save himself for the race. If he's going to have problems, it might as well be then.'

Ben paused for a moment. 'Correct me if I'm wrong,' he said, 'but no one's ever won an Olympic marathon twice, have they?'

'No,' said Niskanen, 'nobody. Not so far.'

'Does he know?'

'If he thinks the odds are against him, he might just give up. If he thinks it's a goal he is able to achieve, then he will push himself to reach it.'

'I guess you're right.'

'I can't just teach them how to run by showing them how. Abebe has to be able to believe in himself. It's what these people lack the most, not water or food or medicine or technology or investment, but the means to believe in themselves. If they believe they are handicapped from the start, they won't even try.'

Abebe and Mamo were waiting in the locker room when Niskanen and Kidaneh entered followed by a Japanese man wearing a blue blazer with the Olympic logo. He bowed low to them; behind him came an assistant carrying an aluminium case, who also bowed.

The Ethiopians bowed in return.

'Mr Bikila, please,' asked the Japanese man.

'I am *Ato*. Bikila,' answered Abebe.

'Mr Bikila. Is my great honour to present gift of shoe.'

He knelt before Abebe while his assistant put the case down and opened it.

Inside was a pair of running shoes.

'Special design for Mr Bikila, barefoot runner, marathon man. Please try. Great honour for my company. Please, you try.'

The assistant passed the Japanese man one of the shoes. With both hands, he held it out to Abebe.

Abebe sat down and extended his feet. The Japanese man unlaced and removed first one shoe and replaced it with the one he had brought, then the other.

Then he stood and bowed low, withdrawing backwards in the same manner as someone concluding an audience with the emperor.

The next day, Abebe wore the shoes for a practice run in the streets of Tokyo. The marathon was going to be run through the streets of the city, but over freshly laid tarmac rather than slippery cobblestones as in Rome. Niskanen hadn't wanted him to do too much training in the Olympic facility. He said it would be a good idea if Abebe got the feel of the real conditions, as they had done in Rome. And so, over a week, they covered the marathon course in a series of short legs. As well as preparing him, Niskanen was protecting Abebe. They had lost the element of surprise; Abebe was now the one they all wanted to beat, and Niskanen didn't want the other marathonians to see any signs of weakness in their main opponent.

The place where they removed his appendix was still hurting, but Abebe just grimaced and pushed himself on. He was content with the shoes, made by the Japanese firm of Asics. He decided he would wear them, partly out of courtesy, but also because not to do so would be disrespectful to their hosts, not to mention the affront it might cause to the local spirits.

42

Behind his desk, the talk show host waited for his cue. On a sofa next to him Professor Carleton Coon squinted in the glare from the studio lights, which he joked were hotter than the sun over the Serengeti. He was still wearing his bush jacket, but he had donned a bow tie for his appearance on television.

'Good evening, and welcome back, America,' began the host. There was applause from the audience in the small studio.

'A physical anthropologist such as my guest tonight could ask for nothing more in the way of a field study than a visit to the Olympic stadium in Tokyo this week. There, he would have the world's most varied assortment of the human species on hand. When you take a close look, as the professor has been doing, performance charts of the Olympic Games do seem to offer an anthropological pattern of achievement.'

As the host spoke, the monitors in the studio showed a montage of Olympic footage: a Chinese gymnast balancing on her hand; a black athlete bursting out of the starting block in a 100 metres sprint; the 1964 US Olympic swimming team, all of them white.

'Orientals have done particularly well at swimming, gymnastics and table tennis, for example. Negroes have been outstanding in boxing and basketball; and now they're taking the lead in the shorter foot races, not to mention the jumps and hurdles. Just a few days ago, we saw Bob Hayes smash the hundred metres record in Tokyo with an incredible nine point nine seconds! Now, all these sports call for quickness of fist or foot and sudden, explosive bursts of effort. White athletes, meanwhile, are complete masters of some sports, like rowing, sailing and fencing. It's a fact that no Negro has ever qualified for the US swimming team, and this year was no exception.'

The montage ended and, as the monitors went black, the host turned to Professor Coon.

'That was our swimming team there. They came away with a brace of gold earlier this week. But if there are few Negroes on the Olympic yachting team, you're saying it has as much to do with opportunity as with anatomy, is that right, Professor?'

'I think that's so, yes. But there *are* factors like lung capacity, bone density and body fat that also have to be taken into account. Negroids have thirty-eight per cent less protective fat than Caucasoids and this would put them at a disadvantage in the cold and in water.'

There was a rustle of tense whispering in the studio.

'Hold on a minute there, Professor. Let's get this straight before we go any farther. Does what we're talking about here have anything to do with superiority – or inferiority?'

'Not unless you believe that being able to run a hundred metres is inferior to being able to swim it!'

The professor let the air settle before he continued.

'A moment ago, you mentioned opportunity,' he said. 'Sport is traditionally one of the few areas where Negro people in America are allowed to achieve success. And I think the reason is that it reassures us. The mind–body dichotomy is something we inherited from the Greeks—'

'Like the Olympic Games.'

'Quite. It suggests a separation of mind and body and, although the ancient Greeks didn't see it that way, we like to suppose that excellence in one means inferiority in the other. As long as black people excel at sports, then we don't have to feel guilty about not giving them equal access to education and employment.'

In the studio, someone applauded, a lone handclap that was picked up by others in the audience, and there was an uncertain moment before the host began again.

'That's quite a theory, Professor. But it still leaves us wondering whether race matters – in sports, I mean.'

He ignored the professor and turned to the camera.

'I'm here with Professor Carleton Coon, an expert in the exciting field of physical anthropology. We'll be back in a moment to find out exactly what that is, and to hear his views on the barefoot runner, Abebe Bikila.'

Abebe and Mamo were running together on the practice track at the Olympic village. Mamo, as he often did, looked pained, though Abebe knew it wasn't the training which was making him suffer. He was feeling the pressure. They had come to Japan with three weeks to go before the marathon, and ahead of them lay the qualifying heats. Abebe would be entering only the marathon, but the major wanted Mamo to compete in the distance races, especially the 10,000 metres. Abebe already had an Olympic medal, but Mamo had never stood on the podium and heard their national anthem played for him. He had come fourth in Melbourne, but that was eight years ago, and he was going to be facing a younger field. Whatever anyone said, they both knew that even if it was enough just to participate, it was better to win.

At the end of August, before his operation, Niskanen had made them run a 10,000 metres race. The results had reassured him; the two of them had covered the 10 kilometres on the road to Debre Zeit in just under twenty-nine minutes and, encouraged by this, the major had decided to put them through a full marathon a week later. Abebe and Mamo came in side by side at two hours and nineteen minutes.

The major had been jubilant as he clocked the time of Demissis Wolde, a younger runner, just two minutes behind them. 'An all-Ethiopian final! What about it?' he had enthused. But that was before the operation. Since then, Abebe had not run more than 10 kilometres.

And so Abebe was forcing the pace, conscious of Mamo hard on his heels. But it was their first day of training in Tokyo and he was conscious too of the stares they were drawing; he wanted to put on a good show, let everyone see how confident they were.

Out of the corner of his eye, Abebe observed the athletes

warming up inside the oval. As they stretched or jogged, their thoughts concentrated on their bodies, oblivious to the foreign surroundings, it seemed to him that they were moving like animals, evolving in their own space and time, coiled up, awaiting the decisive moment, the split second in which the chase was won or lost. Like animals, their catch would depend on speed and grace.

The African and Afro-American athletes recognised the Ethiopian runner at once. They whispered to each other as he passed with Mamo on their series of laps. Though most of them had seen him only in photographs, there was no mistaking the lean torso, the narrow shoulders and long, skinny arms hanging loose, and the look of steady concentration. Their admiration turned to bewilderment, however, when they looked down and saw his feet.

The barefoot runner was wearing training shoes!

Abebe, in turn, was surprised to see that many of the black athletes were barefoot. He pointed it out to Mamo.

Mamo laughed. 'Of course! That's why they are looking at your shoes,' he said. 'It's good. Let them wonder. They won't know what your secret is now!'

After their laps, they went to the canteen to join Kidaneh, who said he had arranged for Abebe to speak to the press the following day. 'Just tell them what you said last time,' he advised. 'Tell them you have recovered from your operation and you're ready to run another marathon.'

They queued with the athletes and received their food on a tray. The cutlery was made of plastic, but the two of them were even more bemused by the sight of a table of Asiatic competitors eating with chopsticks. It was stranger still to be eating with women present: sport separated the sexes for competition but in other respects they mingled in a casual way, a closeness to which Abebe still wasn't accustomed. It was a new world where all that mattered was your sporting performance, not your kin, not your tribe, nor your ancestors, nor even your sex.

'Even if there is only one gold medallist, there is a place for everybody,' Abebe remarked. Kidaneh said it would be a good phrase for the pressmen.

While they were eating, an American athlete came up to their table.

'Hey, Bikila!' he exclaimed. 'Remember me?'

Abebe had not forgotten. He recognised at once the American sprinter they had met in Rome.

Mike was as cheery and direct as before, an effervescence that made Abebe uncomfortable. Such lack of reserve in public was unseemly to Ethiopians, a mark of low origins.

Mike was accompanied by another, younger athlete.

'This is Lee. Hey, Lee, meet the barefoot runner, the man himself! Lee here's always making fun of me for running without shoes.'

'I am pleased to meet you, Lee,' said Abebe, standing and offering his hand.

'The pleasure's all mine,' said Lee.

Abebe introduced Kidaneh and Mamo. 'Where is Wilma?' he asked Mike.

'Wilma ain't here this time. She's back home taking care of her babies.'

'She is married?'

'No,' said Mike slowly. 'She ain't married. That was part of the problem...'

He exchanged a knowing glance with Lee. Abebe was unable to hide his puzzlement.

'Wilma is one brave sister. She's doing it all by herself, see, raising her kids without their father. How about you? Are you married yet? I bet those Ethiopian girls can't get enough of you!'

'I have a family now,' said Abebe.

'Oh, that's great. I'm happy for you, man.' The effusive American smiled and patted Abebe on the shoulder.

'You guys sure caused a big fuss last time. Back home, wherever I go, all the kids ask me about you. Like Lee here. "What's he like? Was he really barefoot?" He was asking me that all the time. And there I was thinking *I* was the star!'

Lee spoke up. 'You were my hero, man! You're an authentic African. You got soul, brother.'

'What is soul?'

'It means... ' Lee hesitated. 'You don't know what it is?'

Abebe shook his head and Lee thought for a moment, struggling to find the definition.

'It means you know where you're coming from.'

Abebe nodded slowly, wondering whether perhaps he had misunderstood. Apparently, for the American Negroes, the matter was far from simple.

'Going for gold again?' asked Mike.

'Yes. I run the marathon again.'

'Attaboy, Abebe! Ain't *nobody* ever won the marathon twice, but if anybody can, I guess you're the one.'

Kidaneh was staring at his food when Abebe looked over at him. They hadn't told him. The major and the others had kept this from him, just as they hadn't told him about the death of the first marathonian. They were treating him like a child. Worse, it implied they thought he lacked the courage to hear such things.

'And you?' he asked Mike, containing his annoyance.

'I ain't no marathon man. Hundred metres, four hundred, sprints and relays; hope I get me some gold this time. Sure be nice to take home some medals, get me a promotional contract, make some money. You must be makin' plenty!'

Abebe was even more confused now. He saw Kidaneh watching, waiting to see what he would say.

Mike had noticed too. 'Who's your manager?' he asked.

'Manager? You mean my trainer? My coach is Major Niskanen.'

'Major, huh,' said Mike, with one eye on Kidaneh. 'Like Elvis and the Colonel? I'll tell you what, Abebe, when you get through with being the emperor's bodyguard or whatever it is you are, why don't you come and see me? I'm serious. You gotta be thinking about your next move. Shoot! Can't run for ever, not even you.'

He smiled.

'The barefoot runner. You take care now. And watch your ass, man. They're all gonna be looking to beat you this time, every last one of them!'

To Abebe's surprise, Kidaneh said that the American was right.

That afternoon, Niskanen took Abebe and Mamo and some of the other athletes to see the Tokyo stadium.

Abebe was awed once more by the scale of the Olympic enterprise and humbly gratified to be a part of it again. It was a brand-new arena, a monumental construction the likes of which didn't exist in their country, with banks of seating swooping back to the sky and a canopy projecting overhead; a mass of metal girders that defied gravity just as the athletes who gathered there defied the limits of nature. A week from now, he would be leading the Ethiopian team in the opening parade. The benches would be full and he would be marching behind the red, green and yellow flag, with the spectators, their faces indistinguishable, blending into one vast, excited mass.

That afternoon, however, the terraces were empty except for Japanese officials wearing dark blue blazers and white gloves checking that everything was in order.

The marathon started in the arena this time, and without any confusion. The stands were crammed with spectators for the key event which, unusually, was taking place before the last day of the Tokyo Olympiad.

The crack of the starting pistol ricocheted around the stadium, momentarily drowning the cheers, and the runners made a lap of the track before leaving the stadium through a tall dark archway and heading out on the 26-mile course along tree-lined streets through the prim suburbs of Tokyo. It was a mild, slightly damp day, reminding Abebe of the freshness of Addis in winter, perfect weather in which to run a marathon.

Number seventeen, the barefoot runner – wearing his Asics shoes this time – trailed at the rear of the pack of competitors; there were more than fifty, a large field, each of whom had him singled out as the man they would have to beat, each of them fired by the desire to take home the gold and the glory for themselves.

Blocked by the pack, he made a lacklustre start, or so it may have seemed to the spectators. In fact, Abebe let them go, sensing they were being pulled along by the Australian, Ron Clarke, who had forged recklessly ahead from the start. Abebe was listening as he ran to the advice of the major circling in his thoughts: don't let yourself be put off; don't be lured into any needless duels; just keep your own pace, the one you always have; you know you can win.

Niskanen had warned him about the Japanese. They were the host nation, so their runners would have the crowds cheering them on, giving them a psychological edge; moreover, above all else, they wanted to win the marathon; it was the supreme challenge, after all, the ultimate declaration of human superiority. The Japanese had fielded three runners, each capable of under two hours thirty, each determined to reach the podium.

In a lounge in the Olympic village, athletes and coaches watched the start of the marathon on a television mounted on the wall, images that for the first time were being transmitted instantly around the world. On the screen, Niskanen, Tessema and Kidaneh saw Abebe trapped at the rear of the pack, blocked by the mass of runners ahead of him.

'He knows,' said Kidaneh. 'The American told him that nobody has ever won it twice.'

It was as if every one of the competitors had decided to get in front and not to let him pass.

Niskanen showed no emotion.

'The marathon is not like other races,' he said. 'The distance runner is not like other runners. He can't see the finishing line. When he begins the race, he doesn't even know if he is going to reach the end.'

They watched as, slowly, steadily, his supple gait showing no sign of any extra effort, Abebe began to catch up with the body of runners.

43

The Hall of Audience was filled with uniformed men. The emperor emerged from his private offices and approached the throne. Led by Ras Kassa, who was wearing ceremonial robes and decorations, the Rasses, senior clergymen and ex-ministers who comprised the Crown Council followed. They had given their views, and Selassie had listened in silence.

The Keeper of the Cushions slid a cushion under His Majesty's feet as he sat and the councillors disposed themselves in a line to the emperor's right. Selassie's eyes, normally so alert, were weary. He had spent the night deep in reflection. Looking around at the faces in the hall, lowered but eager to hear what was about to be said, he pronounced the name.

'General Andom.'

The councillors exchanged surprised, troubled glances. There was a murmur in the hall, and two army officers shot anxious glances at each other. One was an older man who was unable to hide his dismay; the other was General Andom, who did nothing to disguise the flicker of ambition that illuminated his face.

Selassie stood and, as he did, the Keeper of the Cushions slipped the cushion away from under his feet.

The emperor took a long stride forward and drew his sword as the general approached and knelt before him. The King of Kings touched him on each shoulder with the blade.

'I hereby appoint you commander-in-chief of the Imperial Armies,' he announced.

The emperor stepped back, and only when he had sheathed his

sword did the general rise and salute him.

The three pairs of doors opened one after the other and Selassie left the Hall of Audience, followed by members of his family and the imperial court in order of eminence: Princess Tenegneh, the *Abuna* Baselyos, Ras Kassa and the twelve councillors and, lastly, Prime Minister Aklilou, unable to conceal an anxious frown. They were followed by General Andom, ahead of the rest of the army brass.

As the imperial procession passed along the hallway, waiting clerks and advocates bowed their heads low. Then the remaining ministers left the hall and shuffled off in small groups, conferring in whispers.

The emperor was alone except for the courtiers, and he made his way slowly to his private quarters.

Inside, he waited as, on the wall, the cuckoo clock chimed once. He switched on the wireless and listened closely to the BBC World Service transmission. The commentator described how the crowded pack of competitors had left the barefoot runner little room to break through and that now, twenty minutes into the Olympic marathon, the Ethiopian wasn't even among the ten leaders. Elsewhere in the palace, the Keeper of the Cushions replaced the cushion on a shelf in a room piled from floor to ceiling with cushions and pillows of different sizes and fabrics.

His Majesty sighed. So, the bodyguard too was going to let him down. He had promoted him from corporal to sergeant before the departure, to make him feel better after his operation. He wondered now whether the recompense had been premature.

In the lounge, the television monitor showed a lingering close-up of Abebe's face, glistening from sweat but concentrated and steady.

Niskanen put his palms together and, his forefingers touching his lips in concentration, he closed his eyes and silently began to pray.

Abebe was only sorry that Mamo was not running at his side. Not at his side, exactly, but slightly behind, as though deferring to him, the way he'd been doing since Rome. When he asked him about this,

Mamo said it was because he didn't want to get in the way of the cameras that were always pointing at Abebe. He would have wanted to be there, Abebe knew, but Mamo had been exhausted after the 10,000 metres and the major had decided there was no point in entering him. He had been in the lead for a while in the 10,000; he ran a good race, said the major, but he was overtaken by a Tunisian named Gammoudi and the American, Mills. Even though that was five days ago, the major had said it would be better if he sat out the marathon this time. Abebe would have liked to have been running with Mamo. They all knew he might not get another chance.

The Australian Clarke, who had started the marathon so swiftly, had been deceived, perhaps, by his own success in the 10,000. He had won the bronze and it must have gone to his head. He must have forgotten that he was running a marathon this time. The other runners had kept up with him but, by covering the first 5 kilometres in just fifteen minutes, he had set a trap for them and perhaps also for himself. He couldn't maintain the same pace.

One by one, the rest of the runners had fallen back; one after the other, Abebe had passed them.

A red light went on over one of the cameras and the host turned again to the professor of physical anthropology.

'Can white people and Negroes compete on an equal basis? You seem to be telling us they can't, Professor, that physiology makes a difference.'

'Most observers attribute the domination of certain athletic disciplines by certain populations primarily to cultural and sociological factors, but there are physiological factors as well. That's not to say that it's a question of race, however.'

'But that is what your field – physical anthropology – is all about, isn't it: race?'

'I'm interested in the natural history of humanity. Despite what some people might think, I myself don't see that history as a ladder, with a single superior species at the top, but more like a tree with a common trunk and many branches.'

The host turned to talk to the camera.

'Right now – out on one of the branches, you might say – is Abebe Bikila, the Ethiopian runner who won the last Olympic marathon barefoot.'

Images appeared on the monitor of Abebe running.

'As if that wasn't enough, he's trying to repeat his success in Tokyo, though I understand he *is* wearing running shoes this time. Let's go over to the marathon race now with live satellite coverage from Tokyo.'

A close-up of Abebe's face appeared. The Ethiopian guardsman was unaware that he was being filmed by television cameras and that his likeness was being transmitted by satellite around the globe; he had no inkling that TV had penetrated his runner's solitude, stealing his thoughts and sending them around the world. From far away, the camera focused on him, transmitting his anguish and also his concentration.

'…The Ethiopian highlands are situated at over four thousand five hundred feet and the air is relatively thin at that altitude. A few days ago we saw Kip Keino, another distance runner from Kenya, which is also at a high altitude, come in sixth in the five thousand metres race. Proportionally, the Africans have been doing so well I think we have to look for a reason.'

'That's very interesting, Professor, but tell us, what does it take to make the barefoot runner run like that? What has he got that the others don't have?'

'Oh, natural ability, I should say – and the determination to make the most of it.'

In the Olympic village, Niskanen opened his eyes and looked up at the monitor. He saw Abebe's face and recognised the expression. All of a sudden, he knew his prayers were going to be answered.

Abebe had advanced unperturbed. At the 10-kilometre point, there were only three runners ahead of him.

He knew he would be able to catch up with the Australian, who had managed to conserve the lead but who was surely going to have to slow down after such a rapid start. And even if he didn't, at their present rate, Abebe knew he would be able to outrun him. That left two others, one of whom was an oriental. Despite the major's warnings, he wasn't afraid of the Japanese athletes. The only adversary he truly feared was Rhadi, who had pushed him to the hilt in Rome, but once he had been assured that the Moroccan wasn't among the competitors, his confidence knew no bounds.

The pressmen had asked whether he was in better shape this time around than for Rome and he had answered yes. He told them he had experience and self-confidence now, having learned from the marathon in Boston. He was four years older, it was true, but he still weighed the same – 56 kilos – and he could run even faster!

Behind him, he could hear the breathing of another runner, a white, though he didn't know from where, trying – and succeeding – to keep hard on his heels. Ahead, he watched as the Australian fell back, coming closer to them. Together, Abebe and the white runner soon passed the Japanese runner and, as they went by, the local people at the kerbside fell silent. He heard the cheers for the Japanese runner resume only later, as they caught up with the Australian in the lead. Abebe could see him better now, and he knew he was named Clarke because he recognised his style from the 10,000 metres race. He felt a twinge of regret as, just after the 15–kilometre point, he passed him, but at least the Australian wouldn't be going home empty handed like Mamo.

Now Abebe was in the lead, and all that remained for him to do was shake off the white runner dogging his heels.

He had known all along that he was going to win – he had even said as much to the pressmen and they had laughed at him, pretending to scoff – and by the time he reached the halfway point, he could no longer hear the panting of the white athlete.

He was alone. The marathon was his race.

He ignored the curiosity on the oriental faces lining the roadside. He could see only the tarmac unrolling underneath him, a dark, majestic causeway. He could feel the iron in his legs, propelling him onwards.

44

The food they brought him in the hospital had no taste, but he was too grateful to tell them. It came on trays under metal foil, like army rations, but it was grey and had no smell. Abebe longed for the sour, fiery taste of a shred of *injera* dipped in a spicy stew, but he didn't know how to ask for it and, in any case, he would not have wanted to offend his hosts. He was amazed and humbled by their kindness and their preoccupation with his well-being.

Already, it was astonishing to him to be there in the hospital with the other patients, a privilege he would never have imagined would be his due. No one in his family had ever been in a hospital before, unless it was a field hospital, to die. His sporting victories had given him this privilege, but it bothered him that, although he had brought glory to Ethiopia, he had done nothing to change the circumstances of his people, not like the major. There were too few doctors and nurses, and most of them were foreign volunteers in the Red Cross. He had been given rewards, but there wasn't enough to share, and, while Mamo might be right in saying everyone shared in his triumph, he had never imagined that victory could be so solitary.

So he ate the tasteless food without complaining, pleasing the nurses by finishing his plate. And he swallowed the little pills they gave him with a glass of water. He was lucky, he had medicine and he had enough to eat.

He had travelled too; but his journeys to America, to Japan and now to Britain had merely shown him how far Ethiopia still had to go to develop. He thought he understood now what Mengistu meant when he ranted in the prison about progress. The general was an idealist, Abebe had concluded; he wanted everyone to have the same privileges, but was this not what His Majesty wished for too? Mengistu had been mistaken to think that killing members of the royal household and the government would hasten progress.

What had puzzled Abebe the most, though, was his demand for justice. When Mengistu said he wanted justice for all it made no sense to Abebe. There was justice in Ethiopia, dispensed by His Majesty, the King of Kings. You could pray for the intercession of Mariam, mother of Christ, or the *Abuna*, but you were responsible for your cruelties and for your kindnesses and for all that they brought. That was why his situation – immobile in a comfortable bed, unable to get up, unable to run or even walk – was so distressing.

What had he done?

Abebe had searched his memories, his conscience, for a cause; for something that would explain why he was there, the world's greatest runner, they said, unable to feel his legs. He didn't want to believe in the *zar*, the troubled spirits that surrounded the village, killing cattle and poisoning wells. They frightened the children and the old people, but not him; he simply dismissed them. He preferred to believe that he had committed an unpardonable act, and that his plight was the just sentence of the Lord; that it was the emperor's will that he should be deprived of his mobility, as they called it in the hospital (no one ever mentioned running) – even this was acceptable; though it was a harsh punishment for failing his country after all he had done.

The race in Tokyo had been so easy. He had run as never before, fleet as the wind.

He couldn't forget the Japanese runner, however. He couldn't forget the agony of his effort to win, the pain in his body, and the humiliation on his face...

A little over an hour after he passed the Australian, having slowly out-distanced the other white runner, Abebe came through the archway and back into the stadium with nobody else behind him.

As he turned right and on to the track, however, he was met by a stunned silence. He ignored the eyes of the 100,000 spectators, among them those of the legendary athletes Jesse Owens and Emil Zatopek, who Niskanen told him would be in the stadium, and concentrated on the 350 metres that remained for him to run.

For a moment he thought something was wrong, that he had taken the wrong route and come in late. There were expressions of dismay on the faces of the white-hatted Japanese officials waving him around and on to the track. Then he realised that the silence was the sound of the entire stadium, full as it was on the opening day, holding its breath. When the cheering started, it was muted at first, but grew louder as he came around on to the final straight and raised his arms to let the rope burst across his chest.

He knew he had a good lead, though he couldn't be sure of how much because beyond the 35–kilometre point he hadn't been able to see anyone pursuing him. He found out later it was four whole minutes; he was nearly a mile ahead of the Japanese runner Tsuburaya and the Englishman Heatley, who were battling neck and neck for second place.

As he raised his arms to pass the line, the roar that went up for him from the stands was so intense that his senses swam and he feared for a moment he would lose consciousness. Yet he couldn't stop running even as he glanced up at the ranks of spectators to his right and shrugged off the officials wanting to smother him with blankets.

Still jogging, he slowed to a halt and bent over to touch his toes, sending a peal of astonishment through the crowd; then he stood to attention and raised his arms straight, palms outwards in salute. He finally stopped on the track and turned slowly around, gazing up at the stands, quenching his thirst with the enormous, unprecedented praise. A hushed expectancy overcame the spectators. In that instant, Abebe was at the centre of the world, the greatest runner, king of the marathon. He wanted to acknowledge the cheers somehow, but didn't know what was expected of him.

He sat down and, rolling on to his back, began to lift his legs slowly, keeping them straight, knees together and toes pointed, as he had been taught by the major all those years ago. Then he began to pedal his legs in the air and the entire stadium clamoured with delight.

He stood up again to relish the cheers, both palms raised high towards the sky. He had achieved the supreme victory, setting a new world record as he became, for the second time, an Olympic champion. Looking around, he saw a startled young Japanese girl waiting with a wet sponge. He took the sponge and wiped his brow and, at that instant, he heard the spectators drawing their breaths again as his closest rivals came through the arch and on to the track.

Tsuburaya was leading, but only just.

Abebe turned and saw the Japanese runner. Right alongside him was the Englishman, Heatley, making a final, desperate effort.

As they came around into the last straight, with less than 200 metres to go, the Englishman put on a final burst and, before his eyes, the two of them crossed the finishing line at what seemed like the same instant.

There was a terrible hush as the spectators awaited the judge's decision. Finally, the scoreboard flashed the result, and the long silence was broken by a deep moan of disappointment when it was announced that the Japanese runner had won the bronze medal.

The British runner had beaten him to the silver by two seconds.

Niskanen watched on the television screen as Abebe leapt on to the podium. The tears he had been crying, tears of pride, turned to tears of laughter.

The greatest runner the world had ever seen, his Olympic champion, his discovery, his protégé, still had a spring in his step.

It was as though he would run for ever!

In the palace gardens, Selassie was feeding the imperial menagerie. The old lions had been replaced with younger beasts, more ferocious but less trustworthy. He could still hear the commentator jabbering with excitement on the radio inside.

'Incredible!' he said. 'An almost superhuman victory! The Ethiopian runner Abebe Bikila has become the first African – indeed, the first man – to win the Olympic marathon twice!'

A smile of satisfaction crossed the emperor's lips as he watched the great cats chewing on the meat.

'Not only that, but he's set a new Olympic record of two hours, twelve minutes and eleven point two seconds!'

Selassie breathed a deep sigh.

His reign, his glory and his kingdom would endure.

45

Niskanen finally reached Abebe in a corridor of the stadium where he was being carried by an ecstatic human tide: athletes, pressmen, everyone who ever dreamed of surpassing themselves.

He hugged Abebe. Photographers and pressmen were crowding around them and he wanted to give a dignified account of Ethiopian success, but he couldn't help himself. He couldn't let go of his runner, his discovery. Abebe had outrun everyone who had ever competed in a marathon; his victory was complete. It belonged to all of them, yes, but especially Abebe – and to him.

'Hey, Bikila, hey!' shouted one of the pressmen. 'Can we have a word? How do you feel? You look like you hardly broke a sweat out there...'

'Good,' said Abebe. 'I feel very good!'

'There was a possibility that you wouldn't run. You were recovering from an appendix operation.'

'Yes. It's true. Look...'

Abebe was enjoying himself, lifting his vest to show his scar from the operation.

'I had operation six week ago. I keep the scar and give medal to doctor,' he joked. 'He has made a good job, no?'

'After your achievement here today, do you expect another promotion when you get back to Ethiopia?'

Abebe explained that he had already been promoted to sergeant. He didn't see how his win could lead to any advancement; he already owed his career, his success, indeed his life, to the emperor.

The medal, the honours, everything belonged to His Majesty; although he didn't say it, he wondered whether it would be enough.

'Think you'll try to make it a hat-trick?'

'A trick with my hat?'

Kidaneh saw that the reporters were laughing at Abebe now. 'It means winning three times,' he interjected.

'They say no man from Africa can win a gold medal, but I win. They say no one can win Olympic marathon twice, but I win. Now you say I cannot win three times?'

This time, it was Abebe who laughed as the reporters scribbled.

One of the reporters turned to Niskanen and asked him whether he thought Abebe was going to be able to win a third time.

'Of course! You can never be surprised about anything with Abebe! But he's not the only one.' He was always careful to encourage them all. Abebe was a fine example for the other athletes, but he wouldn't be if they thought his achievement was exceptional. 'We have plenty of new talent in Ethiopia like Bezabeth and Demissis, and you still haven't seen what Mamo Wolde can do. I think we're all very confident for Mexico. Ethiopia is going to be an important athletic nation in the future, I promise you.'

'Do you think the altitude at Mexico City will give your boys an advantage?' asked the reporter, and everyone listened for the answer. It was no secret among the sports journalists that Ethiopia's altitude played a part in Abebe's victories. But nobody was sure what the explanation was.

'Ethiopia's runners don't need any concessions,' said the major. 'But I expect they'll be able to give their best at that altitude and I predict you'll be in for more surprises! Why should we stop with the marathon? There's the five thousand, the fifteen hundred, plenty of medals waiting!'

Later, when they were back in their quarters, Tessema chastised Abebe for behaving improperly.

'You were playing the clown for them,' he said. 'It's not the dignified way an Olympic champion should behave. You are an ambassador for our country now. And that show in the stadium was dangerous and foolish.'

Unexpectedly, Kidaneh came to his defence. 'You are right,' he said, 'but what he did was only natural. I have the impression that sports and media are creating heroes of a new kind, individuals like the American boxer, Cassius Clay, who speak for themselves and for humanity, not just for a nation.'

Abebe had been right about his fate, at least. He returned to a hero's welcome, and then to the barracks, where he became once again a member of His Imperial Majesty's bodyguard.

He decided to hold a party at his house, however, a celebration to which he invited everyone he knew, the way the major sometimes did.

Niskanen came with Ben and Helen. He brought flowers for Yewibdar, which he picked from his garden, and boxes of Lego bricks that he had arranged to be sent from Sweden for Dawit. He found Abebe with the new baby in his arms, a little girl. Abebe said her name was Tsige.

'You are a lucky man. You have a lovely wife and fine children.'

Abebe was embarrassed by his good fortune, but even more so by the sadness behind the major's compliment. He would have liked to be able to ask after the health of his children too. He decided to venture a suggestion.

'You should take another wife,' he said. 'Then you would have children too.'

The baby on his lap began to cry and at once Yewibdar came to retrieve it. Niskanen was grateful for the distraction.

'You're like my children,' he said. 'You know that. You and Mamo and the others. Anyway, it's too late. I don't think any woman would be able to put up with me now.'

Abebe saw that Helen had been listening to their conversation.

Later, she approached Niskanen and impulsively smoothed the lapel of his sports coat.

'I remember that jacket,' she said. It was one he often wore, a pale blue woollen blazer with, on the breast pocket, the crest of the Idrotts sports club in Sweden. 'You were wearing it at the party when we first met. I thought it was very smart. I didn't know what to make of you then. What with the war, you couldn't really tell what people had been through.'

She looked at him. 'What happened,' she asked, 'to bring you here?'

'I always wanted to travel,' he said.

'I'm serious. You're so secretive. You live alone, you never give anything away. Come on...'

So Niskanen told her how he had come to Ethiopia because of Count von Rosen, the great aviator whom he had met in the Red Cross.

'That's all?'

It wasn't all, but he didn't know how to tell her the rest, how he could never be happy in Sweden, how he felt he would never be accepted. She was waiting for him to continue, however, so he did, relating the general truth, if not his own.

'My family is from Finland. That's where I was born, but my parents moved to Sweden, where I grew up. When the Soviets invaded Finland at the start of the war, I wanted to do something for my country, so I joined the Red Cross and got involved in fund-raising. The Finns were badly outnumbered but we fought Stalin's armies through the winter and halted their advance. There was a truce.'

'Go on...'

'Then they attacked again and we were forced to make an alliance.' He hesitated, hoping she would understand.

'Finland made a pact with the Germans. Nobody else would help us. We received German guns and planes. Their officers came to the command meetings. The truth is, they were our friends.'

'The Nazis? You fought with the Nazis?'

'I didn't fight with them. We weren't Nazis, we only allied with them against the Soviets. It was called the Separate War.'

'I'm sorry,' said Helen. 'I wasn't saying you were one.'

Ben had said something about not trusting Swedes, especially ones with Finnish names. Still, she found it hard to believe. She tried to look into his face, to be sure, but he turned away.

'We didn't know anything about what they were doing to the Jews in Poland,' he pleaded. 'All we wanted was to stop the Soviets, and the Germans were fighting Stalin too. It wasn't until afterwards that we found out about the camps, about the Final Solution, about what that meant...'

He looked about the room, which was full of Ethiopians, many of them his close friends. 'The Nazis would have considered these people an inferior race! I wanted no part of that. When I found out, I felt sick, physically sick! How could they have treated human beings like that?'

'But you *weren't* part of it, not personally...'

He had his eyes lowered but he could sense Helen staring hard at him, and finally he looked at her.

'After the war, you know, when the Germans lost, people treated us differently. It was hard to say you were a Finn. But in the Red Cross, at least, nobody mentioned these things, you just got on with helping people. I suppose I thought that helping the Ethiopians would be a way of making amends.'

'And was it?'

'At first, I wanted to improve this country. In the beginning I thought I could make it better for them, help Ethiopia to develop. Now I've given up that idea. My obligation was not to Ethiopia, I see that now. These people wanted nothing of me except for me to teach them some sporting exercises, for which they paid me a salary. The truth is I needed them more than they needed me.'

She smiled tenderly at him.

'What if there was someone?' she asked. 'I mean, someone who needed you?'

Niskanen turned away.

46

After lunch in the hospital, it was always the same routine. They brought him to the room full of gleaming metal contraptions hung with ropes, pulleys and weights like a chamber of torture, except that he could feel nothing below his waist and so there wouldn't be much point in torturing him. He thought in his darker moments that they might as well cut his legs off.

The nurses laid him on a table and turned him on his stomach, then the osteopath went to work, kneading the vertebrae on his back, searching for a response with her bony fingers.

She was a young woman who wore a white coat and glasses, and she always had a serious expression, just like the Red Cross nurses in Ethiopia. Her frowns made him uneasy; it was as though she was as accustomed to the plight of the infirm as the nurses at home were to the suffering of the poor. Unlike the male nurses who watched him as they lowered him into the pool, she was able to conceal her disappointment, at least. She made no sound as she pressed her fingers into his back; her breathing remained constant as she ran her knuckles against his spine. Once, she had spoken of his body as a powerful machine, but it was broken, she said, there in that room full of strange contraptions, and they would have to find a way to repair it. He wondered whether a human body was as easy to fix as a lorry or a sewing machine. He doubted it.

That day, however, she seemed unusually glum. He thought she would speak again about the war in Biafra. 'They can put a man on the moon, why can't they do something about all the children starving in Biafra?' she had asked once.

Another time, she said it was part of her job to hope for miracles.

After massaging his back for fifteen minutes, she spoke.

'Do you feel anything?' she asked. 'Any sensation at all?'

'Where?'

'Anywhere.'

'No. What should I feel?'

'No warmth, no tingling, pins and needles; you know what I mean?'

'Like cramp, yes...'

'Yes. But you can't feel anything?'

Abebe was looking away from her and he couldn't see her expression.

'You know, Abebe, perhaps we ought to be thinking about a different sort of treatment,' she said. 'It's been nearly six months now and there has been no response so far. We mustn't be discouraged; sometimes it takes years and you just have to be patient. Meanwhile, well, you just have to get on with things.'

He didn't understand what she meant by getting on with things.

'What things?' he asked.

'Life.'

He wondered how many things might be left for him.

'It's not the end, you know. Life goes on.'

Since coming to the hospital, he had thought about little else, though he had said nothing. He had been considering just that: the ways in which his life might continue.

'In my country, my people, we believe that each man must pass through different stages in life. He must learn when he is a boy, then he must become young warrior and he must go out and defeat other young warriors. Then, when he has conquered lands, he must take a wife. He must become a father; he must protect his family. Then he will become an elder. He will settle disputes. His advice will be sought. He will tell of all the things he knows.'

She had stopped massaging him and her warm hands lay on his back as she listened.

'I have been a bodyguard and a father. If I can no longer run, it's because I have finished running. No one can say I did not run as far as I could!'

'That's the spirit,' she said, wiping her hands with a towel.

'I am lucky,' he said. 'I have run far. I have brought honour to my family, my village, my people, and to His Majesty!'

'We can only do so much, you know. After that, it's up to you.'

Not for the first time, he thought about Tsuburaya, the Japanese runner. After the Games had ended, he had returned to his village and, unable to bear the shame of losing the race in the final few hundred metres before the very eyes of his emperor, he had committed hara-kiri. He had taken a long knife, slashed open his bowels, and bled to death.

The marathon was not like other races, the major always said. The marathon runner can't see the finish, he never knows whether he's going to make it...

'Thank you, Doctor,' Abebe said to the osteopath. 'I know you have done your best.'

Whether it was the restless *zar* of Tsuburaya, or any of the other shamed, exhausted or broken marathonians, or the race itself, a jealous mistress who took every and any tribute as her due, there was nothing the Englishwoman could do about it.

His life belonged to the King of Kings. Surely he had done nothing to bring dishonour to His Majesty?

47

The curtains parted silently to reveal a map of Ethiopia, hand painted and studded with flashing lights. Like so much that was locally made, it looked to Niskanen like the work of children. It was an uncomfortable sentiment, but one he could never dispel. Ethiopian goods had the variable finish of handicrafts, sometimes fine and impressive in their patient detail, the mark of the artisan, but never perfect, never uniform. Ethiopians themselves, he had noticed, preferred the machine-made things from abroad, which, in their view, were properly designed. Their traditional skills, it seemed to them, could never equal Western engineering. He had come to understand that, in almost the same measure as their discourses were bloated by national pride, they suffered from feelings of inadequacy.

The lights on the wall map blinked unevenly. Beneath was the year, 1968. With his baton, the emperor tapped the lectern to call to attention the foreign dignitaries. Many of the visitors were African, and they had been convened by the emperor for an informal reception. Selassie wanted to share with them his feelings about development.

'Development is the key!' he insisted. It was a theme Niskanen had heard many times. 'Develop and surpass, that is what we must do! Our people are hungry for development. Like our great athlete Abebe Bikila, they are running a marathon, a race that we shall win.' He announced that he had added to his schedule the Hour of Development, during which he would be able to discuss new projects for the advancement of the country and ensure that he was up to date on the progress of projects already under way. 'This—' he tapped the painted map with his baton '—is the Haile Selassie bridge. And this is the Haile Selassie dam project.'

In the room, there were nods of approval and then a round of applause. For what? wondered Niskanen. Nothing had been finished, nothing was accomplished.

Niskanen was there with Spencer and Ben. He was obliged to oversee the spending of charitable funds from Sweden; over the years, the sums had grown to colossal levels, and the Ethiopians had become accustomed to the aid. There were always new projects looking for funding from charities, from development agencies or – in exchange for concessions and permits – from the Americans and the Soviets.

Ben leaned close and whispered to Niskanen.

'His Highness has added the Police-Army Hour to his day too. He feels he needs to pay special attention to the problems of his loyal soldiers and police. Each year, he appoints more of what he calls his "personal people" to the administration, like that one over there...'

Ben nodded discreetly at a burly man in a suit and sunglasses.

'He hand-picks them from the rabble in the Mercato.'

Niskanen had long ago realised that, since Ben was there essentially to buy His Majesty's favour, he took a jaundiced view of imperial motives. Niskanen, on the other hand, thought Selassie was sincere in his wishes for progress, but knew also that the emperor was as cunning as a fox. If the Americans wanted a base in Ethiopia, he would make them pay the best price he could get.

A few days later, as he was leaving the physical education department at the Haile Selassie I university – one of the few projects that had been completed – Niskanen heard a different speech being made. Under heavy skies, on a lawn screened from the road by eucalyptus trees, a young man was addressing a group of thirty or so students seated on the grass. Most of the students were dressed in the casual Western clothes that their professors wore, but some ostentatiously wore their traditional *shammas*, a new trend among the young men on campus.

'How can anyone talk of development in the midst of utter poverty?' the young orator was asking. 'What sort of development is it when the whole nation is being crushed by misery, when entire provinces are starving, when only a handful of His Highness's subjects can read and write, when there are no hospitals or physicians, when ignorance and illiteracy hold sway?' His tone grew agitated. He was older than the rest of the students, and Niskanen recognised him behind a newly grown beard as a former alumnus. 'Barbarity, humiliation, despotism, exploitation, desperation! What manner of development is this?'

There was a rumble of thunder, followed by a sudden downpour. The students scattered for cover under the trees and Niskanen dashed to his car.

It was the start of the season of heavy rains that turned the unfinished streets of the capital to rivers of mud.

As he turned the key in the ignition, he felt a shiver of foreboding. Change was coming to Ethiopia – the emperor was in his seventies and Prince Asfa was unlikely to be the victor in any battle for succession – but where would that leave him and his athletes?

It was late at night in the offices of the Red Cross. Niskanen was sitting at a typewriter, slowly punching the keys. He lifted his glasses and rubbed the bridge of his nose. A stack of letters still remained beside him. He fed another sheet into the typewriter and resumed typing.

He was unaware at first that Helen had entered the office, the sound of her footsteps hidden by the constant gentle drumming of the rain that had been falling for weeks.

'Hello,' she said.

He peered over his glasses. She was carrying a bottle of whisky and it looked as if she might have taken a couple of swigs before entering. She approached him with exaggerated confidence, her hips swaying in that uncontrolled way of women who exercise little.

He stood up and came around from behind his desk, bowing slightly. His manners were a defence, old fashioned and somewhat stiff, but impeccable. 'What are you doing here?' he asked. 'Why aren't you at the reception?'

'Another reception,' said Helen. 'You don't attend them any more, I notice. So I decided to find out what you were up to.'

Niskanen had long since tired of the formal occasions, the dinners and galas that the emperor seemed to feel were necessary for prestige, and the endless ceremonies that His Imperial Majesty loved to perform, rituals that seemed to reassure him more than serving any other purpose.

'We hardly see you any more these days,' she said.

'I have all this paperwork to do for Save the Children,' he said. 'I know it's a weak excuse...'

'No, it's not a weak excuse, it's a very good one. At least you're doing something worthwhile.'

'Was it a good party?'

Helen shrugged.

'Who was there?'

'The usual crowd. Everybody. Spencer wanted to know where you were, so I decided to find out. I wanted to see you.'

'I had to answer these,' said Niskanen, indicating the letters. 'Swedish donors like to know where all their money is going.'

Helen slumped in the chair in front of his desk. Niskanen sat on the edge, wanting to appear casual, ready to listen. Clearly, she wanted to talk.

'You're so good, aren't you? Save this, save that. You write personal letters to all these people.' She nodded at the correspondence and then looked up at him. 'What about saving yourself? What about saving me from all this?'

She looked at him pleadingly. Then it happened, as he had feared. She got up and came around the desk. Without any hesitation, she put her arms around his neck. She brought her face close to his, looking into his eyes.

'What about... I mean, you're married!' he blurted.

'To hell with my husband! He doesn't care. The Good Lord doesn't care either, otherwise he wouldn't have let me marry him.' She slid her hand down the front of his shirt. 'And he wouldn't have sent you here.'

Niskanen closed his eyes. He was suddenly aware of the rain falling outside, beating harder than ever as she kissed him, trying to force her tongue into his mouth. It had been a long time since he had been kissed by a woman. He found that sport – physical exercise – took away most of his desire. The rest he kept to himself.

After a while, she pulled away, licking her lips with a look of puzzled dismay.

'You don't want to, do you?' she said. 'What is it? Don't you like me?'

'It's not you,' he said. His heart was pounding like the rain; hammering from the fear that he wouldn't be able to give her what she wanted. It wasn't something he could express.

'What would people say?' he pleaded lamely.

'You don't have to worry,' she said, drawing back. 'I won't tell them.'

48

Abebe was relaxing in the sauna with Mamo and Negussie Roba. Over the years, he had come to look forward to sitting in the wooden cabin full of hot steam at the end of a training session. The heat took away the aches that came of running, the pangs he tried to ignore as he ran but which grew more insistent with the years. After Rome, the major had received funds for a large sauna at Debre Zeit, big enough for more than a dozen athletes. With the next Olympics in Mexico City coming up, the Ethiopian team came together there regularly. Sitting in towels in the steam, they discussed running and planned race strategies.

Negussie had been recounting his sojourn in Czechoslovakia, where he had seen the Eastern Bloc athletes at work. The Czechs were dedicated to sporting achievement, and he warned everybody that they would be hard to beat. The facilities there were the best, everything up to date, he said. As well as the coaches, there were scientists who studied the athletes and measured their performances and chemists who prescribed them special diets, food that came in powders, or which you sucked from a tube. He said they had wired him to machines and taken blood samples from him several times a day. 'And I was the one who was supposed to be learning from them!'

The Czechs were interested in studying runners from the highlands, from Ethiopia and Kenya, Niskanen told them. He had joined them with Tessema after a game of tennis in which the former footballer had once again lost to the Swedish ace. 'It looks as though you do have a physical advantage because of the altitude.

They're saying so now at the institute in Stockholm too. It's something to do with oxygenation of the blood. Oxygen in the bloodstream is what carries energy to the muscles,' he explained. 'Because you live at altitudes where there is less oxygen in the atmosphere, it seems you have an advantage over other runners when you descend to lower levels. Your lungs are used to delivering more oxygen, and therefore more energy, to your bloodstream, and so to your muscles.'

Tessema said the federation had been receiving requests from athletes to come and train at Debre Zeit. Americans, Russians, British, they all wanted to come, hoping that whatever it was, the magic would work for them too. Niskanen said they would probably be wasting their time. It wasn't simply running at that altitude which made a difference, as they had previously thought. You had to be born and raised there at least. And probably your forebears too.

The Ethiopians all laughed at this – all except Abebe.

He could understand how science could help him: Niskanen's training methods were scientific, after all. But he was dismayed that science could explain his wins, reduce them to simple circum-stances. What about all the training we've done, all the preparation? he asked.

'That's right,' said Niskanen. 'We did do a lot of preparation, didn't we? If it was just a matter of oxygenation, everybody would have medals. Mamo here would have plenty of gold.'

Niskanen slapped him on the back and they all laughed, even Mamo.

Tessema said he was going to have to turn down the requests because there weren't enough facilities for Ethiopians, let alone visitors.

But Abebe was still upset. It hurt him to hear that his gold medals might not be the rewards for his own efforts, that nature – not even nature, an accident of geography – had given him an advantage. It was unfair to all the other runners from around the world and it was unfair to him. It meant that winning the Olympic marathon twice in a row was a fluke.

There was only one way to prove them wrong.

'I know what everybody is saying.'

Abebe had heard the talk in the Mercato.

'Three times is impossible, I know this. Everywhere I hear them saying it will be impossible for me. But I will run. I will win!'

Demssie and Wehib, two younger runners, looked at Abebe in shock. It was unimaginable: the marathon hero had acknowledged that there could be doubt! Wehib Masreha had run in the marathon in Tokyo, proud to be competing in the same Olympic event as the barefoot runner. Inspired by Abebe, he had run a national marathon in 1960, his first ever race, and come third. But in Tokyo he would have been unable to keep up, even if he had wanted to beat Abebe.

Mamo was silent. He had come close to the podium; he had achieved fourth place in Melbourne, but that was more than ten years ago. He had never felt the surprising weight of an Olympic medal around his neck. He and Abebe would soon be forty years old; they were already past the age at which most athletes retire. If that was what they were saying about Abebe – that he couldn't go on much longer – what were they saying about Mamo?

Mexico would be his last chance.

'Abebe, my friend, you must not listen,' he said. 'They are jealous. They want to see you lose because they have never won anything themselves. They don't know what it is to train and to race, to struggle and win!'

Niskanen jumped in.

'Of course you will win. They said Africans couldn't compete at international level. Look at all of you. Nobody ever won the marathon twice before; they said it was impossible. Now they say you can't win a third time? Hah!'

He grinned and the others nodded.

But Abebe could feel the pain when he ran. It had started one day while he was training. He wasn't even exerting himself, just a few miles, a gentle slope... But the pain had come, and it came slowly this time, unlike before. It wasn't the sudden stab of a muscle tightening or tearing, it was something else, an ache he had never known in the past, and it wouldn't go away.

'Why do we run, Major?'

It came back to him in an instant: the fatigue you think you can't overcome; the sublime surge of the second wind, the perfect emptiness as you ran. He didn't say so, but running, for Niskanen, was a way of forgetting.

'It's a question of potential, I suppose, of achievement,' he said. 'We are trying to reach a peak – and then go beyond that peak.'

'When I run,' said Abebe, 'I think that I am running across the plain near my village... In the distance, I see Debre Birhan. The name means light. The mountain of light is shining for me, like a flame. This is my Olympic torch. When I see it, I can run for ever. Nothing will stop me.'

'Nothing,' repeated Niskanen.

'If I don't run, there is no flame.'

49

In the locker room of the Mexico City stadium, Abebe and Mamo were lacing their shoes when a man entered, an athlete wearing a tracksuit topped off with a fashionable black beret.

'Hey, man!' he said in the loud way of Americans, his stern face cracking into a wide grin. Abebe, taken aback, exchanged glances with Mamo.

'You don't dig me? I sure dig you.'

'Yes,' said Abebe, 'I know. Your name is Lee.'

'Lee Evans. How're you doing, brother?'

'I am OK.'

'Sure you are. You're an African!'

His smile vanished. 'Not interrupting, am I? 'Cause we need to rap.'

He sat down on the bench and leaned forward conspiratorially.

'See,' he said, 'we're Americans, and we got a problem.'

Abebe was perplexed.

'You used to be my hero, man, my sporting idol. Nowadays my heroes are community leaders, brothers taking a stand, setting an example. And that's what I'm here for. We want your help, see.'

Abebe did not see as yet but said he would help if he could.

'Me and some of the brothers got something in mind; we figure it's time to make a statement.'

He raised his fist in the Black Power salute.

'You know what that means?'

Abebe looked at Mamo. He had been in Korea along with

American soldiers. Perhaps he would understand.

Mamo shook his head.

'It means we're black and we're proud of what we are. You proud to be black, Abebe Bikila?'

'Am I proud to be black? I am proud, yes. Why should I not be proud?'

'Right on, brother!'

The American was excited. Abebe exchanged glances with Mamo. Then Abebe spoke: 'I know what you want. You are segregated. You want to tell the world that you are a prisoner in your own country.'

Lee lowered his eyes.

'Yeah, slaves of Uncle Sam. Right on, except it ain't about desegregation this time, it's about respect. We want respect, like you got respect. It ain't a white man's flag you gotta salute every morning. It's your flag, man.'

The American shook his head.

'I guess it ain't your problem, African man.'

He smiled at Abebe and, standing up as straight as a guardsman, gave the Black Power salute again.

'Tell you what,' he said, 'do me a favour. Make it a hat-trick, huh?'

They had been in Mexico City for three weeks, confined to the Olympic village because of rioting students, smelling the tear gas and hearing sirens and machine-gun fire as they trained.

Mexico City was situated at 2,300 metres, about the same elevation as Addis. There was 30 per cent less oxygen at that level, and Niskanen wanted to find out how it would affect results. By the time the Games started, he was fairly sure the thin air wouldn't penalise the Ethiopians, and might even give them an advantage. It was evident that the other athletes, who were unused to the altitude, tired more quickly. The only danger he could see was the Kenyans. The Kenyans, he knew, had been posting some impressive times in local events. They too lived on the high plateaux of the Horn of Africa and their British trainers were extremely competent.

Once the heats got under way, he turned out to have been right to be concerned. Kenyans won gold and silver medals in the 3,000 metres steeplechase; their best runner, Kip Keino, won a gold medal in the 1,500 and a silver in the 5,000. Clearly, Kenyatta, the erudite Marxist president of Ethiopia's southern neighbour, had decided to make it his business to show Selassie what it was to develop and surpass.

The 10,000 metres had turned into a fearsome duel between two runners from the Horn of Africa: the valiant Mamo and Kenya's Naftali Temu. Mamo had struggled to take the lead but the Kenyan had snatched it back from him in the final lap. At least Mamo finally had his medal, however, a hard-won silver in a race that had left Ron Clarke, the Australian, collapsed on the ground with serious breathing problems, due, probably, to the altitude.

With the marathon now just one day away, they were faced with a difficult task.

Niskanen had discussed it with Negussie Roba, who as the team trainer was officially the one who had to make the decision. Abebe had been complaining of pains in his right knee and Niskanen was worried that he might not even be able to complete the course, let alone take home another gold medal. Mamo had to prepare himself. A couple of days after winning a silver in the 10,000 metres, he was going to be lining up for the marathon. He wouldn't be there just to encourage Abebe, however. Mamo was going to have to find somewhere inside him the incredible resources a marathon demanded. It was a matter of competition psychology; he might be their only hope.

Negussie asked, 'Do you think he can do it?'

'I don't know,' said Niskanen. 'He must still be feeling those ten kilometres in his legs.'

'You remember Rhadi, don't you?'

Niskanen recalled only too well the heroic performance of the Moroccan in Rome. Rhadi was just 2 metres behind Abebe until the last kilometre. If Rhadi had not run the 10,000 two days earlier, he might well have had the reserves to win.

'Look at it another way,' said Niskanen, 'winning second place in a ten thousand like that will have boosted his confidence.'

If he knew anything, he knew that the Ethiopians were capable of confounding his estimations. He remembered how amazed he had been by Wagkira's performance when the thirty-seven-year-old came in seventh in the Rome marathon. Mamo was the same age as Wagkira now; perhaps he could still manage it.

Niskanen was surprised to find he didn't feel too sorry for Abebe. He had had his hour of glory, after all. For eight years, he had been the Olympic champion. Remarkable, legendary; those were the things people were always saying about him, and Niskanen couldn't help wondering whether it was given to legends to surpass themselves. Abebe had already done it once, in Tokyo. He had been telling the reporters he would make it a hat-trick, but the major sensed that, like everybody else, he knew that the chances were not great.

When they told him about Abebe's knee problem, Mamo lowered his head and cried. Not for himself, Niskanen knew – even if the pressure on Mamo, participating in his fourth Olympics, was greater than it had ever been – but for Abebe.

Abebe understood the eventuality of defeat. It was in the nature of sporting competition, like the cycles of life. He had been a warrior and then a father, soon he would enter a new phase. Records never endured; always, eventually, there was someone faster, fitter, younger.

He had listened to Tessema telling how, after twenty-seven years, he had been gently relegated from the St George's football team. One day, as he was lacing his boots in the dressing room, the hero of Ethiopian football, who was also the captain of the team, was handed a list of the players selected for the match – and he saw that his name wasn't on it...

Before the race, Abebe told Mamo that he hoped that if he couldn't make it, then it would be Mamo's turn to win.

'If I don't finish, it will be up to you,' he had said sternly. 'You must win. For His Majesty – and for me.'

Mamo told him not to be foolish, that he would complete the race and, furthermore, that he was going to win the hat-trick.

But after they passed the ten-kilometre post Abebe wasn't sure how much longer he would be able to go on.

The pain in his knee was getting worse. It wasn't a cramp that jabbed suddenly like a knife, and it wasn't like the pain that had enveloped him before they removed his appendix, but he could feel that something was wrong. Instead of the iron in his legs, he felt a stiffness that was growing and wouldn't leave him. He didn't know whether perhaps he had pulled a muscle. But what did that feel like? He had never suffered a sporting injury and he speculated that he may have torn a ligament. He had seen such calamities occur to others, however, and they instantly collapsed from the pain, so it probably wasn't that. He couldn't understand why he was feeling so tired. He was overwhelmed by a weakness he had never known before, a fatigue that made his body heavy, dragging him downwards...

The Mexican people and their families lining the route cheered and waved, their faces full of encouragement. He had taken the lead without any particular effort but, despite his elation, he doubted it could be so easy: what was wrong with all the younger runners?

Of course, he knew that they were letting him set the pace. They wanted to see what he could do, find out whether he was still the world's greatest runner. They were all waiting to make their move, as surreptitious as cubs watching for the moment when the old cheetah would stumble and fall.

He was in the lead still but he started to pray that Mamo wasn't far behind. He prayed too that Mamo would have it in him to take over.

Abebe had watched him battle the 10,000, a hard race, to the end. Mamo had caught up with Naftali Temu and the other Kenyan, Kip Keino, and, just 200 metres from the finish, those short, powerful legs of his had propelled him into the lead. But Temu had put the pressure on and, in the final moments, just as they reached the line, he had pulled in front.

Abebe was satisfied for Mamo none the less: he had won a silver, his first Olympic medal.

He wondered whether Mamo knew, whether Negussie had told him...

When he glanced behind – something he had never before needed to do – he saw no one he recognised. Wehib wasn't anywhere in sight. More worryingly, where was Mamo?

In the palace gardens, Selassie was feeding the imperial lions. Near by, a servant nervously held the silver tray with the radio on it.

'Incredible!' shouted the Ethiopian reporter, the same one who commented on all the football matches, his voice rasping over the airwaves from the other side of the world. 'Abebe Bikila seems to be having difficulty with his right leg. He's holding his knee and he looks as though he's in pain. Oh no! This is incredible! He's dropping out! He's hobbling off the road. He's holding his knee and bending over. Abebe Bikila is out of the competition!'

Hearing the burbling panic in the voice of the commentator, Selassie froze. He tried to assess the significance of the runner's failure.

'The great Abebe was leading the race, he was on his way to winning a third Olympic marathon, but he has dropped out at the fifteen-kilometre post!'

So, Corporal Bikila had fallen. His promotion had been undeserved. But who would take his place?

The beasts he had been feeding roared hungrily.

Abebe lay on a stretcher in the ambulance, wondering only whether the pain would go away, a cruel trick, or whether it would overwhelm him finally and completely. He had felt anger at first as his body had given up and dragged him down; then regret, sorrow, pity for himself, and finally shame.

He had failed His Majesty, to whom he owed his life.

'It's all right,' said Tessema. 'You will be OK.'

Tessema had stayed with him while Niskanen had gone on ahead with an Ethiopian reporter in one of the official cars.

But Abebe wasn't worried about himself. 'What about Mamo?' he asked. Mamo would have no way of knowing he had dropped out; he might even assume that Abebe was still somewhere ahead of him.

'They are following Mamo,' said Tessema. 'They will tell him what has happened.'

Abebe was relieved.

'We must pray for him,' said Tessema.

Mamo was now Ethiopia's only hope and, as he thought of his old friend, willing him on, Abebe began to forget his pain.

It hardly mattered what the medics were saying: his knee was swollen, that it was too bad, but it probably wasn't serious, just an inflammation.

The time passed slowly as they listened on the transistor to the commentator shouting as he followed the race leaders. Abebe had never realised a marathon was so long: 42 kilometres; 26 miles; a whole lifetime.

But the commentator said nothing about any Ethiopian runners apart from repeating Abebe's name and the news that he had been in the lead until the fifteenth kilometre when he had suddenly dropped out owing to fatigue. It annoyed Abebe to hear him say that the reason was fatigue. If his strength had evaporated like that it was because he was ill, and he wanted to correct the reporter and tell everyone that it would be all right, that he would race again. It wasn't a question of fatigue. But the reporter kept on repeating that Abebe Bikila, the barefoot runner, the two-time Olympic champion, was out of the Mexico marathon.

He said nothing about Mamo, however, and Abebe and Tessema waited tensely as he described how the leader was the indefatigable Australian, Clarke, who liked to train by running up and down the sand dunes in his native country.

At the twenty-fifth kilometre, the Australian abandoned the race – stricken by God for his temerity, thought Abebe – and there was a new leader.

It was Temu, the Kenyan who had vanquished Mamo in the 10,000 metres race.

The news was depressing. Tessema and Abebe looked away from each other, neither wanting to accept failure, as they listened to the reporter describing the scene as a fresh challenger moved up into third place, then second. He was being followed by a car with a man leaning out, shouting and waving the Ethiopian flag!

Finally, the commentator identified the challenger as Mamo Wolde, teammate of the legendary Bikila.

Mamo was catching up!

By the 30-kilometre post, Mamo had reached Temu and they were running neck and neck. A few days before, Mamo had been bested at the finish by Temu. It was going to be his chance for revenge, thought Abebe; this would be the motivation he needed.

They didn't have to wait long. For ten minutes, the reporter jabbered excitedly about the two marathonians running neck and neck. He said it was an incredible duel between two athletes, both natives of the high mountains of the Horn of Africa. Then, as they passed the thirty-third kilometre post, he cried that Mamo had gone into the lead.

Abebe knew that Mamo would not abandon the lead now. Nothing would stop him. This time, Temu was not going to be able to catch up.

He smiled as he thought of his friend, of what it was like to be running the race of your life. The race it is only given to you to win once, if God is pleased with you.

Thirty-two minutes later, Mamo passed the finish and the pain in Abebe's knee lifted. His Majesty would be content; an imperial bodyguard had won a third marathon victory for Ethiopia. But Abebe was gratified, too, for the major, and overjoyed, most of all, for Mamo. At last his friend, who had run beside him for so many miles, would know how it was to hear the anthem played for him.

50

The awards ceremony did not take place in the palace grounds this time. There was no parade along Churchill Avenue, no day-long feast for hundreds of thousands prepared by the staff of the imperial palace. Perhaps this was a mistake. Selassie knew he should have given the people their celebration, but the coffers were empty and this time there was what his new advisers called a security risk. They said opposition groups might seize the opportunity to exploit popular fervour. So the ceremony took place inside the military base at Debre Zeit.

Abebe and Niskanen sat on the dais and watched as His Majesty decorated Mamo with an Imperial Order.

Abebe held his cane at his side. Thankfully, the painful swelling in his knee had gone down and the doctors said an operation would probably not be necessary. He could walk again, though he still needed the cane. It surprised him that they didn't know what it was: it could have been a circulatory difficulty, they said, or it might have been an infection, bacteria in his knee joint, and fighting it had made him weak and feverish for many days.

Later, Abebe told Niskanen that it was during the ceremony, watching Mamo receive the Star of Ethiopia from the emperor, that he had made his decision.

'Do you remember that I asked you why we must run?' he asked the major. 'And one of the reasons you said was simply that we are good runners.'

'Yes.'

'Is that all we are good at?'

Niskanen was taken aback. He turned to his protégé. 'No. Of course not,' he said. 'That's not what I meant.'

'Then I have made up my mind.'

Abebe was staring at the distant mountains.

'I have decided not to run any more.'

'Just because you had a problem in Mexico it doesn't mean you can't go on running. I thought you said you could never stop!'

'I must stop running now. There should be new runners, like Wehib and Miruts. They are young, they are fit; they are the ones who must run now.'

'What are you going to do?'

'I want to teach others to run. I would like to become a coach, like you. I've learned many things. Now I want to teach these things to others.'

Niskanen didn't know what to say. He knew such a moment would come, but he had never thought about his response. He was surprised to find an emotion welling in him greater than any he had ever felt at Abebe's victories. He was warmed by a jubilant sense of satisfaction. It meant at least that he would leave behind him something more in Ethiopia than just a few gold medals.

At the same time, though he had no way of letting him understand what this meant, he was increasingly aware that Abebe had become a hero for poor people around the world. In America, they wrote that he was an example of what they were calling black pride, not as vociferous as Ali, maybe – Abebe was far too humble, and he would never think of using the podium as a political platform – but a hero none the less. Though people didn't really know much about him, and they knew even less about life in Ethiopia, his barefoot triumph had symbolised African achievement.

Niskanen felt proud to have been a part of this too. He had come to realise that Abebe's marathon wins were greater than just sporting triumphs, greater than Olympic gold medals. Abebe had shown everyone that, with determination and courage, you could overcome impossible odds.

Ras Kassa bowed slowly before the King of Kings, and Selassie watched him from the throne as he straightened his ageing body, still tall but increasingly stooped, as though from the worries of the age they were living through. Times had changed for them; nearly ten years had passed since the Ras had proved his loyalty and cunning by slipping away from the assassins who came for him in the night and alerting His Majesty to Mengistu's plot.

'You are getting old, my friend. You should take more exercise.'

'Yes, Your Highness,' said the Ras, surprised by the emperor's concern.

'Well, what is it?' asked the Negus.

'Your Majesty, the Crown Council has decided that, in order to encourage support for the institutions of the monarchy among our rebellious student factions, a pro-government march should be held in the capital.'

The emperor laughed, a creaky, unfamiliar sound.

'But who is going to take part in a pro-government march?' he queried.

'The police.'

'The police?'

'The march will be led by police officers disguised as students.'

'Are you Rasses so senile you believe anyone will be fooled by this? Call off your march at once!'

The elderly Ras looked around nervously at the other Rasses.

'We cannot,' he said. 'It's taking place this morning. They are marching as we speak.'

'This is folly!'

Outside in the capital, along the avenue that led to the Haile Selassie I University, the police officers dressed as students carrying placards with the emperor's photograph met a barrage of real students, their arms linked, blocking the way. The fake demonstrators halted and there was a moment of tense quiet as the two groups measured each other. Stones flew from the ranks of the genuine students and they pitched into battle.

They were soon joined by real police, who fired on them with real ammunition.

***

Paul Rambali

Abebe always liked driving his white Beetle through the streets of Addis. The car had been a gift from His Majesty, after his return from Tokyo. Not many people owned cars and he enjoyed the attention he drew. It was never long, as he advanced fitfully through the multitudes in the streets of the capital, stopping regularly for the passing herds, before someone recognised him as the Olympic champion from the bodyguard. Although its cause hardly mattered, the excitement would spread like fire through the crowd and everybody would soon be cheering while those closest peered dumbstruck through the Beetle's windows. Eventually, people at the front of the throng would self-importantly push the others back to let the car and its driver through, as though making way for royalty.

That day, however, the roads were strangely empty. Abebe was on his way to Debre Zeit as usual, where he was now a sports instructor, a special assistant to Coach Negussie.

He was driving past the university when he saw a gang of students running across the road, chased by older men and by police officers.

There was shouting and the sound of gunfire.

Suddenly – out of nowhere – three students ran out in panic in front of the Beetle and Abebe was forced to swerve.

He turned the wheel hard, intent only on avoiding the screaming, blood-covered young men, and he didn't see the ditch until it was too late. The Beetle pitched over, almost flying into the void.

The heavy car rolled sideways, turning twice, and ended up on its roof, rocking gently, its wheels spinning in different directions.

Abebe was trapped inside, upside down, his neck twisted, his head jerked awkwardly to one side and pressed by the weight of his body against the roof.

He could see blood. When he tried to move his hand to touch his head, to find out whether he was the one who was bleeding, he was stricken by a pain so great he slipped into unconsciousness.

Niskanen picked up the telephone. He had heard the shooting and knew something was wrong, but he also knew it was better not to go out into the streets until there was an all-clear. He was relieved the telephones were working again, and he expected the call would be from someone at the base telling him there had been another attempted coup, perhaps a successful one this time, but it was Kidaneh.

'It's gone quiet outside. What's happening?'

'Never mind. Abebe is at the hospital. He had an accident – in his car.'

'Is it serious?'

'The physician said it's his back, his spine has been damaged...'

Niskanen sat down, staring uncomprehendingly at the telephone.

Kidaneh's words had plunged him into a dark abyss. He hoped it was just a nightmare and that he would wake up and find that everything – the shots, the phone call – was merely his fear playing tricks on him.

'They're saying he can't...'

There was a silence on the line.

'They say he might not be able to walk!'

Niskanen composed himself. 'I'm coming over to the hospital,' he said. 'Wait for me there.'

'No. You can't go out. You must stay where you are. It's dangerous out there. A curfew has been announced and it will be dark soon. They are going to be out rounding up the students.'

The emperor received Niskanen informally in his private office. The decor had changed and Niskanen thought to himself that here, at least, there was progress: the old-fashioned English furnishings had been replaced by functional modern items.

His Majesty said he had summoned him to the palace for news of Abebe. Niskanen was obliged to relate that the Russian doctors were pessimistic; they were saying he was unlikely to regain the use of his legs.

When he had finally reached the hospital the next day, he found Abebe lying with his legs in splints and a brace around his neck. His eyes had followed Niskanen as he came into the room. Nobody else would look at him. The nurses and doctors all bowed their heads. He asked Niskanen why he couldn't feel his legs...

There was a glimmer of hope, however. 'I've been in touch with physicians at Stoke Mandeville Hospital in Great Britain,' Niskanen told the emperor, 'and they've offered to treat him. They warned that he might be in re-education for some time, but they're optimistic. They say they'll do whatever they can.'

The emperor brightened. 'Then we shall provide an aircraft to take him there at once,' he announced. Niskanen had wondered what His Majesty's attitude would be after Mexico, but the suggestion that Abebe could be treated abroad appeared to revive the imperial spirits.

'I was extremely sorry to hear about the accident. The problems with the students have been a great strain. And now this...'

Selassie broke off. He was silent for a moment, and when he resumed, it was like another person speaking.

'Abebe is an example to the people of Ethiopia,' he said. 'At this time, we need examples of courage and loyalty, examples of duty and service to one's country. We are facing another rebellion – in the Gojam province again. The people are complaining that the Rasses are taxing them too heavily. What is your opinion, Major? Are they right to complain?'

Niskanen was about to ask whether he might speak freely, to suggest that it might be unwise to tax people who had so little, but the emperor's question had been rhetorical. He already knew the answer.

'They are right, yes!' he said. 'Of course they are. They want progress, but they are given only stagnation while the Rasses fill their own coffers. I have tried to put new men in charge, men of the people...'

Selassie's voice trailed off again.

'But we must not give up hope, eh?' he said. 'Abebe shall walk again. I am sure of it!'

The emperor stared at Niskanen, his eyes, once hard and bright, now clouded with uncertainty. He confided that the destiny of Ethiopia – 'our destiny', he said, meaning both the nation and himself – was entwined with that of Abebe, and that the loyal bodyguard's near-fatal accident was a distressing omen.

It worried Niskanen that, in this difficult time, Selassie was taking comfort in superstition, but his reign couldn't last for ever: despite the mythology, the Lion of Judah wasn't immortal. He was more than seventy years old, and the world of which he was once lord and master was slipping from his grip. Once, the people were cowed by his very name, but now, in the bars and restaurants of Addis, they laughed at his pompous displays. Feudal loyalties were eroding, and His Majesty was right that Abebe's popularity was part of it. But only a part. Ethiopia was considered the most modern country in Africa: away from the big hotels and the offices of the international agencies, however, people lived and died like dogs.

Nevertheless, His Majesty remained the incarnation of a supreme and increasingly paranoid power. Niskanen had always admired the emperor's shrewdness and determination but – though he had long ago decided he couldn't judge Selassie by his own standards – the cruelties that sometimes resulted made him shudder.

51

Lifting himself up in the hospital bed, Abebe tried to bow. He was sitting up, and he leaned forward in reverence, but the emperor raised his hand, excusing his subject.

'No,' he said, his fierce eyes filled with sorrow. 'It is I who should be the one to salute you.'

He smiled at Abebe and asked him whether he was well.

'Thanks be to God, I am well.'

'And how are your sons?'

'Thanks be to God, they are also well.'

'Do you have everything you need? Is your pension sufficient?'

'It is more than enough for my humble household.'

Selassie nodded. He studied Abebe, then turned to stare out of the window at the orderly fields. When he turned back, he smiled again at Abebe.

'I expect you think that we are the one responsible for your misfortune,' he said.

Abebe lowered his regard.

'You are wrong.'

He had been dreading this encounter, yet the moment His Majesty had entered the room, his apprehension had vanished. Whatever the cause of the accident, he knew then it was not the emperor's displeasure. The very fact that His Majesty was there, in his lowly presence, sufficed to tell him he had nothing to fear. Why would the omnipotent emperor seek vengeance against him? Why would he want to see Abebe a cripple? If he had been angry with him, then His Majesty – who had the power of life and death over every one of his subjects – would not have chosen this way of manifesting his displeasure.

'You became the hero of the Mercato, it is true. You were the inspiration of our people. You were the one they wanted to worship, to imitate; and as they did, they forgot how to serve us.'

At last, Abebe dared to lift his face.

'The people complain now, they are no longer satisfied with our victories; in the university, they clamour for rights. But that is not your fault.' The emperor looked pitifully at Abebe. 'You are not to blame, Sergeant. You have always been loyal.'

The imperial gaze became dispassionate for a moment, and then it grew angry, dark as a storm.

'We have given them everything, and they reward us with betrayal,' said the Negus. 'They reward us with treason,' he moaned, his voice a frail monotone, like the voice of a priest, 'and there is nothing we can do. We are helpless.' He was contemplating Abebe's legs, immobile and useless under the blanket. 'Helpless as you are, Sergeant Abebe.'

Perhaps it was the doctors and nurses and their belief in accidents; their conviction that fate could be reversed by patience and by therapies. Perhaps this had encouraged him to view his plight dispassionately. Nevertheless, Abebe couldn't quite bring himself to believe that there really was such a thing as an accident. That would be too unbearable. It meant that chance could be crueller than the most terrible tyrant.

No, it was all willed, ordained, if not by His Majesty then by others – and if not them, by his unseen enemies, then by God.

Then he heard the emperor's words, and he was struck by a terrible premonition...

The emperor straightened.

'We have a new post for you, Sergeant,' he announced, shrugging off the gloom that had entered the room like one of the large black crows that lurked in the fields outside.

'We have decided to make you Ambassador for Sport. We want you to travel to schools and to meetings at home and abroad. We want you to remind them that we are not inferior when it comes to sport. Your example will serve to show them that Ethiopia can catch up and surpass!'

'Yes, Your Majesty. I am most grateful. Thanks be to God.'

Abebe bowed again as best he could.

His Majesty nodded slightly, signalling that the audience was at an end.

He departed without another word.

Whether it was the plain white walls of the hospital room which had stripped the emperor of his power, or the ordinary dark suit he was wearing, or the absence of servants to bow and scrape at his feet, Abebe couldn't say, but a blasphemous impression struck him: for an instant, he saw the King of Kings as a short man with a ferocious, pained expression.

The next morning, Abebe woke and stared for a long time out of the window at the grey sky. It had been the same colour ever since his arrival in Britain, always grey, like a veil that had fallen over the days so that they never fully dawned.

He was looking forward to the visit from Rita, the only thing that cheered him up in the hospital. Boisterous and jaunty, she had none of the shyness of the women of his country, and she raised his spirits when she told him about Jamaica, about her large family over there planning to come to England, how they were mad about a sport called cricket that he could never understand – though when she tried to explain it, it sounded like *Gena* to him, the game he used to play in the village.

After the emperor had gone, she had come to see him and they had talked for a while. She clicked her tongue – *tsk, tsk* – when he told her how all the young men in his village wanted to go to Addis, how they all dreamed of entering the bodyguard. She told him about the time His Imperial Majesty had come to Jamaica. 'Everyone make a big fuss,' she said. 'Rastafarians come down from the hill beating they big drum and chanting. Haile Selassie, he can't even see them, don't know what it all about!' He hadn't grasped what she was saying at first. He explained to her that Ras Tafari was His Majesty's name before he was crowned emperor, at which time he took the name of Haile Selassie. She said she didn't know about that, but the

Rastafarians were always talking about going back to Africa on the *Black Star* liner. She explained that black people had been taken from Africa to work as slaves in the plantations of the Caribbean, but that slavery had ended a long time ago. 'Is that so?' she said, raising her eyebrows when he told her it was His Imperial Majesty who had abolished slavery in Ethiopia.

'Good morning, Abebe,' she chirped, bustling through the door with her tray as usual. 'How are we doing today?'

'I am doing very well, thank you, Rita. How are you?'

'Oh, not so bad. They takin' good care of you, now?'

He saw her looking at the wheelchair parked against the wall, exactly where it had been for days.

'You still don't take a ride on that thing?'

Abebe shook his head.

'Want to try?'

He said nothing at first, then he told her that he didn't want to try.

'You can't stay here in bed for ever. There's a lot of people waiting for that bed, you know. You gotta start getting out and about.'

'No, I can't,' Abebe stammered.

'You can't? Or you don't want to try? I know you was a running man. Is going to be hard for you, but some people, they never win a race like you, they never run like you and win a gold medal; they walk all they life, to they job they walk and then they walk home. You get a medal for running. Now you are going to have to win another medal with this.'

As she was speaking, she pushed the wheelchair alongside the bed. Then she cranked the handle to raise the back of the bed and with another lever lowered it to the level of the wheelchair.

Firmly, with greater strength than he would have imagined in such a heavy person, she put her arm under his shoulders, lifting him. He helped her by pushing himself up with his arms and was shocked at how little he weighed, how easy it was for her to lift him off the bed. He held his head stiffly upwards. His body was limp inside his pyjamas.

'That's right,' said Rita warmly as he gripped the wheels.

Abebe sat in the chair and his body relaxed.

'Soon be getting around just like before.'

He threaded the wheels through his hands and the chair glided smoothly forwards. He tried to manoeuvre it, aware that it was his new means of mobility, discovering its possibilities. Slowly, he inched towards the window.

52

Christmas festivities were in full swing in Tore's house. Bing Crosby was singing of sleigh bells and a log fire was burning, although the weather was mild – about 7 degrees – and damp, not the kind of crisp, icy cold the Swedes liked. Most of them preferred to return home at that time of year, but Niskanen usually stayed. More than anything else, this underlined to him as the years passed that Ethiopia had become his home. Luckily, there were still plenty of his compatriots left in the country to keep up the traditions. Tore and Anna made a point of inviting him to their party to eat the special Christmas ham that Anna prepared and drink *glugg* made with the strong local spices.

It troubled him to be there with Helen, however, especially in the presence of her husband Ben.

'I'm glad you came,' she whispered. 'I've been thinking about you.'

He had tried to forget her kiss, afraid that it would happen again. He didn't know what to say to her, how to explain how uncomfortable he felt when she was near him, and how uneasy it made him to be unable to control his feelings. He hoped that Ben was unaware of what had transpired, as he wouldn't have known how to tell him it was an accident. For that was what it was; not a kiss. But Ben seemed to be oblivious. He was absorbed with the usual talk, drinking brandies with Tore, Kidaneh and Spencer, the Englishman who counselled the emperor.

Warily, Niskanen joined their group, but Ben reacted as if nothing had happened, and perhaps this was the case. The certainties of male company soon reassured him. He was taken aback, however, when Ben announced it was going to be the last Christmas he would be enjoying with all of them.

'That's it for us,' he said. 'We're pulling out of Kagnew. Can't fight the communists in South-East Asia *and* in the Horn of Africa at the same time. Washington has decided His Majesty is not a priority.'

'We'll be sorry to see you go, Ben,' said Spencer, though Niskanen couldn't tell whether he meant it.

'The emperor was counting on our support, wasn't he?' Ben asked.

'I'm afraid so, yes,' Spencer answered.

'Too bad. But I'll be honest with you. The Arabs don't like it, they think the Christian Amhars here are persecuting their brothers, and the Arabs have the oil. What has Selassie got?'

Kidaneh said nothing.

'I suppose we shall just have to get used to drinking vodka,' said Spencer.

'Let's hope that is all we are forced to swallow,' said Kidaneh.

They stared at their glasses.

It was a relief to all except Niskanen when Helen joined them, breaking the silence. Spencer, ever the gentleman diplomat, complimented her on her dress, and Ben wandered off, saying he would return with refills.

'Happy Christmas,' said Helen. She was looking at Niskanen.

He told them how, earlier, just as darkness was falling, he had gone to Abebe's house and, wearing a Father Christmas costume with a bushy white beard which he had ordered by post, he had knocked on the window. The looks of fear and delight on the faces of Abebe's boys had reminded him of his own excitement as a child. His hearty laugh had frightened them as he handed out the presents from his sack – more boxes of Lego bricks for the boys, a silk tie for Abebe, leather gloves for his Yewibdar – and he was careful not to stay too long lest the children see through the disguise. He had told them in a booming voice that he still had many children to visit, 'all the little children in Ethiopia!'

'It would be nice if it were true,' said Helen.

'It was always a mystery to me as a child how Santa could visit all the children in the world in one night,' said Niskanen.

Helen smiled gently at him. 'Perhaps that's the reason you do all the work you do for Save the Children,' she said.

Niskanen blushed. He said that in Scandinavia, Father Christmas was called Tomten. 'He's an old man who lives in the forest. He's sort of like the spirit of the woods and we were very afraid of him. If he was angry with us for some reason, it meant we would have nothing to eat in the winter. We had to be very respectful. When he came to bring us presents at Christmas, we had to put a bowl of porridge outside the door for him.'

There was a silence and then Kidaneh spoke. 'We have a story about the forest too,' he said. 'It's a parable, really. Would you like to hear it?'

He related how a lioness, a cheetah and an oryx, who had come together on a long journey, decided one day to confess their sins to each other. As Queen of the Forest, the lioness was the first. 'She told the others that, once, after she had finished off a big buck, a zebra came by. "It looked so sleek and tender," she said, "that I couldn't resist pouncing." But she was too full to eat it! "I had wantonly dispatched a fellow beast for no purpose," she said regretfully. The cheetah reassured her. "Why should you, Queen of the Forest, be remorseful about the skill that has made you the greatest hunter of us all? You are to be forgiven." Then the cheetah told how, one day, he had spied a fat ewe and her two lambs. Hungrily he had pounced on the nearest lamb, but the mother had begged him to spare the remaining lamb and eat her instead. "I agreed," the cheetah said, "but I was so hungry I then ate the ewe and the other lamb too!" Even though she was a mother herself, the lioness forgave the cheetah since he was so beautiful, sleek and strong. Then they turned to the oryx. But the humble beast could think of nothing he had done wrong. "Come now," they said, "we are all mortals, surely there must be something that troubles your conscience?" The oryx thought for a moment and answered that, once, after walking all day along a hot desert trail, he had spied a clump of grass. Famished, he stopped and ate it.

'The lioness and the cheetah looked at each other in disgust.

"You have committed an unpardonable crime and do not deserve to live," they growled. And they pounced on the oryx and devoured him.'

Kidaneh glanced quickly around.

Niskanen saw that he was embarrassed and lifted his glass, proposing a toast.

'To progress,' he said.

'To justice,' added Kidaneh.

53

Selassie was silent. Aklilou sat opposite him in the private office, waiting for His Majesty's attention. The King of Kings was hoping, somehow, to avoid hearing what his prime minister had to say. He was well aware that the rebellion in Gojam had escalated to worrying proportions.

Aklilou went ahead none the less.

'The people are refusing to pay the new taxes,' he said. 'They are smashing the skulls of tax collectors, hanging policemen and trying to expel the Rasses! There are no crops to harvest and so they are using their machetes to hack government people to pieces instead. The army is powerless. They report that the peasants prefer to die. And the students have begun to praise the rebels' courage.'

'The students?' queried Selassie. 'Why are they not studying?'

There was no answer.

'We have given them a university, the first in our country. Why are they not at their desks, learning the things of which Ethiopia has need if it is to develop and surpass?'

'But...' said Aklilou. He was taken aback by the question. 'After the disturbances...'

He paused, unsure of whether to go on.

'After the students rioted, His Imperial Highness ordered that the campus should be closed for a year.'

The dining room of the Hotel Ghion had been turned into a temporary press room. Flowers and a bowl of fruit had been set on a long table, and chairs had been arranged in rows facing it. Sitting in the chairs and milling about the room, journalists were conversing noisily. They had been convened by the palace, a rare occurrence. Many of them were visiting the country for the first time and were busy gleaning information from their local colleagues.

Niskanen was there for Save the Children. As the drought had worsened, he had been asked to file daily reports to the centre in Stockholm. But even with what he was able to learn at the air force base at Debre Zeit, the situation was confused.

He had received a telex from Sweden that morning about a BBC television programme, asking whether it was accurate. It was because of the programme that the press conference had been called.

Aklilou entered with two government officials, neither of whom Niskanen recognised. The prime minister took a position at the centre of the table, facing the reporters, flanked by the two officials.

'Gentlemen,' he began, 'allow me to welcome some of you to Ethiopia for the first time. I am well aware of the purpose of your visit, and I would like to begin by telling you categorically there is no famine in the north. The reports of your colleague Mr Dimbleby are greatly exaggerated.'

According to the telex from Sweden, the BBC programme juxtaposed film of Haile Selassie on a visit to Disneyland in California, enjoying a ride with his little dog Lulu on his lap, with other film of starving Ethiopian children, their bones protruding from sagging skin. The telex quoted the words of the commentator: 'In the mountain kingdom of Ethiopia, famine has struck. While Emperor Haile Selassie I, the so-called *Negus Negasta*, or King of Kings, has become known as the flying monarch because of his frequent trips abroad, hundreds of thousands of his subjects are dying. Here in the Horn of Africa, in what is one of the poorest and most underdeveloped nations in the world, starvation is rife...'

'Can we go there and see for ourselves?' asked one of the reporters.

'I would very much like to be able to grant your wish,' replied Aklilou. His tone implied that reconciliation of everyone's needs was his only concern. 'But I am afraid it would be too dangerous at this time. We would not be able to guarantee your safety. As you know – and I would like to take this opportunity to signal once again the unfair treatment of Ethiopia by the international community – we are in the midst of a war against Marxist rebels. Encouraged by certain Islamic states, the Eritrean People's Liberation Front has been waging a campaign of disruption. They have been receiving arms and logistical support from the Soviet Union.'

A second reporter stood up to speak.

'You say there's no famine, but what about this?'

He brandished a photograph of a starving child. The empty, desperate eyes of the dying infant had stared out of magazine covers around the world that past week.

'This photo was taken in the northern provinces last month. Do you deny that starvation is widespread there, and that this famine is in part the result of Rasses and officials hoarding grain?'

'Where did you get that photograph?'

'Answer the question, please.'

'I repeat that there is nothing that could be described as a famine in Ethiopia. There are some problems in the north because we are having to devote scarce resources to fighting the EPLF, which I repeat is backed by Moscow and supported by Libya. His Most Supreme Majesty attaches the utmost importance to these problems.'

'What measures are you taking, specifically?'

'His Majesty will announce in due course his intended royal decisions, assignments and directions. It is not fitting for ministers such as myself to do so.'

He paused and, in that instant, he seemed to be touched by an inspiration.

'We need help and the Americans refuse us,' he said. 'I would like to use this opportunity to call on the assistance of the international community.'

Fortunately, Niskanen's house was a villa, all on one level. The maid had answered the bell when Abebe rang and she had helped him up the few steps in the wheelchair. He wheeled himself adroitly forward into the living room and halted when he saw Niskanen on the veranda. The major had his back turned, occupied by his thoughts.

'Major,' interrupted Abebe. 'Am I disturbing you?'

Niskanen turned and was unable to hide his surprise. He hadn't seen Abebe in a while. His former star athlete had put on weight and grown a thin, wispy beard.

'No, no.' He had been listening to the church bells. They all sounded together at regular hours, the echoes rippling over the hills. 'How did you get here?' he asked.

'I wheel. Is that what you say?'

'Huh?'

Abebe pushed the wheels with his hands, surging forward dangerously.

'Like this!'

'That's great,' said Niskanen. 'Well done.'

'Something is wrong, Major?'

'Nothing is wrong. I was just thinking.'

Abebe's arrival had disturbed his contemplation. It had become a ritual for him to listen in the evenings until the last peal faded away. Though most of them were simple mud-walled huts topped by a straw roof and a high *Maskal* cross, no other land could claim as many churches. So many churches – and so little mercy.

'You came all the way here on your own? It must be – what – five miles?'

'I am going to win the marathon again! I have been training in this. I will race in my wheelchair!'

He grasped the wheels of the chair again and Niskanen laughed.

'Do they give gold medals for racing in a wheelchair?'

'I can't say,' responded Niskanen. 'They certainly should!'

Abebe watched the boys running, remembering what it was like to run, to surge ahead of your rivals.

Four teenagers were racing around a track roughly painted with lanes. Every school in Ethiopia had improvised a running track and every boy in Ethiopia dreamed of equalling and surpassing the barefoot runner. The boys were running a relay race, carrying their markers aloft, and the spectators, families and friends of the runners, plus all the people of the town and the surrounding hamlets, cheered as the athletes handed on the torches to the waiting team members. Later, as guest of honour, Abebe would be the one who gave the medals to the winners.

When the race was over, Mamo wheeled him back to the schoolhouse. Mamo sometimes accompanied him on these trips, sharing in the glory and also in the chore of telling everybody, over and over again – for it seemed that nobody ever tired of hearing about it – how it was to take part in an Olympic Games. Mamo had begun to study history. He told Abebe Galla was a language of the Oromo, a people originally from the southern part of Ethiopia. For the Oromo, each eight-year cycle of a man's life brought different challenges and responsibilities, Mamo explained. 'First we were children, then we were warriors; in our case, warriors of sport. Then we became fathers. Now we have duty to instruct.'

They reached the schoolhouse. An official was waiting, a local dignitary who stared at the Star of Ethiopia pinned to Abebe's jacket. He shook their hands and then explained that he would be making the introduction. Abebe was going to speak in the school hall, which was hot and crowded already with people who wanted to hear what he would say. The official wanted Abebe to join him onstage but Mamo interceded, saying that Sergeant Bikila was tired and it would be better if he waited in the wings where it was cooler. Reluctantly, the official accepted.

He made a lengthy speech about the need for unity and hard work and loyal service to His Majesty. Mamo looked at Abebe and shook his head. It was often like this. There was always a functionary, someone who had never run a race but relied on flattery and favours for their position, who was keen to associate with them. Mamo had once said darkly that when everyone said their medals were a victory for Ethiopia, they were trying to claim them for themselves. 'It should be a victory for Oromo, not Amhar,' he had said. 'We are Galla, not good enough to be anything more than blacksmiths in the market, but when we win medals, suddenly we are Ethiopians, like them!'

Abebe didn't know whether he was right. One thing, though, was true. He had certainly listened to many long speeches, especially when he travelled abroad as Ambassador for Sport. Abroad, it was different. Though he might not be able to understand everything that was being said by the politicians, they treated him like royalty, like a god. He had shaken the hands of the men they called the architects of modern Africa: Jomo Kenyatta, Joshua Nkrumah, Julius Nyerere. These educated men in their horn-rimmed glasses and dark suits had clasped his hand in theirs and said he was a hero to the people. They said he had shown the world what Africa was capable of and now all the boys in their countries wanted to run like him! Someone said it was a good thing, otherwise they would have no idols other than the gunmen who rode around in their paramilitary vehicles.

The official had finally finished and he waved his arm to introduce the barefoot runner, Abebe Bikila.

Abebe wheeled himself forward on to the stage of the packed assembly hall. He had visited more than a dozen African countries, discovering his continent: the tin-roofed shanty towns, the unfinished, muddy roads, the daily desperation. But there was also the hope, the excitement his presence created wherever he went.

There was applause from the crowd seated in the hall as he approached the microphone in the centre of the stage.

'Thank you,' he said.

The clapping continued, growing louder as some of the audience stood up from their seats.

'Thank you,' he repeated.

But the applause didn't stop. Now the entire hall was on its feet.

Abebe bit his lip, overcome. He raised his arms for silence and leaned towards the microphone.

'Once, when I was a child,' he began, 'I could not walk. But then I learned to walk. Then I became a boy,' he continued. 'And I learned to run.'

He paused, waiting for the cheers of the crowd to subside.

'Now I cannot run any more. But I am able to speak. And I am here to tell you to run – run for me. Run in my place. Run to win, run to succeed!'

54

Niskanen was among the many who relayed Aklilou's request, and within weeks an international aid effort was under way, an outpouring of charity on a scale no one had ever seen before, unleashed by televisions that brought stark images of hitherto distant and unseen suffering into the comfortable homes of the First World. On the quay at Djibouti, crates marked with the names of Oxfam and other aid agencies began to pile up. Amid much shouting and bustle, the crates were loaded on to lorries by Ethiopian soldiers, to be distributed to the starving peoples in the north. It seemed as if the images had accomplished something extraordinary; in the same measure that they shocked, they were going to help to avert a humanitarian disaster.

Niskanen, however, had heard disturbing news.

He was received by Aklilou in his office in the palace.

'Thank you for seeing me at such short notice.'

The prime minister shook his hand warmly.

'Not at all, Major. You are one of Ethiopia's oldest friends, after all. Won't you have a seat?'

Aklilou returned to the large swivel chair behind his desk. 'Now,' he said, bringing his hands together, fingertips spread apart, to signify his consideration. 'What can I do for you?'

'I'm not sure exactly where to begin... As you know, I am a voluntary officer with a number of charity organisations. We've been getting reports... The field workers say the aid isn't getting through.'

'Not getting through,' repeated Aklilou, and Niskanen knew immediately it wasn't the first time he had heard the suggestion.

'I'm sure there's some misunderstanding.'

'The field workers say it's being stolen.'

'Stolen? That's absurd!'

Aklilou rose from his seat and walked to the window. He gazed out, as though pondering the idea.

'The foreign aid is in the hands of the army. How could it be stolen? Perhaps there is confusion here. One of the conditions under which we accepted foreign aid was that the government would have control over the distribution. We didn't want it to fall into the hands of the rebels. And, as you of all people must know, things are not done in Ethiopia with quite the same dispatch as they are in your country, Major. Your donors will have to understand that.'

'I received details of all the shipments and I checked with the field workers. It appears that barely a tenth of the famine relief is reaching the people who need it!'

'They will have to be patient.'

'Those people are dying.'

Aklilou began to pace the room.

'What is hunger to our people? They are used to the pain in their bellies. Even with all these shipments, there is still not enough grain. You are shocked, but that is how things are.'

But Niskanen was not shocked. He had grown accustomed to the fatalism of the ruling class in Ethiopia. He remembered how Mengistu, the leader of the failed coup, had said the same thing to him when he first came to Ethiopia.

He stood, preparing to leave.

'Perhaps, then, it is time for things to change.'

Aklilou looked him in the eye. It was the first time the major had made such a statement, but he had been unable to check himself.

'Perhaps,' Aklilou concurred. 'In the meantime, your allegations will be investigated. You have my word.'

As he was leaving, Aklilou clapped him on the back.

'Patience,' he said.

Nervously, Yewibdar opened the door. Her husband had warned her not to admit anyone she didn't know. But it was only the major. He was wearing his uniform as a precaution against marauders. She let him in hurriedly.

Inside, Abebe was playing a game of cards with his two children. Dawit, the eldest, was nearly eight years old and Tsige was six. They were lean and lithe; Niskanen could already see the runners in them.

'How are you?' he asked them.

Dawit and Tsige were too shy to reply.

Their father told them not to be rude.

'Very well, thank you,' they said, as Abebe had taught them.

'They are learning,' he said proudly.

Niskanen placed his hand affectionately around Dawit's shoulders. Then he watched them leave. He was struck, as always when he saw Abebe's children, by how much they had grown, how quickly time passed. Looking around to hide his emotion, he saw alongside the trophies and cups on the shelf some letters stuffed under the frame of a photo of Abebe running along the empty roads of Debre Zeit. On one of the letters was a royal crest.

Abebe saw him staring at them.

'There is one from the Queen of England and one from President Nixon of the United States,' he said. 'Since the accident there have been many letters. They all say kind words: the American president writes that he wishes me a speedy recovery.'

Yewibdar returned carrying a tray with glasses and a jug. Niskanen accepted a glass of *hydromel*, though he had never quite become used to the bittersweet taste of fermented honey.

'Thank you, Major, for everything you have done for us,' said Abebe.

'You did it all yourself, Abebe.'

'God has spared my life and I am grateful to him.'

He wheeled himself backwards a few inches, his spine straight, as if to demonstrate that there was nothing more he could rightly ask.

'There is only one thing I would like.'

'What's that?'

'I would like to be able to help my people.'

'Help them in what way?'

'They come here all the time asking me for favours, begging me to ask the emperor to help them and grant their wishes. They think that because I am Ambassador for Sport, I can do this for them, but I cannot.'

'Who are these people?'

'They come from my province, they are my relations. This is how it is.'

'What's the situation like up there? Have you had news from your village?'

'There is food in my province. They are not in danger.'

'Good. But I don't think there's much you can do about your relations.'

'I know. But how can I tell them? They don't believe me, they think I am lying.'

'You've been an example to your people. That's helped them more than you could ever imagine.'

Abebe nodded.

'There's nothing more you need to do.'

Abebe nodded again. The major still had much to learn about the way things were in Ethiopia.

'Anyway, I came about you,' said Niskanen. 'I've received an offer for you to participate in a special kind of competition.' The thought of what he was about to say made him smile. 'You know what you said once about getting a medal for being able to get about in your wheelchair? Well, they are organising a meeting in Norway, a series of competitions for handicapped people – those with physical disabilities – and they would like to invite you to be there to take part as a guest of honour.'

Abebe was perplexed. 'This is not like the Olympics?' he asked.

'No, it's not the Olympics, but I suppose it is a kind of Olympics. They've heard about what you've been doing as His Majesty's Ambassador for Sport and they would like to give you an award.'

'An award for what?' Abebe asked. 'I have not won anything. First, I will have to compete!'

'You're absolutely right! Who ever heard of receiving an award without any effort? I shall tell them!'

They both laughed.

'What do you say? It's taking place in Scandinavia and I would be honoured to invite you to visit my country. You can bring your family too, if you want. I'm sure there'll be no problem.'

55

The palace was immersed in an eerie quietness, as though there were nobody left to conspire in the deserted hallways.

The lawyer sidled nervously up to Niskanen.

'What have you come for?' he hissed, his voice reduced to a paranoid whisper. 'There is no use in coming here any more.'

He was like a ghost now, still haunting the corridor, without clients, forgotten and hence unseen. But the lawyer kept himself informed.

'The students are kicking up a fuss and the Derg is arresting everybody. They accuse them of corruption and throw them in jail. Once it was called privilege, it was what you aspired to; now they call it corruption.'

He snorted.

'What choice did we have? How can you share a privilege?'

There was a sudden commotion in the corridor.

Niskanen watched as Aklilou was led from the prime minister's office by soldiers. He was handcuffed and the rough-hewn soldiers had their rifles pointed at him.

Niskanen stood up as they approached but Aklilou shook his head.

The soldiers passed, ignoring Niskanen and the lawyer, who stared blankly ahead as if he knew they could come back for him too but was determined not to see them.

After they had passed, he spoke again.

'Soon the jails will be full. And then what?'

Niskanen had come to see the emperor. He waited, wondering what the arrest had meant, with the loquacious lawyer offering no clear reasoning, until finally a soldier came to summon him.

Inside his private office, the emperor was waiting in silence. He was not alone, and seemed uneasy. General Andom was ensconced comfortably in an armchair and he stood when Niskanen entered to salute him.

The emperor invited the major to sit down, but it was General Andom who spoke.

'We have been looking into this business about the aid,' he said, 'and I'm afraid the reports of your field workers turned out to be true. Some of the aid was being...' He paused, searching for the right word. '...*misappropriated* by certain officers, who were supposed to be overseeing its delivery.'

Niskanen noticed that, with the subtlety he had always known in his Ethiopian hosts, the general had failed to specify which sort of officers, army or government. Given the presence of this army man in the private chambers of the emperor, he concluded that the balance was turning in the military's favour.

'I see,' he said. It was important to Niskanen only that the aid got through and so he didn't press for details.

'I think our donors would like to know how you intend to ensure that it doesn't happen again,' he said.

It was the emperor who spoke this time.

'Luckily, not all elements within the army are so ungrateful. Rest assured, the guilty will be punished. You have my word.'

General Andom did not allow the emperor to conclude.

'An ad hoc committee has been formed to investigate this and other instances of corruption,' he said.

'I have given the committee sweeping powers,' interjected Selassie.

'And the famine relief effort?' asked Niskanen, his patience fraying at this charade. 'Who is going to see that the aid gets through?'

General Andom exchanged glances with the emperor.

'His Imperial Majesty has agreed to allow foreign observers to accompany the aid.'

The Negus snorted with irritation and Niskanen wondered whether it was because the general had spoken on his behalf. He saw him suddenly as a grumpy old man.

'They have betrayed us,' exclaimed Selassie. 'It was not only the foreign aid they stole. They took the pay rises that I awarded to their men during the Army and Police Hour. I dedicated this hour in my day to their problems, and they stole the money. I promoted them and this is how they rewarded me – with disloyalty! They stole the pay from their own men!'

Now General Andom was uneasy. 'Will that be all, Major?' he asked, interrupting the emperor.

It seemed to Niskanen that the army man was impatient with the sentimentality of the emperor's outburst as much as with what it revealed. Hitherto, it would have been unthinkable for anyone to cut him off.

In the gardens outside, he heard the lions growling, and he hoped that the new masters of the palace hadn't forgotten to feed them.

56

The twelve Rasses stood in a line, with Ras Kassa at the centre. Wearily, His Majesty descended from his throne – the Keeper of the Cushions adroit as ever at whisking away the cushion from under his feet – and walked up and down before the Rasses, appraising them with a fierce glint.

Finally, he stood back.

'We of the aristocracy must set an example. We must be fit to rule,' he said.

The ageing members of the Crown Council looked at one another in confusion.

'To rule, we must be fit.'

Ras Kassa had stepped forward to speak when there was an interruption. The doors of the Hall of Audience burst open and they saw the page, whose duty it was to announce visitors, wearing a helpless, frightened expression.

Without waiting, General Andom entered. The councillors froze in amazement at this disregard for protocol.

The page followed the general into the Hall of Audience and spoke quickly.

'In the name of the Derg, General Andom requests an audience with His Imperial Highness.'

The emperor was the only one who was not perturbed by the intrusion. He paused, none the less, before replying.

'We shall grant General Andom his request,' he said.

Selassie held the door of his private office open for the general, who passed the line of councillors, presumptuously making eye contact with them.

The emperor closed the door behind him and, without moving, the councillors turned to Ras Kassa.

The elderly Ras was rooted to the spot.

He remained there for a long time, and as long as he did, none of the others dared break rank.

The numbers of foreign reporters waiting for news in the Hotel Ghion had grown steadily. In the lobby, as well as journalists and the television crews, there were other strangers, and it was with one of these men that Kidaneh was talking.

He was telling the man that, what with all the fuss about the famine, it was becoming difficult to get seats on the flights – but that if necessary, he could start right away.

Kidaneh saw Ben and excused himself. He caught his sleeve as he passed and drew the American aside.

'I thought you'd left,' he said.

'We'll be going soon. It's falling apart here. What about the major? What's he going to do?'

'I haven't seen much of him lately. There hasn't been a lot of time for sport. The major is busy coordinating the relief effort. The Athletics Federation has been turned into the headquarters of Save the Children.'

'And Abebe?'

'Abebe is safe. They won't harm him. They need the people's hero too, even if he is a guardsman.'

'Still, it's getting dangerous. What about you? What are you going to do?'

'Oh, they won't bother with me. I have nothing to fear. I will get an exit visa...'

He reflected for a moment.

'What do you think we did with all those shoes?'

'I don't know.'

'We gave them away.'

Kidaneh spoke quietly now.

'I could have sold them in the Mercato. In a country without shoes, can you imagine how rich I would be? Instead, I am forced to flee. Who would believe that I did not enrich myself the way anybody else would have done?' He shook his head. 'Nobody would believe it.'

'I guess not.'

The curtains were kept drawn all day, shrouding the Hall of Audience in a gloomy darkness.

Selassie sat alone on the throne, silent and unmoving. He had abandoned the Hours that once measured his day, although he had given no instructions, issued no edicts; the people had simply stopped coming to ask for his judgements. Eventually, he concluded that someone else was making the decisions.

Apparently Ras Kassa, too, felt free to defy protocol. He barged into the hall, followed by the other councillors.

The emperor showed no surprise at their arrival. Though he no longer had informants to keep him appraised, he knew that the wrath and, therefore, the fear of the councillors would be growing.

'As chief of the Crown Council, I have been delegated to enquire what His Imperial Highness intends to do about the recent arrests.'

'Do?' answered Selassie calmly. 'I shall do nothing.'

'The Derg is making arrests in the name of His Majesty. How can this be?'

'The anti-corruption committee is doing a fine job of cleaning up our public affairs.'

'That is not the opinion of the Rasses.'

'You have nothing to fear. You have always acted loyally.'

'This is impossible!' exclaimed Ras Kassa.

Selassie flinched, as though woken from a dream.

He descended from the throne and, kicking away the cushion from under his feet, for the Keeper of Cushions had gone, he approached the tall Ras. Though he stared up at him he still somehow possessed the regal authority to dominate.

'We have decided that the members of the council shall undergo a programme of physical education.'

The councillors were bewildered. They looked at each other, not knowing how to interpret what His Majesty had said. Was the emperor talking in riddles?

'Surely,' queried Ras Kassa, 'His Imperial Highness cannot be serious!'

'We are perfectly serious,' said Selassie. 'How can we rule if we are not fit? You shall begin training at once!'

57

Helen had deliberately put off saying goodbye. She had been unable to face her feelings and, so that she wouldn't change her mind, she had forced herself to wait until there was almost no time left.

She arrived at the offices of the Athletics Federation to find that they had been taken over by aid workers, mostly Swedes and young Americans with the Peace Corps. She told one of them she was looking for Major Niskanen and he said the major had received a message from the emperor and had gone to the palace.

It took some time for Helen to reach the palace. The streets were full of refugees in search of the makeshift kitchens. Many of them were mere skeletons, empty sacks of sagging flesh. Without the strength to go any farther, they slouched against the walls or lay dying in the gutters.

In the palace grounds, Niskanen was standing in front of the ageing dignitaries as the emperor looked on.

He turned to Selassie, who made a sign for him to begin.

The major bent down to touch his toes.

The members of the Crown Council looked at Ras Kassa, who continued to stare stonily at the King of Kings.

Finally, the tall Ras bent over slowly and stiffly and painfully attempted to touch his toes.

When he straightened, Niskanen saw that tears were welling in his eyes.

Niskanen was uneasy. He knew it wasn't the physical effort which distressed the Ras but the humiliation. He looked around at the emperor before continuing, but Selassie was frowning. Niskanen raised his arms in the air and the councillors reluctantly copied his gesture, too loyal or too irresolute to refuse.

Helen arrived at the palace and hurried unannounced along the corridor that used to be so busy with dignitaries, lawyers, clerks and hangers-on, but was now deserted apart from a few dusty, shadowy figures. These pages and grooms were the only remaining attendants. Helen saw them bowing low as a woman in white robes passed, a member of the royal family.

It was Princess Tenegneh, the emperor's daughter. She halted in front of Helen.

'I assume you're looking for the major,' she said.

'Is he here?'

'He is outside with my father. He's showing the royal councillors how to keep fit.'

Helen was bewildered.

'Look for yourself,' she said, nodding towards the wooden trellises that lined one side of the corridor.

Through them it was possible to see the gardens and, once Helen had focused, she realised that the figures in the grounds were performing basic physical exercises. Before them, she saw the major bending sideways with one arm at his side, the other stretched straight up.

The councillors were performing the same movements.

Helen turned to the princess.

'It was His Majesty's wish,' she said.

'Why? What does he think he's going to achieve by this?'

The ageing princess tried to preserve imperial dignity.

'My father is someone who believes in progress, in keeping up. He brought the first automobile to our country, and the first aeroplane. He brought justice to our people. Do you know what justice meant before he came to the throne? Imagine living in a country where, at any moment, they might grab you and chop your arms off just because someone accused you of theft! My father gave Ethiopia a constitution, he gave the nation a parliament...'

She looked away, too stern to allow tears to come. Helen saw that she was the one who had inherited her father's rigour.

'The councillors are stubborn. They refuse to condone the work of the anti-corruption committee. But my father is someone who believes in progress, he won't try to stand in its way. If we can't push through reform, then soon we will all be gone.'

The princess had been watching Niskanen and the councillors exercising as she spoke.

She turned to Helen.

'Please,' she said cordially. 'They will soon be finished. You may wait, though I'm afraid there's no one here any more to bring you coffee.'

Helen thanked the princess and told her it was unnecessary. She stood alongside her, observing Niskanen in silence.

In very little time, the councillors were exhausted. They could barely follow the demonstration and Niskanen was acutely uneasy. Finally, Ras Kassa straightened and stared straight ahead as though on parade, unable to put up with the charade any longer. When Niskanen began to repeat the series of exercises, he refused to follow. The disobedience of Ras Kassa seemed to waken the emperor from his reverie.

'I think that will be enough for today, Major,' said Selassie.

Niskanen thanked the Rasses and turned to walk back to the palace, his head lowered.

Helen hurried down the corridor, leaving Princess Tenegneh watching her father dismissing the councillors, a decrepit old king making empty motions before his tired, elderly governors.

Helen caught up with Niskanen just as he entered the corridor. She saw the defeat in his face and took his hands in hers, pulling him close.

'We're leaving,' she said.

She couldn't help herself.

'Come with me. Let's go now. I don't want anything to happen to you.'

Niskanen shook his head.

'I can't leave. Ethiopia is my home now. Whatever happens here, I must stay.'

'I need you now. I need you more than they do.'

'Ben needs you. He's your husband. You must go to him.'

Niskanen embraced her, and then held her away from him.

'You want forgiveness. I forgive you,' she said.

He shook his head slowly.

'But who will forgive you?'

Except for a few cowering courtiers, there was nobody left in the palace. In the Hall of Audience, the emperor sat brooding as Princess Tenegneh walked anxiously back and forth.

Abruptly, the emperor addressed a nervous page.

'Where is Ras Kassa? Where is the council?'

The page seemed dumbfounded by the emperor's question. He stammered, unable to speak.

Princess Tenegneh answered for him.

'They have been arrested. They were detained by the Derg this morning – in the name of His Imperial Highness.'

'I see,' said the emperor. He reflected for a moment. 'Then everything is as it should be.'

58

Aiming just above the target as Niskanen had shown him, Abebe drew back the heavy bowstring and let the arrow fly. It hit the middle of the circle with a thud, quivering in the moment's silence before the applause rippled from the stands like birds fluttering upwards towards the heavens. The sound was nothing like the thunder he had experienced in the Olympic competitions, great waves like a blast that swept him aloft, but it was satisfying none the less.

Next to him, another archer pulled back his bowstring, a blind man from the United States.

Abebe had been practising for months with the bow and arrow, learning how to hold the bow, how to aim, how to pull the bowstring back with his elbows high and his arm straight. He had been pleased to find the strength in his arms increasing since he began to use the wheelchair; one part of his body compensating for a deficiency in another. Even if he could no longer run the way he used to, he still had to strive, and there were still prizes to win.

One of the other competitors had said to him that whatever your abilities, you had to make the most of them. These people without limbs, some without sight, some with terrible deformities, had humbled him. The important thing, he knew, was not to win, but to take part; but it was a victory for the disabled just to participate. They had fought enormous battles with nature, much harder than the ones he had faced.

The blind archer released his arrow next, and as the shaft struck the target with a shiver it was Abebe's turn to applaud in wonder someone who had surpassed nature.

He didn't win any trophies that day, but resolved to practise when he returned home. Archery reminded him of his boyhood, when he and his friends would pretend to be hunters stalking animals on the plain with their home-made bows. If he couldn't run the distances, the arrow could traverse them, and patience and a true aim became the important skills. Niskanen said it was a bit like golf, which was fast becoming the major's favourite sport. He would soon be turning sixty, he had told Abebe, and he was looking forward to having the time to improve his swing.

Once the round was over, Abebe's son Dawit wheeled him back to the clubhouse, a wooden pavilion that glowed ochre red in the sunlight. He had been disappointed not to see the snow, but Niskanen told him they would have to return in the winter. Abebe didn't mind: the daylight that lasted all day and all night was astonishing enough.

In the clubhouse, Niskanen was waiting with Yewibdar, who held the new baby in her arms. The little girl was crying, and Yewibdar rocked her gently, singing an Ethiopian lullaby.

Niskanen took Abebe aside.

'I'm worried about the situation back in Addis,' he said. 'I've been thinking I could apply for you to be given asylum in Sweden, you and your family. You would all be safe there.'

Abebe shook his head.

'I could not leave. Ethiopia is my country.'

'There's going to be a change. The emperor won't be able to last much longer, I'm afraid, and it won't be like before.'

'Perhaps that will be a good thing. Perhaps then it will be better for the people.'

'I understand.'

'What about you, Major? What will you do?'

'I don't think they'll be giving me a new mandate, but that's OK. I'm happy to be back here in Scandinavia. I've been away a long time, so long that I didn't even realise I missed it.'

'It is very comfortable here. People have everything that they want.'

Niskanen contemplated the circuit, the oval running track that had been his passion and his life.

'You know, the thing you want most of all is to be able to make a difference. That's what you gave me, Abebe: the chance to make a difference. I cannot be grateful enough to you.'

'What is this, Major? I am the one who should be grateful to you.'

He looked down at his legs, the frail and now inert limbs that had carried him to the Olympic heights. He was satisfied merely to participate in the archery contest, but he couldn't help gloating over his one victory.

A few days earlier, he had won a silver medal in one of the wheelchair races. The trick was to lean forward at the same time as you tipped the wheelchair back with the weight of your body, so you were almost cycling on the two big wheels. The track had a 200-metre straight, making it easier for him, but he resolved to practise tipping his wheelchair too. Some of the Americans were able to take the bends on one wheel. Once you'd mastered that, you could go as fast as you dared.

The world's greatest runner grinned at the thought.

Abebe Bikila's treatment at Stoke Mandeville Hospital, England, failed to improve his condition. He died from a cerebral haemorrhage in October 1973, having turned forty. He was buried in the grounds of St Joseph's church, Addis Ababa, in the presence of Emperor Haile Selassie – the last public appearance of His Imperial Majesty. His son Dawit and his daughter Tsige both became runners.

Haile Selassie I died in 1975 in the Guennet Lal Palace, where he was held prisoner by the military junta.

Onni Niskanen eventually retired to Sweden, where he died in 1984, aged seventy-four. He was awarded medals by the Ethiopian government, by the Radda Barnen Save the Children Organisation and by the Swedish Red Cross Society. He never remarried.

Mamo Wolde went on to win a bronze medal in the 1972 Munich marathon, his fifth Olympic participation. When the *Derg* was overthrown in 1991, he was one of 5,200 former officials charged with murder, war crimes and genocide. He was held without trial until 2001. He died shortly after his release.